Organization
RENEWAL

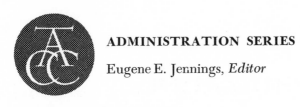 **ADMINISTRATION SERIES**

Eugene E. Jennings, *Editor*

Organization
RENEWAL

Achieving Viability in a Changing World

GORDON L. LIPPITT
The George Washington University

APPLETON-CENTURY-CROFTS
EDUCATIONAL DIVISION
MEREDITH CORPORATION

New York

This book is dedicated to the women in my life—
my mother, Lois G. Lippitt
my wife, Phyllis
and my daughters, Anne, Mary, *and* Connie

PREFACE

This book is written and published at a time when many of man's organizations are faced with dissensions, stress, turnover, strikes, and conflict. Evidence is seen in newspapers and newscasts that schools, hospitals, voluntary agencies, businesses, government agencies, trade associations, unions, churches, communities, and industries are trying to cope with some of the most difficult issues that either new or old organizations have faced since their beginning.

The challenge to most of these organizations is their relevancy to the age in which they live. Powerful changes in social responsibility, moral standards, economic pressures, educational requirements, and man's search for identity are but a few of the forces causing disequilibrium in today's organizations.

I feel that at no other time in my lifetime has there been more need for organization renewal. The need for organizations to re-examine their objectives, review their structure, improve their relationships, and to rediscover their responsibility to their members, clients, or employees is very evident. The organization that will remain viable, creative, and relevant must engage in the process of search that the renewal effort involves. Such renewal will not take place by chance. It must be a purposive effort that embodies more than good intention. An organization renewal process takes time, energy, money, and skill.

I have attempted in these pages to share some research, experiences, and challenges with both the practitioner and the student of organizational life. I feel that there are many persons in organizations that can be the creative renewal stimulator so needed in today's organization world. It might be an executive, a professional employee, a staff specialist, the organization development office, the training officer, a key supervisor, or some other concerned person. This is not, therefore, intended to be just a textbook, nor a "how to do it" in oversimplified terms. Implementation of organization renewal will require all we know about organizations and individual behavior to be mixed with the best of experimentation in practical application.

In writing this book I have wanted to present a frame of reference for initiating and maintaining organization renewal processes. In doing so, the reader will find that I have blended the utilization of behavioral and management science with my own experience in government, education, voluntary agencies, and industry. My experiences as an administrator in all of these types of organizations hopefully will lend a note of reality. My practical failures, successes, and frustrations were helpful ways to test and clarify my own research and that of my colleagues.

While any author must take responsibility for his own writing, I want it known that I am indebted to many others for bringing me to that point in life where I feel I have some thoughts, ideas, and experiences worth sharing. Ten years of my early career were spent in helping develop and build the National Training Laboratories Institute for Applied Behavioral Sciences. In such a position I was privileged to work with Leland P. Bradford, the Director of NTL, who contributed more than anyone else to my professional growth. The association with NTL Fellows and Associates at numerous laboratories, consultations, and programs these past twenty-five years provided a continuing stimulus for which I am indeed grateful. The ten years I have spent at the George Washington University has provided an opportunity to pursue research and teaching with faculty and student associates who have made it possible for me to test and refine the ideas expressed in this book.

My experiences as a founder and first president of Leadership Resources, Inc., gave me a chance to practice some leadership skills in the practical world of business rather than serving only as a consultant, teacher, or researcher. My pre-NTL experiences as an administrator with both a government and a community agency developed my interest in organizational dynamics. In addition to my associates at NTL, the George Washington University, and Leadership Resources, Inc., I want to acknowledge the value to my learning in serving for five years on the Board of Directors of the American Society for Training and Development. My association with professional training and educational practitioners in the United States and overseas was informative, rewarding, and helpful.

These relationships and my own interest and skills have made it possible to consult and work with numerous clients who have tolerated both my successes and failures. These experiences have provided another testing ground for the ideas and actions I have felt are important in the area of organization renewal. To work with such varied organizations as the Westinghouse Corporation, International Business Machines, American National Red Cross, National League of Cities, Goodyear Company, U.S. Department of Labor, National Council of the YMCA, Girl Scouts of America, Champion Papers, Inc., Department of Defense, American Public Power Association, Mead Corporation, and many others, were actually opportunities to apply the organization renewal process.

I also want to express my appreciation to the professional journals, books and magazines from which I have been allowed to use revised portions of my own writings which first appeared in their pages.

I am especially indebted to Warren Schmidt, Coordinator of the Integrated Masters of Business Administration Program, and Assistant Dean at the Graduate School of Business Administration, at the University of California at Los Angeles, and Leslie This, President of Projects Associates, Inc., for their friendship, encouragement, co-authorship with me of some earlier writing ventures, and detailed critique of the early drafts of the manuscript.

I should also mention Forrest Belcher of Pan American Petroleum Company, Patrick Farbro of Radio Corporation of America, Robert Dawson of Equitable Life Assurance Company, Eugene Jennings of Michigan State University, Andrew Daly of International Business Machines, Shirley McCune of the American Association of University Women, and my faculty colleague, John Rizzo, of the George Washington University, for their invaluable assistance in reviewing the final draft of this manuscript prior to publication.

A sincere expression of gratitude goes to R. E. Stivers not only for editing the complete manuscript and considerably improving its readability, but also for contributing to its rationale. As important as anyone else is my everwilling and overworked secretary, Mrs. Patricia Guy. Last but not least, as they say, a word of thanks and much love to my wife for her patience and encouragement during the many occasions when this effort created fatigue, impatience, and moodiness.

G.L.L.

CONTENTS

PART ONE

Organizations as Socio-Technical Systems

PART TWO

Organizations as People at Work

PART THREE

Process of Interfacing

PART FOUR

Conditions, Skills, and Actions in Organization Renewal

PART FIVE

Resources for Organization Renewal

Organization
RENEWAL

INTRODUCTORY NOTE

The field of organizational systems theory, research, and practice is a relatively new area for the researcher and student. While much has been written in the behavioral and management sciences about individual and group functioning, it has been only in the last decade that major attempts have been made to study the complexity of the total system as well as those that benefit the individual and group in the organization. As a consequence of these developments, many new concepts and words have been used in different ways by different writers and advocates of one approach or another. In light of this fact, I feel it may be helpful to the reader to have a glossary of some of the words and concepts I have used in discussing the relatively new field of organization renewal.

ORGANIZATION RENEWAL is the process of initiating, creating, and confronting needed changes so as to make it possible for organizations to become or remain viable, to adapt to new conditions, to solve problems, to learn from experiences, and to move toward greater organizational maturity.

RENEWAL STIMULATOR is a person or group that initiates an action, process, or activity intended to bring about planned change contributing to organization renewal.

BEHAVIORAL SCIENCE is concerned with the study of the problem-solving behavior of man. Such study uses primarily the findings and insights from the disciplines of psychology, sociology, and anthropology, but it may also include the behavioral aspects of economics, political science, and biology.

SOCIAL SYSTEM refers to the system of sub-systems within an organization made up of individuals, dyads, and groups having common social elements.

SOCIO-TECHNICAL SYSTEM is the organizational concept emphasizing that both human and nonhuman factors—including technology, structure, and process—interact to determine individual and organizational functioning.

ORGANIZATIONAL DEVELOPMENT is the strengthening of those human processes in organizations which improve the functioning of the organic system so as to achieve its objectives.

ORGANIZATIONAL GROWTH refers to the concept that organizations are complex organisms that have a life cycle with stages of development commencing with birth, and progressing through survival to later stages of maturity.

CHANGE is any planned or unplanned alteration of the status quo in an organism, situation, or process.

PLANNED CHANGE is an intended, designed, or purposive attempt by an individual, group, organization, or larger social system to influence directly the status quo of itself, another organism, or a situation.

ORGANIZATIONAL CHANGE is any planned or unplanned alteration of the status quo which affects the structure, technology, and personnel of the total organization.

INTERFACING is primarily a process by which human beings confront common areas of concern, engage in meaningfully related dialogue, actively search for solutions to mutual problems, and cope with these solutions purposefully. Interfacing may also involve the confrontation between human beings and machine processes or technological systems.

PART ONE

Organizations As Socio-Technical Systems

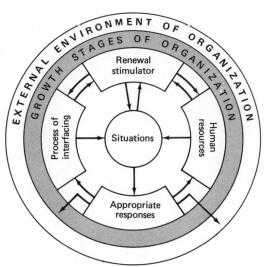

Organizations consist of social, technical, and economic components woven into a system designed to accomplish multiple purposes. Herein lies the basis for focusing on the socio-technical aspects of organizational life.

Chapter 1 presents a basic theme and develops a circular concept of appropriate renewal processes. Chapter 2 presents the stages of growth of an organization, and Chapter 3 examines the social system elements of organizations to provide a background for the human and technical aspects.

1 CIRCULAR PROCESS OF ORGANIZATION RENEWAL: A CONCEPTUAL MODEL

> Life cycle patterns are found in human artifacts, such as automobiles, buildings, and so on. The concept is less applicable to social organizations which often have the capacity for self-renewal. Neither organizations nor civilizations are under the necessity of aging, although this does sometimes happen. The fact that people die, however, means that organizations can renew their youth as the old occupants of powerful positions die off and younger occupants take their place. We do not seem to be able to do this with neurons.
>
> KENNETH E. BOULDING, 1910–

The buildings, real estate, typewriters, computers, and financial resources of modern organizations are no more than useful tools, the material side of enterprise. These tangibles could be dispensed with and there could still be an organization. This is because basically an organization is made up of human resources—people. In a way this is paradoxically both fortunate and unfortunate. On one hand, the prospect of an enterprise that could function endlessly and efficiently without human guidance is the substance of nightmares; on the other hand, the greatest obstacle to the successful functioning of man's organizations is the all-important asset that is man himself.

No one denies that few tangible evidences of organization last forever—that, for example, there usually must be a purchasing schedule for new machinery. Every personnel director is plagued with the realities of employee turnover. In the language of ancient adage, philosophers and physicians warn that all work and no play make Jack a dull boy. Peculiar to themselves, of course, the necessary processes of replacement and restoration contribute to organizational needs for revitalization. However, they are not ordinarily applicable to another essential form of renewal which has to do with the manner in which an organization undertakes decision-making or the way it deals with the world around it. The renewal of people and tools is, at best, incremental; renewal of attitudes, aspirations, and purposes, because they rest basically on the will and ideas of human beings, involves the interrelationships of people with people, and of people with situations. In other words, the human side of enterprise.

Perhaps the latter can best be illustrated by mentioning some of the sought-for results of organization renewal:

1. Continuous examination of the growth of organization, together with diagnosis of the multiple internal and external influences affecting its state of being.
2. Improvement in the manner in which problems are solved at all levels of the organization.
3. Development within the organization of formal and informal groups which are effective and communicative.
4. Development of leadership which is appropriate to the situation facing the organization at any given time. /
5. A way for people within the organization to learn from their experiences of success or failure.
6. Maturity of individuals and groups within the organization as well as maturity of the organization itself.
7. Development of a climate that encourages and channels creativity by people throughout the organization.
8. Development of a system to which all employees of the organization feel committed, thereby securing their motivation.

All of the above involve *change*, which is a word much used in organizational theory, but often misunderstood in context. Organizations are goal-seeking complexes of human resources. Stability within such a complex is not synonymous with growth. Growth of such a complex, in terms of mere numbers, is not synonymous with maturity. Change occurs within an organization—or it should occur if survival is to be achieved— as from time to time its goals and circumstances vary. These variances cause the human resources of the organization to engage in problem-solving as they seek reorientation and try to adapt to new environmental influences.

Organization renewal, therefore, affects the organic functioning of the system, confronts a real situation, and helps the organization mature while being responsive to the environment. The many programs of management and organization development may contribute to and be a crucial part of organization renewal, but successful renewal is a *total* response by the human resources of the organization. Organization renewal enables these human resources to become increasingly viable, to cope with the future, and to contribute to it in a relevant manner.

It can be understood, therefore, that organization renewal is concerned with the manner in which an organization's people, first, confront situations and search for solutions to them, and second, cope with facts and circumstances in implementing solutions. Solutions can be, and not infrequently are, found without appropriate processes, being achieved by vaguely intuitive or haphazardly venturesome actions, and with little understanding of what really has happened once the dust has settled. Or they can be accomplished by one of the formally structured methodologies based on directive or participative management currently espoused by different organizational theorists. Intuitive solutions, while occasionally unavoidable, are sometimes as harmful as wishful bookkeeping and seldom add to the understanding of cause and effect. Solely directive or participative management is sometimes patently unsuitable in the face of certain circumstances and, therefore, discouraging.

During the past thirty years I have gained an insight into the renewal process through actual line responsibility in widely different organizations. Interspaced with these employments, I have consulted with troubled executives and leaders, conducted research in group and organizational dynamics, and taught behavioral science as it relates to human functioning within organizations. From these associations and the learning they have afforded, I have derived a theme from a combination of the empirical and practical, as well as the behavioral sciences.

Experience and study, therefore, have demonstrated to me that between the two extremes of guesswork and formula there is a middle ground on which most leaders operate. Here they recognize occasions which demand situational leadership—appropriately autocratic or laissez-faire—and other occasions which permit the integration of human resources with conscious renewal processes. Organization renewal can live quite comfortably and effectively in this middle ground.

While every organization has some elements common to a social system, not all organizations are socially or purposively the same. The management of a military unit and a research-oriented electronics firm, or of a youth organization and a steel industry, must necessarily be different in structure, technology, and human interrelationships. Organizations do go through stages of growth, but they occur at varying speeds and in varying orders, and instead of growth there can be retrogression, not only in sales volume but also in the facility of problemsolving. A new, fast-moving research enterprise specializing in computer services may reach spectacular volume quickly, but never reach mature management; whereas a company manufacturing farm equipment may take fifteen years to reach a similar financial position, but enjoy problemsolving maturity within a relatively short period of time. One reason for this lies in the personality and understanding of the principals. But organizations are also affected in many complex ways by external forces, not the least of which are kaleidoscopic economic patterns, governmental regulations, population trends and mobility, community tension, international conflict, and competition. Such forces will have increasing effect on organizations in the nineteen-seventies. These factors often require reaction that some pseudo human relations advocates would disparage as nonparticipative. Still, survival should not be sacrificed willy-nilly on the altar of nonarbitrary decision-making.

Most businessmen soon come to know that it is neither possible nor particularly desirable to involve everyone in everything. It is advisable to distinctly separate "need to know" from "need to involve," to make the areas of "freedom" and "nonfreedom" clearly understood so that individual roles, functions, and actions are encompassed within a framework of reality. I am convinced that few organizations can function very long, or very effectively, as "one big happy family" or as a "well-oiled machine." They cannot even provide all possible information to their participants; all their employees do not even care to know all there is to know. Without at all deprecating the values of productive group interaction, I must admit that there are some things groups cannot accomplish, some things they should not be asked to try.

It is practicable, however, to take into account that individuals, dyads, and groups within organizations are "systems" in a biological, psychological, sociological, and anthropological sense, and that organizations themselves are social as much as technological systems. The concept of the organization as a socio-technical system is entirely valid and, rather than urge the democratic overtones of participative management upon every situation, leaders would do better to take advantage of *all* the contributions that management and behavioral sciences have made to understanding how and why a socio-technical system functions best. We know, for example, that the human organism is a lot tougher than we give it credit for being, that the individual can absorb more punishment than we ordinarily suspect, and that he is not always injured by not always being involved.

I cannot agree that any one style of leadership characterizes successful leadership. Generally speaking, effective leadership is that behavior which is most appropriate to the situation at the time. Rather than assuming a predetermined leadership mode, the leader must respond to, concurrently, the nature of the problem, the needs of his organization, the interacting environmental forces, and the capabilities of all the individuals concerned. Nor can I deny the efficacy of sometimes treating symptoms while diagnosing the long-range nature of organizational problems. It may well be that employee thievery or strident discontent over parking spaces are symptomatic of deeper troubles, but the damage they cause should not be ignored in favor of pursuing only underlying dissatisfactions.

Another unwarranted shibboleth is the implication that organization renewal concerns itself exclusively with the relationships between top management and nonmanagerial personnel. We are closer to beneficial truth when we dispel the feelings of worry, impotence, and insecurity that haunt those in middle management. In the same vein, the rapid growth of professional positions and roles has made it imperative to accept and encourage multiple loyalties as a way of organizational life. Loyalty to, and interest in, a profession for its own sake, within reason, is an avenue that generally leads to individual growth of far greater value to an organization than strictly corporate loyalty can hope to develop.

For many decades we believed that effective decision-making was the essential goal of leadership, ignoring the now rather plain truth that an unimplemented decision, no matter how correct, is meaningless. The mere dropping of a signed directive into an "out box" is too often conceived as being similar to rubbing Aladdin's Lamp rather than, realistically, as only a fractional step in the total process of problem-solving.

"But," says a leader, "that's really all I have to do. My organization is so organized and trained that everyone operates as a member of a team." It is easy to see why this well-intentioned but thoughtless leader may come a cropper on the shoals of teamwork, training, and communications —because he does not truly understand their actualities and potentialities.

Teamwork, of course, is desirable, but in itself it does not solve problems; it only makes it possible for groups of persons to relate to each other as they confront problems, and thus get to work more quickly because they do not have to have "warm-up time." Training in skills alone is exceedingly sterile when it comes to organizational improvement. The best training in the use of a typewriter, machine tool, or slide rule cannot provide a capability to reason in situational response. Problem-solving, therefore, requires that individuals and groups be so developed as to achieve adaptability to organizational climates, crises, and procedures. Two-way communication within an organization may be, and often is, deceptively superficial, lacking the practices of "leveling" and "confrontation." There is a multitude of subterfuges to be found after passing through a policy-ordained "open door."

I have so far brushed lightly by several things that are too frequently misunderstood or taken for granted by leaders of organizations. They are not altogether to blame, however, because one or more of these aspects of organization renewal somehow has been overlooked by many of our contemporary organizational theorists. It is my intention to discuss these things in detail in succeeding chapters. First, however, it may be helpful to present an overview of my concept of the cyclical or loop-system nature of organization renewal. As suggested by Figure 1-1, the growth stages of an organization are an outcome of the way situations are confronted by organizational management. For the sake of clarity, keep in mind that the word "growth," as used here, does not have the same meaning as it does in the market place. It does not refer to growth of stock or capital assets. The concept here is that of progressing toward a potential capacity to achieve organizational objectives, to maintain and improve the organization's internal systems, and to adapt to the external environment. In its various stages, this resembles the mental and psychological growth of an individual from boyhood to manhood, with correspondingly increased maturity not only in physical actions but also in reasoning out problems, making ideas known to others, judgment in thoughts and reactions, and getting along with people. This comparison is satisfactory, however, only if we remember that it is the people making up an organization who solve the problems, not the organization itself. When these people, working together, gain maturity in reasoning, communication, wisdom, and rapport, it can be said that the organization they form is achieving growth.

While we might think of growth of an organizational system as relatively orderly, like that of the human organism, it must cope with internal ineffectiveness, external forces, and various forms of crises that confront it at each stage of growth. These crises bring into focus the multiple deficiencies in the system. If an organization does not cope with these confrontations or crises, it may not move upward to the next stage

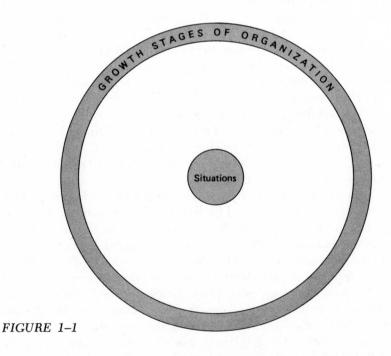

FIGURE 1–1

of growth—it may retrogress to a lower stage of growth. The stages of growth and maturity through which an organization might pass are discussed in Chapter 2.

In using the word "situations" as the focal point of the circular process of organization renewal, it is intended that the multiple and complex nature of such words as "problem-solving," "confrontation," "crisis," and "everyday decision" be included. More will be said about the differences in the various degrees of situational intensity, but let it suffice in this conceptual model for us to recognize that "situations" may refer to such things as the death of the leader of the organization, inadequate cash flow to maintain financial stability, an embarrassing error in an annual report, or the pickets posted at the main gate when a strike is in progress.

Since people constitute "sub-systems" of the larger organizational system—as discussed in Chapter 3—our next step is to indicate diagrammatically that they solve situational problems and contribute to the growth stages of the organization of which they are a part (see Figure 1–2).

The reality of social systems is well annotated in behavioral science research on organization. Besides the typical superior-subordinate rela-

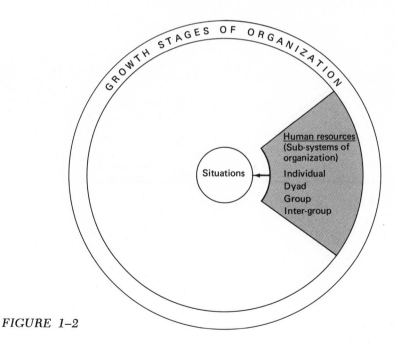

FIGURE 1–2

tionship, the work group behavioral phenomena with the powerful effect of group norms and cohesion, and inter-group conflict between one group and another, there is the well-known reality of informal structures in any modern organization. In addition, organizations are finding it necessary to utilize temporary human sub-systems to achieve goals. These "task forces" or "project groups" are providing new ways of linking appropriate human resources together to achieve results. Such organizational forms will become more prevalent as organizations strive to adapt to new needs and responses in our changing society.

The way human sub-systems accomplish the objectives of their organization, maintain the internal systems, and deal with its environment involves dialogue, confrontation, searching, and coping. This interfacing process is discussed in Chapter 7. It is enough now to advance our conceptual diagram with this in mind (see Figure 1–3).

The use of the word *interfacing* is intentional. It is not enough to utilize the much abused word "communication" as being adequate to describe the *process* by which an organization can realize its potential for renewal and growth. Every organizational system has within it the potentiality for either bringing about its own death, maintaining the status quo, or growing into maturity. To adequately cope with these

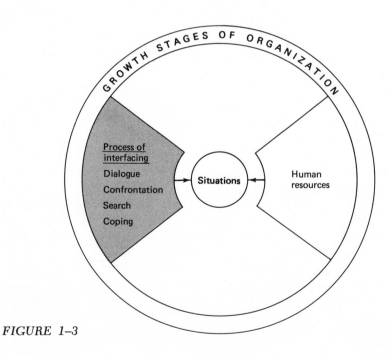

FIGURE 1–3

alternatives, and hopefully to choose the latter, the people in the organization must realistically confront each other, search for ways of finding the meaning of the confrontation, and then deal with the problem or situation under consideration. Such a process will achieve authenticity when the individual can trust the reality of what he feels, reads, and hears in the organization. The process of search will lead toward congruence and credibility of those involved in interfacing, but more important, it will seek the common attitudes, skills, and means by which the coping process may take place.

Although I will frequently refer to effective decision-making and problem-solving as elements of organization renewal, dialogue among the organization's human resources is evidenced when dealing with situations. Decisions are made with respect to situations, rather than situations creating decisions. A situation is not always a problem, but problems are always caused by situations. Situations will test whether individuals and groups are really able to meet many kinds of needs. It is through working on situations and examining the subsequent failures and successes that organizational systems discover the worth of their selection procedure, interfacing process, training program, communication efforts, and development activities.

It is relatively foolish, even in theory, to believe that all responses to situations can be based on predetermined plans, conscious strategy, or objective action. There are occasions when a situation calls for and effectively produces unplanned response. While a great deal of the recent writing on behavioral science and organizational theory has focused on planned change, there is a place for spontaneous action, the seemingly instinctive response, or emotional reaction. It would seem that some of the experts in organizational management wish that all situations could be approached with the kind of rational and unemotional behavior once advocated by a founder of organizational theory—Max Weber. (See Figure 1–4.)

As we examine the process of change in Chapters 7 and 8, I will borrow from the three-step concept of change presented by K. Lewin [1] which encompasses the process of "unfreezing" existing forces, changing the forces, and "refreezing" them at a new level of equilibrium. The way a manager "unfreezes" the forces in a situation may be well planned, based on proper diagnosis of, involvement in, and adherence to the steps in planning change. On the other hand, it may also be appropriate for a manager to utilize his "on the spot" judgment and react with spontaneous competence that is derived from extensive experience, professional education, and training. Both kinds of responses may lead to either appropriate or inappropriate action or change.

Normally, an apparently appropriate action will solve a problem by eliminating or altering a situation. But not always. It can happen that insufficient information has caused misjudgment of the situation. And sometimes—perhaps just to prove the case for human inconsistency— apparently inappropriate action surprises us by somehow dealing with a situation satisfactorily, although it may not contribute to organizational growth. These aspects of organization renewal are discussed later in this book. Either way, however, the action taken or change effected will feed back to block or introduce further organizational growth. U.N. Secretary General U Thant [2] has described this revolution:

> . . . the central stupendous truth about developed economies today is that they can have—in anything but the shortest run—the kind and scale of resources they decide to have. . . . It is no longer resources that limit decisions. It is the decision that makes the resources. This is the fundamental revolutionary change—perhaps the most revolutionary man has ever known.

Organizational situations, goals, and tasks to be accomplished are today more than ever complicated, technical, and unpredictable. Actions and decisions require the collaboration of many persons and cannot flow from the energy or intelligence of any one man, no matter how competent he may be. It is against this setting that we must necessarily evaluate the appropriateness or inappropriateness of responses to situations.

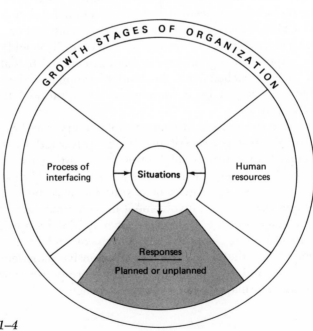

FIGURE 1–4

Another criterion by which to measure the appropriateness of an action is to assess the way it relates to the external environment within which the organization exists. Most attempts to examine organizational dynamics tend to ignore the interrelationship between environmental forces and organizational response. Every organization is embedded in a total environment that conditions its form, decision-making process, and the way it utilizes the resources of the organization. The technological, civil rights, political, economic, and knowledge revolutions are all examples of this modern environment. In appropriately responding to situations, an organization should manifest an awareness of its responsibility to the larger external environment (see Figure 1–5).

An example of the relationship between environment and organizational response is the work of P. Lawrence and J. Lorsch [3] who examine the effects on organizations of an environment which is characterized by rapid rates of technological and market change, and a high degree of uncertainty and unpredictability. The way the managers in a quickly changing environment (such as an electronics industry) will respond is quite different from the way those in the more stable environment of a public utility will.

An industry may be in a quasi-governmental partnership where con-

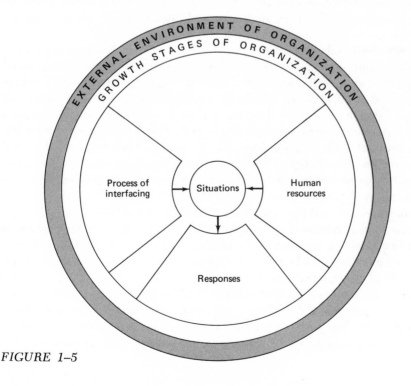

FIGURE 1–5

trols on wages, profits, and processes are important factors in the environment. On the other hand, a new and highly competitive field (such as the plastics industry) is confronted with the need to keep costs at a minimum, react quickly to changing markets, and be constantly alert to the cash flow balance in the corporate budget. This is equally applicable to a volunteer agency (such as the YMCA) which finds its services to a middle-class suburban area not completely relevant to an economically stunted and culturally deprived urban area. If it wants to remain relevant to its constituency and viable as a system, sensitivity and adaption to its wider environment should be a prime consideration for any organization.

Appropriate response, therefore, is defined as those actions which will contribute to improved interfacing in the organization and effective utilization of human resources, and result in growth of the organization and positive adaptation to the environment.

A circular model of organizational functioning emphasizes the need for the organizational system to re-examine its goals, evaluate its performance, and renew its spirit; and it demonstrates that the ability of the socio-technical system to cope is an essential element. The quality of situational coping, therefore, may be aided by a renewal stimulator —an organizational development office, training director, group manager, or some other kind of change agent. In Part Four of this book attention will be given to the role, methods, and qualifications of the renewal process.

Man's continual search for compatibility between his organized relationships and personal growth is being constantly explored by social scientists and practitioners. That kind of organizational system which manifested itself early in history frequently exhibited a high degree of control by managerial coercion that no longer meets the needs of today's organized society or of the individuals in it. The rapid changes in society have brought with them changes in organizational systems, and the need for even greater change. One of the most apparent changes has been control through benevolence and persuasion. Whether viewed from the paternalism of large organizations in the thirties in the United States, or the more recent "sell-the-other-fellow" approach used by some sales and pseudo human relations advocates, such control has been very much in evidence in the leadership of industrial, governmental, social, and welfare organizations. In fact, some writers [4] give a great deal of credence to this kind of organizational leadership.

There is, however, a third way by which at least one other author [5] in the management field believes influence and power can be manifested in organizational life. With him I feel that an *existential pragmatism*, taking into account—as the situation exists at the present moment—the interdependent nature of renewal for individuals, groups, organizations, and environment, is the appropriate managerial response for the viable organization of tomorrow.

In referring to this existential pragmatism as an "E Concept," I am purposefully building upon the clarity with which Douglas McGregor challenged the field of management with his two contrasting theories. The concept represented in his Theory "X" was the traditional way in which management or managers "controlled" the human resources of an organization, based upon the assumptions that man is inherently lazy, unwilling to assume responsibility, and resistant to change. Here, the values underlying the bureaucratic organizational model imply that man is not fully utilized, growth is inhibited, and his motivations not fully released. In his Theory "Y" he bases his concept on some assumptions about the humanistic values deeply rooted in the nature of man. Here we see the application of those values and beliefs that indicate that man does wish to grow, to influence and control his own destiny, and to maximize the human worth of himself and other people. While McGregor did not intend to dichotomize the field, it frequently has this effect on those who argue for one position or the other.

In advancing an "E Concept" of managerial leadership, it is not my intention solely to compromise or integrate McGregor's two managerial theories. It is my belief that as we complete the twentieth and enter the twenty-first century, the character of few men will fit exclusively either Theory "X" or Theory "Y," as later pointed out by McGregor himself in his book, *The Professional Manager*.

Let me first indicate that like Harvey Cox,[6] I am a strong believer in the reality of organizations as a way of life. We cannot, and should not hanker after Thoreau's Walden Pond. As Cox states:

> We must first realize that the organization is here to stay. There is simply no other way to run a world brimming with three billion people in the midst of an industrial epoch. Unless a nuclear war returns us to a culture of hunting and gathering tribes, our world will be increasingly organized as the decades go by. If we choose to live responsibly *in* the world, then we must face the issue of how we can harness organizational power for authentic human purposes.

Many people today have become anti-organization thinkers and want to develop a society wherein only individuals or small groups mature and grow. I do not feel this is an acceptable alternative to our present degree of inability to utilize human resources collectively and creatively in organizations. The very nature of modern organizations places a requirement on the nature of those who manage them, and the evolving and relevant social system in today's world certainly offers a number of choices for maximizing human effort.

Cox indicates that while today's organizations are characterized by *anonymity* and *mobility,* these may not be completely negative forces. He elaborates the thesis that present-day organizations are marked by these four attributes: [7]

1. The organization is *flexible.*
2. The organization is *future-oriented.*
3. The organization is *secularized.*
4. The organization makes only a *limited claim on its members.*

I find a ring of truth in this presentation. If circumstances demand it, every organization I have known could be reorganized, merged, or disbanded. Tradition is secondary. Organizations are formed to achieve certain future goals, managers are selected on the basis of their ability to solve the resultant problems, and nepotism belongs to a past generation. A modern organization is not bound by rituals or taboos; it makes use of professional and technical capabilities as each situation demands, and this invites the moving of individuals from one organization to another. Lastly, organizations are interested only in a limited claim on the life of an individual. Its power over the lives of its personnel is relative. People have additional loyalties and responsibilities; all of their activities cannot be wrapped up in the organization by which they are employed.

This brings into focus the suitability of the existential or pragmatic manager. He concerns himself with actually working out a problem or an idea. He is interested in tackling situations confronted by the organization and in what will change them; he sees organizational life as a set of problems, not as a mystery, or a set of absolutes, or a systematic ideology. He sees the organization as a resource which should be equipped to respond appropriately to the task or problem confronting it. He encourages and lives with provisional solutions. His existential approach sees the potency and capability of the system to solve problems, even though he recognizes no simple, all-encompassing approach. There is a confidence inherent in this pragmatic and existential approach:

> . . . the fact that we approach life today without feeling the need for a big key that fits everything together as one great whole, and are able to concentrate instead of isolating particular issues and dealing with them as they come up, shows that we have a basic confidence that the world is held together, is strong, is self-consistent, has regularity in it, and can be put to the test without everything in life going to pieces.[8]

This kind of confidence enables us to accept McGregor's Theory "Y" assumptions about people. However, it also places emphasis upon organizational viability, as well as on individual growth and development. Thus, we can see the role of the *renewal stimulator* as bringing the

potentials and complexities of organizational problem-solving into pragmatic focus in the "here and now." In other words, renewal improves
the organic functioning and growth of the system (see Figure 1–6).

The expression "existential pragmatism" as a response pattern by managers is not intended to imply that just any response which works is
adequate. On the contrary, it implies a professional response based upon
effective diagnosis by the manager of the situational forces and persons
in the situation. The situation will encompass environmental forces, including the nature of the problem, organizational requirements, and
the interrelationship of multiple forces.

The manager will need to take into account the needs of the persons
in the situation, and what they can best contribute to the situation as he
releases their potential.

The underlying assumption of Concept "E" management is that the
managerial response will be appropriate when it solves the problem
situation, at the same time strengthening the human resources and the
process of interfacing, and when it contributes to the growth of the
organization while responding realistically to the external environment
(see Figure 1–7).

Some of the ways by which the manager can accomplish this will be
discussed in Chapter 6. It will require the manager to be open in his

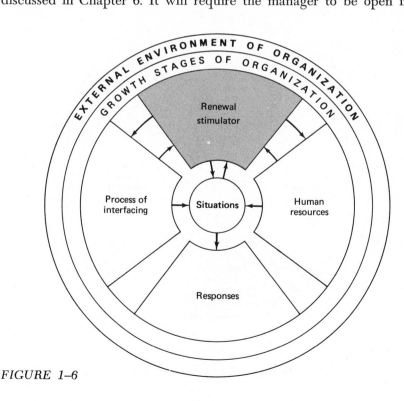

FIGURE 1–6

behavior, professionally responsible in his attitude, and cognizant of the interdependency of his acts.

The expression mentioned earlier, "renewal stimulator," is a generic term inasmuch as it might be instigated, stimulated, and maintained by different people. It might be the chief executive officer of the organization, or the top management trainer, or the head of a particular division or unit.

In many cases we are seeing a training or organizational development office as the source of leadership:

> . . . there was always the correction and the ability to make the training and development department the leading edge, the catalyst for organizational change and adaptability. Rather than performing the more traditional role, these groups became centers for innovation and organizational revitalization, and their leaders emerged as change agents, the new managers of tomorrow's organizations.[9]

In some instances the personnel manager or some part of the manpower planning unit becomes the initiator of a renewal process. A consultant might serve as the catalyst, but a consultative function should

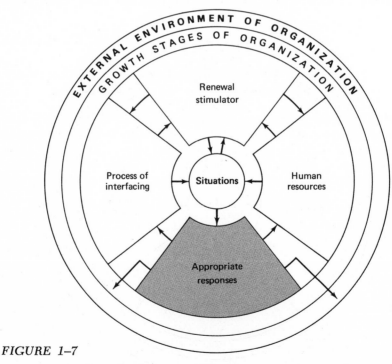

FIGURE 1–7

Circular Process of Organization Renewal

become an integral part of the system itself. The various approaches, methods, and concepts about implementing organization renewal will be discussed in following chapters. It is helpful, however, to highlight at this time some of the questions with which any renewal process will want to deal. These questions are partially based upon thoughts expressed by John Gardner [10] in his stimulating article, "Organizational Dry Rot":

Does the organization have an effective program for the recruitment and development of talented manpower?

Has the organization an environment that encourages individuality and releases individual motivations?

Is there an adequate system of two-way communication in the organization?

Does the organization have a fluid and adaptable internal structure?

Are there ample opportunities and situations where the organization provides a process of self-criticism?

Is the organization able to cope with procedural buildup?

Does the organization have the ability to cope with vested interests?

Has the organization developed effective face-to-face groups for accomplishment of work goals?

Is the organization able to cope with change?

Does a climate of trust exist between individuals and groups in the organization?

How frequently and willingly has the organization evaluated its objectives and purposes, decision-making processes, and goals?

In the past twenty years [11] the behavioral sciences have made an ever-growing contribution to the field of organizational functioning. In the textbooks in schools of business and public administration, in the executive development programs of government and industry, we find constant reference to the mounting importance of behavioral sciences in our understanding of organizational management. One reason has been the increased quality and quantity of research in organizational problems; another, related reason is the increased demand by management for answers to organizational problems that become more and more complex.

Behavioral science and management together cover a vast area. The behavioral sciences are usually thought of as being psychology, sociology, and cultural anthropology. While these may be the three major behavioral sciences, it is well also to include the behavioral aspects of political science, economics, educational psychology, and biology. The behavioral sciences are defined in different terms by different scholars. M. S. Wadia [12] defines it this way: "A behavioral science is a body of systemized knowledge pertaining to how people behave, what is the relationship between human behavior and the total environment, and why people behave as they do.

In a real sense, behavioral science is the study of the problem-solving behavior of man. Using this definition, one can envision readily its importance to the processes, concepts, and practices of management. New findings in the behavioral sciences are relevant to organizations as well as to systems of the culture, but the word "science" should be placed in perspective:

> Pure science is not technology, not gadgetry, not some mysterious cult, not a great mechanical monster. Science is an adventure of the human spirit; it is an essentially artistic enterprise, stimulated largely by curiosity, served largely by disciplined imagination, and based largely on faith in the reasonableness, order and beauty of the universe of which man is a part.[13]

In this spirit, the reader will find that I have related my conceptual frame of reference for organization renewal to the applications of behavioral science. It is obvious that behavioral science research is causing us to re-examine our assumptions about people and their motivation. It is also giving us a better understanding of the behavior pattern of managers and the effects of their leadership within the organization. In this sense, the following implications seem to be most important:

1. THE INCREASED INTERDEPENDENCE BETWEEN THE CREATORS AND APPLIERS OF KNOWLEDGE.   Research coming from behavioral science indicates a need for a closer link between those who do research and create new knowledge, and those who apply such knowledge. A manager who graduated from a school of business administration or public administration ten years ago may now be out of date with respect to his usefulness. Rapid managerial obsolescence emphasizes the need for creative interrelationships between organizational researchers and managers. Their common concerns must be more closely interwoven to stimulate further study and produce mutual benefits.

2. CLOSER FOCUS ON THE EDUCATION OF MANAGERS.   The rate at which managerial knowledge becomes outmoded today makes it almost essential to develop management through both internal and external (to the organization) training and educational programs. Opportunities for managers to acquire new knowledge and skills should have high priority.

3. SITUATIONAL FOCUS ON THE ROLE, SKILLS, AND PRACTICE OF MANAGERIAL LEADERS.   Research on leadership indicates that there is no one concept or simple set of rules for effectiveness. It is increasingly obvious that the manager must examine each situation, and the persons in that situation, to determine the appropriate action. More and more managers are coming to realize the relative importance of focusing on the situation, as opposed to proceeding on the assumption that

there exists a ready-made set of all-weather techniques which guarantee effective leadership.

4. NEED FOR DEVELOPING ADAPTIVE ORGANIZATIONAL SYSTEMS. Research indicates that the organization of the future must remain adaptive if it is to remain viable. It will need to remain flexible to cope with everchanging consumers, services, production techniques, technical skills, changing marketing conditions, social demands, economic forces, and all the other many factors that affect an organization. A particular theory of management suggesting that an extreme of either scientific management or human relations is the right approach will not be adequate. Management needs to recognize that its organization has to meet the multiple requirements of the various social systems to which it is related.

5. GREATER FOCUS ON THE TRANSACTIONAL NATURE OF MANAGEMENT. Research in the behavioral sciences indicates that the quality of personal interrelationships is far more important than their quantity. In searching for quality, the manager of tomorrow needs to recognize the value of confrontation, of search, and of coping in the process of interfacing.

6. NEED FOR INTEGRATING MANAGEMENT AND BEHAVIORAL SCIENCES. Research in the behavioral sciences indicates that separation of productive work requirements and human relations tends to result in ineffective management. Relatively heavy emphasis on one or the other will be inadequate. A manager needs to see the importance of both and become competent in both. People need a sense of accomplishment and achievement. This is best done through effective work achievement, job enhancement, and production. The systems concept needs to be seen in the perspective of both the social and technical natures of an organization.

7. THE NEED FOR A MANAGER TO BE A DIAGNOSTICIAN RATHER THAN ONLY A TREATER OF SYMPTOMS. Research in the behavioral sciences indicates the importance of the manager's ability to diagnose the causes of people's behavior. The treatment of symptoms is not adequate. Absenteeism, turnover, apathy at staff meetings, and similar phenomena are symptoms, not causes. The manager of tomorrow will be required to understand the dynamics of behavior, to diagnose causes, and to improve the appropriate problem-solving skills needed in particular situations.

While behavioral science is making many contributions to our understanding of organizational complexities, it still has a long way to go in giving definitive answers in many areas. The organization is at the same time an open and closed system that has multiple sub-systems and functions. These sub-systems have mutual dependence and interdependence.

We recognize that the organization exists in a dynamic environment consisting of other systems which affect it, and behavioral scientists have learned to look at managerial effectiveness in terms of all the various organizational complexities.

Earlier theorists of organization were content to talk of measuring effectiveness in terms of adequate profits, efficient service, good productivity or effective employee morale. These things are not adequate in and of themselves. Managers of an organizational system need to define its effectiveness in terms of its capacity to survive, maintain itself, adapt, and develop toward its own goals, and in terms of the performance of multiple functions that also affect society.

> If we view organizations as adaptive, problem-solving, organic structures, then inferences about effectiveness have to be made, not from static measures of output, though these may be helpful but on the basis of the processes through which the organization approaches problems. In other words, no single measurement of organizational efficiency or satisfaction—no single time-slice of organizational performance—can provide indicators of organizational health.[14]

It is hoped that my circular concept of organization renewal will contribute to this search. As Douglas McGregor [15] wrote:

> . . . we are today in a period when the development of theory within the social sciences will permit innovations which are at present inconceivable. Among these will be dramatic changes in the organization and management of economic enterprise. The capacities of the average human being for creativity, for growth, for collaboration, for productivity (in the full sense of the term) are far greater than we have recognized . . . it is possible that the next half century will bring the most dramatic social changes in human history.

In Chapter 2 I will present the stages of organizational growth which should be the prime concern of the renewal process. In the nineteen-seventies there will be an increasing stress placed on organizations to be both *viable* and *relevant* to the society of which they are a part. This will demand that more and more organizations confront their present stage of existence and develop further toward the maturity that will permit them to contribute more effectively to the larger society.

NOTES

1. Kurt Lewin, "Studies in Group Decision," in Dorwin P. Cartwright and Alvin Zander, eds., *Group Dynamics, Research and Theory* (New York: Harper & Row, Publishers, 1953), pp. 287–301.

2. Quoted in Robert Theobold, "Need: A New Definition of Work," *New University Thought*, 1963, p. 11.
3. Paul R. Lawrence and Jay W. Lorsch, *Organization and Environment: Managing Differentiation and Integration* (Boston: Harvard Business School, 1967).
4. Robert N. McMurray, "Case for the Benevolent Autocrat," *Harvard Business Review*, January–February, 1958, p. 32.
5. George S. Odiorne, "The Management Theory Jungle and the Existential Manager," *Academy of Management Journal*, Vol. IX, No. 2, June, 1966, pp. 109–116.
6. Harvey Cox, *The Secular City* (New York: The Macmillan Co., 1966), p. 173.
7. *Ibid.*, p. 176.
8. Harry O. Morton, "The Mastery of Technological Civilization," *The Student World*, First Quarter, 1963, p. 48.
9. Warren G. Bennis, "Organizations of the Future," *Personnel Administration*, September–October, 1967, p. 17.
10. John W. Gardner, "How to Prevent Organizational Dry Rot," *Harper's Magazine*, October, 1965, pp. 20–26.
11. The remaining portion of this chapter is a revised version of the author's article, "Implications of the Behavioral Sciences for Management," *Public Personnel Review*, Vol. 27, No. 3, July, 1966. Used by permission.
12. Manek S. Wadia, "Management Education and the Behavioral Sciences," *Advanced Management*, Vol. XXIV, June, 1964, p. 9.
13. Warren Weaver, *Goals for Americans* (Englewood Cliffs, N.J.: Prentice-Hall, Inc., 1956), p. 28.
14. Bennis, *Changing Organizations* (New York: McGraw-Hill Book Co., Inc., 1966), p. 31.
15. Douglas McGregor, *Human Side of Enterprise* (New York: McGraw-Hill Book Company, Inc., 1960), p. 11.

2 GROWTH STAGES OF ORGANIZATIONS

Like people and plants, organizations have a life cycle. They have a green and supple youth, a time of flourishing strength, and a gnarled old age. . . . An organization may go from youth to old age in two or three decades, or it may last for centuries.

JOHN GARDNER, 1912–

In the last half of the twentieth century we have seen the emergence of research and action in applying planned change efforts to organizations, whereas previously planned change tended to be applied rather precisely to individuals and group situations.

Organization renewal, with which we are dealing here, involves planned change. In examining approaches to organization renewal, there have been three models identified by Bennis [1] which provide a frame of reference by which to understand the somewhat new formulation I present:

EQUILIBRIUM MODEL OF ORGANIZATIONAL CHANGE. This approach places value on developing a "conflict free" social structure. It is seen as desirable to release tensions in the organization and try to make sub-systems less defensive. The planned change efforts focus on identifying problem areas and try to alleviate tensions through whatever means of catharsis, group discussion, or problem clarification seems to be appropriate to the situation.

DEVELOPMENT MODEL OF ORGANIZATIONAL CHANGE. In this approach an attempt is made to develop authentic and open relationships among the persons in the organization so that human and interpersonal values are furthered to help the organization maintain itself and grow. The goal here is to develop interpersonal competence among the individual members of the organization so that they can carry out valid communication in the formal and informal aspects of organizational life. The use of T-Group and laboratory training to improve the interpersonal skills, attitudes, and values of persons in the organization is one of the major means in achieving such a goal.

ORGANIC MODEL OF ORGANIZATIONAL CHANGE. A third model of organizational change identified by Bennis rests on the desirability of achieving team management in the organic functioning of the various units of the organization. The work of Blake and Mouton [2] in applying the managerial grid concept to organizational change is a foremost example. The desirability of management acquiring new concepts for teamwork leadership, so that they can solve organizational problems, is a basic premise; and the need for management to be adaptive and collaborative is stressed.

My concept is based on the idea developed with Warren Schmidt [3] that organizations have stages of potential growth in their life cycles, and that each experiences crises and situations demanding certain management and/or organizational responses that are indispensable if the organization is to achieve its next stage of growth. I call this a *situational confrontation model.*

Such a model, closely related to the organic change concept, stresses the need for reality assessment within the organization with respect to its present state of affairs, for identification of the key issues or concerns the organization is now facing, and for planned efforts to confront that situation with those activities or actions which will help cope with the present situation to achieve growth for the people, the process, and the organization. The emphasis on situational confrontation re-emphasizes the relevance of the existential leadership concept discussed in Chapter 1.

This model of organization renewal sees the organization as a sociotechnical system, a term first developed by Eric Trist and his associates at the Travistock Institute, London, England. The organization is thought of in terms of a multifaceted "personality" or organism. For a long time the law has dealt with organizations as if they were persons, and the same viewpoint can be applied to the birth and potential maturity of an organizational enterprise.

We know that many organizations die aborning, or nearly so, while a few, such as Lloyd's of London and DuPont, seem to live forever. Perhaps this indicates that the bedrock of any discussion of organization renewal—whatever the limitations or disadvantages of such an analogy —lies in an examination of what happens when we apply theories of personality development to the creation, growth, maturization, and decline of a business organization. This may be an initial step toward helping us understand and predict organizational growth and give useful answers to some typical introspective questions:

Why don't we have the spirit of excitement we used to have?
Why can't the various departments pull together instead of competing and undermining one another's efforts?

Why do we seem to have so many conflicting pressures and so much confusion?

Why can't our people understand that we have to economize if we are going to survive?

Most managers learn the dimensions and characteristics of *financial* problems within an organization because these kinds of problems are reducible to familiar, inflexible, finite terms. But the problems that are common to organizational growth, being largely derived from *nonfinancial situations*, are more difficult because they are seldom finite, and because they are often a matter of subjective judgment.

As illustrated in Table 2–1, the entire continuum of an organization's life falls within three developmental stages—birth, youth, and maturity. Some organizations succeed in reaching higher stages of development than others, but organizations usually go into decline only because of internal mismanagement or drastic changes in external environment. The objective of organization renewal is to handle the key issues of development in such a way as to achieve higher stages progressively, and to preclude a decline toward a lower stage. Here, since we are not discussing financial status, it is important clearly to understand each of the three basic stages. The birth stage is by no means limited to the level of a "cottage industry," nor is the maturity stage confined to the level of organizational giants. A comparatively small business organization may reach developmental maturity, and a comparatively large one may remain youthful. Thus, the criteria for determining the stage of development of an organization probably are found more in the manner of coping with predictable key issues than in the number of employees, its share of the market, or its managerial sophistication.

From this point of view, an organization is an assemblage of people, procedures, and facilities that is a *socio-technical system* and which, during the developmental stages, experiences at least six critical concerns or confrontations. The fundamental issues posed by these concerns may occur at almost any time, and the problems they create tend to reoccur. The answers are partially supplied every day, directly or indirectly, by precedents set by the acts and words of managers and workers as they conduct the organization's affairs or produce its products or services. Nevertheless, at certain times it is inevitable that one of these issues will acquire exceptional importance, and that the organization must then recognize, confront, and cope with a paramount critical concern. This is similar to the problems an individual must resolve at certain times in his life—the problems of puberty and aging, for example—if he is to have a healthy personality. Renewal—whether individual or organizational—may occur at any time in the growth cycle.

TABLE 2–1

Stages of Organizational Growth

Develop-mental stage	Critical concern	Key issue	Consequences if concern is not met
BIRTH	1. To create a new organization	What to risk	Frustration and inaction
	2. To survive as a viable system	What to sacrifice	Death of organization
			Further subsidy by "faith" capital
YOUTH	3. To gain stability	How to organize	Reactive, crisis-dominated organization
			Opportunistic rather than self-directing attitudes and policies
	4. To gain reputation and develop pride	How to review and evaluate	Difficulty in attracting good personnel and clients
			Inappropriate, overly aggressive, and distorted image building
MATURITY	5. To achieve uniqueness and adaptability	Whether and how to change	Unnecessarily defensive or competitive attitudes; diffusion of energy
			Loss of most creative personnel
	6. To contribute to society	Whether and how to share	Possible lack of public respect and appreciation
			Bankruptcy or profit loss

SOURCE: Gordon L. Lippitt and Warren H. Schmidt, "Crises in a Developing Organization," *Harvard Business Review*, Vol. 45, No. 6, November–December, 1967, p. 103. Copyright © 1967 by the President and Fellows of Harvard College.

The confrontations of an organization, within itself and within its environment, and the questions they raise, are as much a test of organizational growth as individual crises are a test of human fitness. Similarly, the answers which are provided reflect the will and wisdom of its leaders, and organizational maturity, just as an individual's responses to his crises are a measure of his aims, perspicacity, and success. Let us, therefore, examine in some detail the six critical concerns and response patterns in the order in which they are most likely to occur from birth through maturity of an organization.

SIX CRITICAL STAGES AND RESPONSE PATTERNS

1. LAUNCHING THE VENTURE. Here the entrepreneurs confront the crucial question: *What and how much are we willing to risk?* The following two examples typify the extent to which they might be willing to gamble:

> In 1961 two professors of psychology at a well-known Southern university experimented with a new theory of programmed learning in which two learners worked together, each reinforcing the other. The professors created a unique methodology for this. Fascinated by the commercial possibilities of the theory and its potential contribution to society, the men decided to take the risk of abandoning their professorial seniority at the university and investing their savings to develop and promote their idea. Next, they persuaded others to join the venture. Friends put up "faith capital," and their employees took a chance on receiving a salary. An organization was born, but its chance of survival depended on many unknowns. It exists today as a successful enterprise only because all concerned gambled heavily.

The principle revealed in this simple illustration is repeated over and over again in our country. Every new restaurant, dry cleaner, or small electronics engineering firm, of which literally hundreds are born annually, rests on risk. Some of them, if they have taken the right risks, may succeed as the Xerox Corporation has:

> Joseph C. Wilson, then president of a small paper company, learned of a new process for electrostatic copying developed by an obscure inventor. He persuaded his friends and associates to undertake enormous risks to make Xerography a success. Wilson expressed his philosophy in these words: "Great opportunities are given to those who are willing to take advantage of the new . . . [if they are] willing to accept great risk in doing so."

Management must decide how much risk to take in the light of two criteria: the goals by which achievement is to be measured, and the odds against success in reaching them. As we shall see, not only is risk involved in initial investment; it is also involved in each step along the path to full organizational development. But the concern is usually greatest at the beginning.

A man gets an idea for a new product or service. The idea alone is not enough. It must be linked to plans and resources and manpower to become a reality. A socio-technical system must come into being. Many questions must be asked and answered—about markets, competition, location, costs, manpower, and procedures. All of these questions remain hypothetical, however, until this critical question is answered: *Who is willing to risk the dollars, time, energy, and reputation to give this idea a chance to prove its worth?* Once this commitment is made with sufficient strength to give the idea impetus, an organization is born and a new product or service is offered in the market place.

2. SURVIVAL AND SACRIFICE. Now that it is underway, the organization quickly experiences its next crisis—the ability to survive as a viable system—and the question raised for management is: *How much are we willing to sacrifice?* Finding the answer may require agonizing soul-searching, as this illustration demonstrates:

Eight years ago, an organization was created by three leaders in the field of behavioral science, each of whom brought with him several pet ideas for marketable products, in addition to expertise in providing consultation and training for prospective clients. Altogether, the three entrepreneurs attempted to develop twenty-eight new products, including, for example, an audience-reaction measurement device, prepackaged conference setups for hotels, a means of video-taping human behavioral actions in group situations, and a series of self-learning publications for managers. A rapid accumulation of debt and the spending of countless hours after the normal work day trying to cope with unfamiliar problems in production and financing soon forced the leaders to make a hard decision. They came to realize that most of the ideas they had favored were inappropriate to the organization they had created. It was painful to surrender the dreams, and difficult to go back to doing only what they did best. But survival dictated reliance on a hard-core activity of consultation and training, with the sacrifice of all their beloved plans, except the publications. The organization is eminently successful today only because it was willing and able to sacrifice.

It is axiomatic in risk enterprise that each gain, except a windfall, must be accompanied by the deferment of something else. Each gain in the struggle toward organizational development more often than not requires, usually in some combination, a corresponding individual loss of savings, leisure, energy, health, time with family or friends, comfort, or peace of mind. Or the loss may be represented by a deferment of something desired by the individual—for instance, adequate income, a new car, a vacation, or the opportunity to seize a tempting alternative outside the new enterprise. A critical concern develops out of the necessity to make a choice between values. The decision-controlling factors are the length of time the sacrifice must or can be tolerated, and the validity of the sacrifice in terms of survival. Here, as its leaders face difficult decisions while still in the birth stage, there can be exhibited an initial investment in organizational growth. In other words, the way in which these decisions are made contributes to the process of "growing up."

Organizations are born in a climate of excitement and hope; they must survive in a world of test and challenge. A business organization, at any stage of development, is by nature a jeopardized creation. Half of all new businesses in the United States fail to survive their first year of operation, and less than half the remainder continue to operate after the second year. Accounting for this high mortality are many factors, including poor products or services, lack of planning and foresight, unrealistic assessment of the market, inadequate capitalization, and leadership inexperience. Companies which are not mortally weak in these respects still cope with threats to their survival, so that those who bear the risk and responsibility of creation must repeatedly decide whether and how much they are willing to sacrifice. This is a time for soul-searching and constant reassessment of long-range aspirations.

Some organizations remain a long time on a survival plateau, where dedicated effort results only in marginal returns and where continued survival depends on the confidence and commitment of the leadership.

3. ACHIEVEMENT OF STABILITY. If the organization survives, it is then confronted by a third concern which raises the question: *How willing are we to be organized and to accept and enforce discipline?* For instance:

A well-established firm, engaged in filling dispenser cans with liquids under pressure, had a highly effective vice president for marketing. He was young and personable, and most of the clients enjoyed dealing with him. He was, in fact, a driving force, a one-man show, and both employees and clients related to him naturally and by preference.

When the market expanded under the demand for aerosol dispensers for household use, the founder moved up to become chairman of the board, and the young vice president took over as president. There, instead of being a well-liked salesman, he had to be a professional manager. Although he was fully *capable* of filling his new position, delegation and efficiency eluded him because he also attempted to maintain all his former personal relationships. The abrupt withdrawal of so dynamic a leader from day-to-day contacts at the working level would have threatened the organization with chaos, but at the same time, the way things were going, he was threatened with personal failure as chief executive officer. Management consultants pointed out that he simply had to relinquish many of the tasks that he had once performed.

A director of personnel was employed who gradually established rapport with the employees. A new director of marketing was introduced to all but three of the leading clients. A competent administrative assistant acted as a buffer between the new president and the many people who thought he and he alone could make decisions. The storm was weathered, and the organization went on to exceptional success because it was willing to discipline itself.

Similarly:

Two young men conceived the idea of an organization that would offer its customers not only more flavors of ice cream, but also "far-out" flavors. The organization was immediately profitable, but as it grew by leaps and bounds, it became more and more enmeshed in nepotism. Regional franchises and leased outlets went to uncles, nephews, and even to second cousins; wives filled some important executive positions. A few of these relatives were efficient producers; most of them were only so-so.

Troubles loomed large as the organization expanded. It became obvious to the founders that the staff members would have to learn to work with strangers. The moment of truth occurred when a vacant regional manager-ship was filled by an "outsider." Performance criteria were finally established, and all members of the management team participated in specific training. The key phrase became "shape up or ship out." Organizational discipline is hard enough to enforce among veteran employees; it is even more difficult to institute among members of a large family. Nevertheless, it was done, equitably and humanely, and the necessary organizational stability was achieved.

As an organization develops, the original leaders undergo varying degrees of trauma in surrendering personal leadership; the expanding hierarchy breeds factions and results in complicated politics; the maintenance of records becomes ever more burdensome; and there is a certain loss of freedom. It becomes hard to decide between further development, with concomitant stability and resilience, and the retention of close relationships and control.

In the birth stage, there is excitement in creation and challenge in survival. The youthful stage is far less dramatic; the organization is accommodating itself to its environment and adjusting its internal operations. Here is where the socio-technical system becomes functional.

As the outside pressures (e.g., market uncertainties, creditors' demands) on such a system diminish, the internal defects become more evident. Interpersonal or intergroup tensions which could be overlooked in the early stage now clamor for attention. Differing expectations of the founders, managers, and workers are freely expressed. Compensation for sacrifices made earlier is demanded in the struggle to distribute recognition, rewards, and profits. Motivation is complicated by the conflicts between short-term personal gain and long-term organizational gain. Management faces problems of training and retraining personnel, developing a team spirit, stabilizing a core clientele, and developing a long-range plan.

Willingness to accept and enforce discipline means recognizing that expansion is not synonymous with organizational growth. The wisdom required to avoid overcommitment of resources is also involved, for this is a time to solidify gains before launching into larger arenas of action.

4. PRIDE AND REPUTATION. Next the organization is concerned with its relationships with its "public." Executives are confronted with the question: *How much are we willing to engage in self-examination?* Here are two cases in point:

An established youth-serving, nonprofit organization established its reputation on various club and group programs for boys and girls from the ages

of eight through twenty-four years. As it expanded into most cities in the
United States, it began to develop buildings with gymnasiums, swimming
pools, and dormitories. The maintenance of such physical and program expansion required increased financial support from the community, particularly suburban areas. As a consequence, in the late nineteen-sixties, this
organization confronted the reality that it was not serving the youth in the
ghetto and inner city. The organization had built its reputation and pride
on serving "all youth" regardless of race, creed, or color. In light of its
desire to measure up to its own goals, the national policy-making group
and staff set up a process of re-examination of programs and services,
developed new means of reaching the underprivileged youth group, and
directed a major share of its resources in that direction.

A large national airline, well organized and managed, had consistently attempted to establish a reputation of outstanding service to the public. Management recognized that stewardesses were a critically important feature of
this service, and had developed an extensive training program for girls
entering this occupation. When the company undertook an expansion of its
stewardess training facilities, management asked an outside consulting firm
to evaluate the entire training program. This was undertaken cooperatively
with the company's training faculty. The resulting study revealed a number
of inadequacies, as well as strengths, in the content of the program. Disproportionate time and attention were being devoted to superficial aspects of
the stewardess' job while more basic functions were slighted. Teaching
methods were often unimaginative; training facilities sometimes make-
shift. The training faculty frequently felt harassed and unrewarded. On
reviewing the findings, management and members of the training faculty
moved to design imaginative training facilities and to streamline their
entire approach to the program. This effort was costly in time and money—
but the airline's pride and reputation depended on it.

Stability can become stagnation unless the organization's leaders are
prepared to look critically at its products or services, and at its internal
and external operations. The organization's "ego" is now a sensitive
reality. Basking in the youthful stage, and no longer quite as much
threatened, it demands recognition. There is a tendency for leaders to
be defensive when their creation is criticized by outsiders. Executives
and employees want to speak with pride of their organization and what
it does; they want to be respected by customers, competitors, and the
public. Public relations assumes great importance and requires a larger
proportion of time and thought. The budget for promotion is expanded;
but promotional efforts are ultimately dependent on the stability of the
organization, the quality of its output, and the performance of those who
make up the managerial team.

Thus, the issue now at hand is whether management can face up to
the constant need to monitor, review, evaluate, and improve. These
actions may be considered by some of the managers to be an unfair
reflection of their abilities—after all, the organization is successful, is it

not? Any attempt to evaluate is interpreted by them as a threat; any attempt to improve their performance is seen as criticism. Quite often, a manager has capabilities which were sufficient only in the birth stage. Forced to choose between "stepping down" or "getting out," he may choose the latter—and thereby almost invariably cause a shock to the socio-technical system. With executive turnover, new managers must be trained in a climate that is new to the trainers themselves. It is because of this that many organizations go into decline. They are victims of two problems:

a. The turnover of personnel constantly alters the "image" received by clients or customers.

b. The new members of the management team cannot share other than vicariously the original feeling of sacrifice and commitment experienced by the founders.

5. DEVELOPING UNIQUENESS. Having made decisions that resolved the crises of youth, the organization enters the stage of maturity and encounters new crises. The first of these has to do with its adaptability. The question before top management is: *Are we willing to direct the changes necessary to make our organization unique?* To illustrate:

A public school that had achieved a fine reputation in the school district decided to develop a unique "human relations" approach to its educational program from the kindergarten through grade twelve. The superintendent, Board of Education, teaching staff, PTA, and students developed the concept and practice of educational experience as a human transaction in which student, parent, teacher, community, and the present social environment are involved. Through the use of sensitivity training for students, parents, teachers, and administrators, the group discussion process in all subjects and learning areas was implemented. Students learned from fellow students. Parents assisted the teacher. Administration became a resource to facilitate learning—not as a bureaucratic or monolithic system. Older students helped younger students. Teachers helped make learning a quest, not a ritual. As a result this school system became a unique demonstration of what a school organization could become and received the attention of educators, community leaders, and parents across the United States.

A Canadian engineering company, fifteen years old and with nearly 1,000 employees, enjoyed an excellent reputation in the techniques of electrical power transmission. The expansion of hydroelectric systems in Canada confronted this organization with a basic decision. Should it attempt to compete with the gargantuan landline companies which were rapidly taking over with the help of enormous outlays of capital, or should it change to take advantage of the unique knowledge possessed by its engineers in the application of microwave technology?

The latter course was equivalent to starting over, rebuilding the engineering, marketing, and financial structures, and once more taking the risk of failure. On the other hand, chances were that most of the company's talented personnel would eventually relocate, and in time intense competition would force capitulation to its powerful antagonists.

After much painful self-examination, the officers and directors decided the values of uniqueness were worth the gamble. Within a few years, this company was serving the governments of twenty-three developing countries throughout the world—designing, installing and operating noncable, non-wire microwave communications systems.

At this stage, perhaps for the first time, management becomes aware of the basic truth in Peter Drucker's statement: [4] "To manage a business is to balance a variety of needs and goals." Thus far in its development, the organization's goals have been changing but are relatively clear-cut. Now the need is for a kind of corporate "self-actualization" (to use A. H. Maslow's phrase [5] for one level in the hierarchy of human needs). The goal is a more subtle one—achievements dictated not by such criteria as survival, stability, and reputation, but by the desire to make full use of the organization's unique abilities. One might assume that no crisis could possibly arise at this mature stage of development, and that the solidarity created in the latter portion of the youthful stage would be immune to innovation or change. This is not always so. The drive for organizational self-actualization leads to decisions that once more involve risk. Certain reactionary forces within management feel that there is more to be lost than was the case in the initial stage of creating the new organism. They point out that the investment in technical experience, acquisitions, market identification, and goodwill should not be endangered without serious consideration. But such conservatism and a desire to avoid uncertainty leads to various harmful inhibitions.

Hopefully, the leaders will be sufficiently far-sighted to realize that fear of change is the greater risk. To outdistance competition in a fluid market requires a constant search for special capabilities and for ways in which they can be applied advantageously. Thus, research and development—sometimes diversification—are introduced in the hope of establishing relative security in an always uncertain future.

6. CONTRIBUTING TO SOCIETY.   Only a relatively small number of organizations ever acquire "blue chip" security and stature. Most companies remain, often by preference, local firms, with simple organization structures, uncomplicated product programs, and ordinary ambitions. But some social systems do advance one step further. Their managements are confronted, as a result, with a new critical issue, one involving the organization's responsibility to society. The question that top executives must wrestle with is: *What are we willing to give to society without expecting a direct return?* For example:

The president and a few of the top executives of a major automobile manufacturing company determined that their firm should introduce new safety devices on every car. This forward-looking program met with opposition from many of the company's directors and not a few of its sales executives. Those opposed to the idea pointed out that the objective of the organization was to outdo its competitors in price as well as in quality; that bankruptcy would make the company unable to serve society at all; or that the provision of extraordinary safety was essentially a calculated public relations program and therefore reprehensible. The president prevailed in this contest, but the attempt to "market" safety was a flat failure. The public simply was not interested. This company, a year or two later, bitterly opposed the federal government's automotive safety campaign. It had acted independently in its pioneering program, but the experience had been both expensive and disillusioning.

Once orderly internal control and a comfortable financial position are achieved, a company often feels a powerful desire to gain society's respect and appreciation. This desire differs in nature from the external attitudes sought by promotional and public relations activities, which are manifestations of bargaining between the organization and its markets. By contrast, the search for respect and appreciation for their own sake is largely prompted by defensiveness or morality. The search may be self-serving too, but that is not the primary motive.

It is not the manner in which these image-building actions are executed that creates an organizational crisis, but rather the degree of organizational growth and the capacity of that growth to handle properly the soul-searching decision of whether to undertake them at all. The achievement of a particular kind of attitude requires the expenditure of funds and entails some risk that many stockholders and not a few controllers and directors can neither understand nor accept.

Institutional advertising in its pure form, and various kinds of community relations programs, such as publicized anti-pollution efforts, are typical of the defensive methods used by business to forestall the castigation once dealt out to "heedless robber barons" and "heartless trusts." These efforts may also produce indirect benefits in the marketplace, and in a few cases they may help to protect the company against legal threats (for example, more stringent anti-pollution laws).

Because the force behind these image-building actions is often obscure, they are not always conducive to tranquil relationships in managerial hierarchy. There is always another demand for the money, always an investment opportunity somewhere that cannot be exploited if the image-building program is carried out. Lately, however, some organizations have accepted the idea that contributions to the social, political, and environmental welfare of the community, state, and/or nation are good business.

Less defensively oriented but not less self-serving are actions to improve organizational employees as people. Management, in its search for organizational growth, looks inward and asks: *How can we help our executives and workers to develop themselves?* It also occasionally looks outward and asks: *How can we help our community, our nation?* or, *How can we use our resources to improve the quality of human life?*

Positive answers to these questions take many forms. Scholarship programs are originated, educational television is sponsored, executives are loaned to government, key personnel are encouraged to perform civic services, foundations are established. And yet almost all activities of this nature involve some potential risk created by the complications of politics, taste, discretion, opinion, or equity. The severeness of crises generated by efforts to be respected and appreciated as an organization depends on the extent of the conceived organizational need, the organization's financial status, and its own self-image. It also depends on how much the anticipated benefit happens to irritate certain people. There is no intention here to imply that attempts to make worthwhile contributions—for any reason—should not be made by organizations. The truth is that our society is becoming more or less dependent on such contributions, and that a corporate system probably reaches its zenith in development when it finds itself able and willing to so contribute.

The attention of most organizations fluctuates between the six critical needs and issues described above, and perhaps other issues as well, with executives dealing primarily with one now, and then another. Failures do not happen so much because managers do not manage what they know should be managed, but because they do not recognize the significant crises that occur in the organizational life cycle. Or, in John Gardner's words,[6] "Most ailing organizations have developed a functional blindness to their own defects. They are not suffering because they cannot *solve* their problems, but because they cannot *see* their problems."

Recognition of the problem, however, is only the beginning. Problem-solving involves developing a common understanding of the problem and all its implications. If all the members of a management team recognize the developmental stage of their organization, they are better able to understand why certain ambitions must be curtailed while others are advanced, and why and when another need is paramount in importance.

Table 2–2 shows a broad model of some typical results arising from correct and incorrect responses to critical issues. Bear in mind that the crises mentioned above do not always occur in consecutive order; a company may find itself facing an old crisis all over again. For example, new competition, declining markets, or other developments may repeatedly thrust a mature organization or one of its sub-systems into a survival confrontation.

Confusion and intolerance occur in an organization when the true nature of a crisis is misunderstood, and its priority is therefore depreciated. If one group at the management level is striving for organiza-

TABLE 2–2

Results of Handling Organizational Crises

Critical issue	Result if the issue is resolved . . . Correctly	Incorrectly
CREATION	New organizational system comes into being and begins operating	Idea remains abstract. The organization is undercapitalized and cannot adequately develop and expose product or service
SURVIVAL	Organization accepts realities, learns from experience, becomes viable	Organization fails to adjust to realities of its environment and either dies or remains marginal—demanding continuing sacrifice
STABILITY	Organization develops efficiency and strength, but retains flexibility to change	Organization overextends itself and returns to survival stage, or establishes stabilizing patterns which block future flexibility
PRIDE AND REPUTATION	Organization's reputation reinforces efforts to improve quality of goods and service	Organization places more effort on image-creation than on quality product, or it builds an image which misrepresents its true capability
UNIQUENESS AND ADAPTABILITY	Organization changes to take fuller advantage of its unique capability and provides growth opportunities for its personnel	Organization develops too narrow a specialty to ensure secure future, fails to discover its uniqueness and spreads its efforts into inappropriate areas, or develops a paternalistic stance which inhibits growth
CONTRIBUTION	Organization gains public respect and appreciation for itself as an institution contributing to society	Organization may be accused of "public be damned" and similar attitudes; or accused of using stockholder funds irresponsibly

SOURCE: Gordon L. Lippitt and Warren H. Schmidt, "Crises in a Developing Organization," *Harvard Business Review*, Vol. 45, No. 6, November–December, 1967, p. 109. Copyright © 1967 by the President and Fellows of Harvard College.

tional stability while another group believes the essential need is to build a reputation, each group may become highly critical of the way the other spends money or time. The two groups tend to become competitive rather than supportive, simply because they do not understand the basic assumptions being made by their colleagues. It is the function of leadership to clarify such differences and to direct the consolidated efforts of the organization toward the resolution of the basic issue that is paramount at the moment.

Once the organizational leadership has established common understanding among sub-unit managers, it must then remember that the way an organization deals with each crisis inevitably affects its capability and flexibility in dealing with succeeding or recurring issues. This is the essence of organizational growth. For instance:

The way risk is shared by the founders at the birth of a company will thereafter influence expectations, and therefore decisions, during the developmental stages. If one person takes too high a risk at the outset, or if the distribution of risk among several founders is very uneven, the effect may be to hasten and intensify the critical concern of survival during the birth stage, prevent adequate self-examination during the youthful stage, and eliminate any chance of progression to a more advanced stage.

Extraordinary sacrifices made by individuals during the birth stage can become a permanent and discouraging characteristic of their role in the organization, leading key managers to become fearful of further development on the grounds that such sacrifices may have to be repeated.

Efforts during the youthful stage to stabilize the organization and make it more efficient can lead to excessive restrictions and controls, and to the establishment of autonomous groups. The result may be to dampen creativity in decision-making and encourage inter-group conflict.

Certain recognizable, nonfinancial crises occur in the life cycle of an organization. Management cannot control the emergence of these issues; it can only control *how* they are resolved. Effective resolution will involve many different areas of knowledge, skill, and attitude on the part of management as it copes with each critical need. In discussing leadership (Chapter 6), I will try to explain why it is that a manager who is effective in one developmental stage may prove to be quite ineffective in another stage. The growth cycle is only one of a number of factors which influence managerial style, but it should be mentioned that leadership requirements differ at different stages of organizational growth.

The manager who is good at setting short-range objectives and taking great risks at the birth of an organization may be much less useful in shaping long-range plans and laying the groundwork for growth when the organization is seeking stability during its youthful stage. The manager who can act directly and decisively in a crisis of survival may prove to be less than adroit in guiding the search for uniqueness. The managerial capabilities required at various times in an organization's life cycle come into sharper focus when we examine specific issues together with the problems and needs for action which are precipitated.

Of course, management's behavior is only one element of the socio-technical system. Management objectives and actions must be clear to all the members of an organization if they are to be prepared to confront and cope with situations successfully. For this, they need a common viewpoint and frame of reference. It is therefore more important than ever that managers keep asking the kinds of questions discussed earlier—in particular:

What is the critical concern we face now?

How clearly do all our key personnel recognize this concern?

How can we resolve this growth stage confrontation in a way that creates a sound base for dealing with future crises?

What promotes organizational growth?

By asking such questions candidly and resisting the temptation to indulge in sophistic detours in arriving at answers, managers can broaden their capacity to provide effective leadership in an organization. In the practical application of organization renewal, this will require those in leadership positions to provide opportunities for members of the organization to assess "where" they may be in the growth process and the implications of the particular stage of growth which they are experiencing. Methods for implementing such a process will be illustrated later in the book. The organization renewal process is built upon the need for managers and groups in the organization to confront such issues and initiate an appropriate response which will contribute to problem-solving while strengthening the human resources, relationships, and growth of the organization.

NOTES

1. Warren G. Bennis, *Changing Organizations* (New York: McGraw-Hill Book Co., Inc., 1966), Chapter 7.
2. Robert E. Blake and Jane S. Mouton, "A 9.9 Approach to Organization Development," in D. Zand and P. Buchanan, eds., *Organization Development: Theory and Practice* (in press).
3. Gordon L. Lippitt and Warren H. Schmidt, "Crises in a Developing Organization," *Harvard Business Review*, Vol. 45, No. 6, November–December, 1967, pp. 102–112.
4. Peter F. Drucker, *The Practice of Management* (New York: Harper & Row, Publishers, 1954), p. 62.
5. Abraham H. Maslow, *Motivation and Personality* (New York: Harper & Row, Publishers, 1954), p. 102.
6. John W. Gardner, "How to Prevent Organizational Dry Rot," *Harper's Magazine*, October, 1965, p. 20.

3   SOCIAL SYSTEM ELEMENTS OF ORGANIZATIONS

A social organism of any sort whatsoever, large or small, is what it is because each member proceeds to his own duty with a trust that the other members will simultaneously do theirs.

WILLIAM JAMES, 1842–1910

Man has *always* searched for compatibility between his organized relationships and his individual growth. For centuries, the control of his organizations has been characterized by managerial patterns which are now considered by many management and behavioral scientists to be no longer adequate for the needs of most organizations or of the individuals in them. In other words, until comparatively recently the organization has not been viewed as a social system with growth characteristics, much less a system of systems; nor has it been recognized that the sub-systems making up an organization have certain things in common. Today, our conceptual grasp enables us better to understand that:

Organizations are extremely complex systems. As one observes them they seem to be composed of human activities on many different levels of analysis. Personalities, small groups, inter-groups, norms, values, attitudes all seem to exist in extremely complex multidimensional patterns. The complexity seems at times almost beyond comprehension. Yet it is this very complexity that is, on one hand, the basis for understanding organizational phenomena, and on the other, that makes life difficult for an administrator.[1]

The modern organizations of man are becoming ever larger. We live and work in an environment of big organizations: business, government, labor, agriculture, religion, voluntary agencies. Such large scale, usually rationalized, frequently formalized, and hopefully efficient types of organizations are a major reality of the twentieth century.

Some of the significant effects of "bigness" are *specialization, fragmentation of knowledge, coordination*—the bringing together of human and other resources to achieve certain conditions in organizations, to produce a product, to solve a problem, to do a job—and, finally, *integration.*

There are some significant effects of living in and through big organizations. Some of these are the feelings of remoteness, powerlessness, and impersonalness. There are the feelings of isolation and of conformity—emphasized by incompatible and anti-maturing demands.

We need to understand organizations better. In them we find many of our satisfactions and frustrations; in them we achieve or fail, individually and as a society. Through organizations we realize our aspirations or are manipulated into the realization of alien goals.

Basically organization means regularity and predictability in people's relationship with each other. A collection of people may have all the trappings of organization but have no real organization in the sense of regularity and predictability. Regularity can be achieved formally by making explicit rules, regulations, and procedures—and informally by developing a regularity that comes from living and working together. Therefore, an organization is not a thing, but a way of relating human beings so as to work toward shared objectives.

In observing organizations we are frequently in the predicament of the blind men and the elephant. The phenomena of organization, and particularly of individuals in organizations, are too many and too complex to be observed in total and all at once. When one or two people have a job to do, there are no serious problems in knowing what the job is and being able to communicate about it. When many people try to work on a larger job, there will be less understanding about the job and difficulties in communicating accurately about it.

Our solution to this problem has been to ask one person to stop working directly on the job, and *coordinate* the work of other people so as to reduce the duplication of effort and make sure all parts of the job are being accomplished correctly. This arrangement produces more effective use of the total energy of the people even though one person, the coordinating person, is no longer directly productive.

When a group asks a person to plan and coordinate their efforts they give him *the right to make decisions* about their activities. They say, in effect, that it will be easier and more efficient for him to make certain decisions for them while they concentrate their efforts on the task itself. Coordination of work, when many people are involved, requires delegating to certain people a power of decision and giving them *authority* over others.

Organization is the arrangement of people in patterns of working relationships so that their energies may be related more effectively to the large job. The need for organization arises from the problem of dividing labor and decision-making in relation to large tasks, and the need for coordinating both with respect to available energies and resources.

Some attempts have been made to examine organizations as populations of individuals in their proper place and function. This approach emphasizes how organization affects the individual, how the individual achieves his goal in organization, and how the personality of a leader influences the organization. Another way of looking at the organization has been to see it as a population of overlapping groups. Here the emphasis is on characteristics of group cohesiveness and the allocation of group effort (e.g., building the group and getting a job done).

I am inclined to look upon the organization as a system or totality. But as a system or totality of what? As I mentioned above, I see the system as an organism with birth, growth, and decline stages and, upon casual examination, several familiar variations in viewing the organization come to mind:

A SYSTEM OF AUTHORITY. The organization is viewed in terms of conventional management theory—organization as a device to do a job too large for one person, as a division of labor with emphasis on processes of production and work flow.

A SYSTEM OF LIKES AND DISLIKES. Here the criterion is personal preferences (whom we like and whom we don't like); the emphasis is on the "informal organization" as a friend or foe of the formal.

A SYSTEM OF COMMUNICATION. Hence the criterion is who talks to whom, for what purpose, and with what effect.

A SYSTEM OF POWER AND CONTROL. The emphasis here is on relative distribution of the total amount of power the organization can mobilize, and on the bases of power (rewards, coercion, legitimate, expertise or personal) among members and leaders.

Other categories of systems could be listed that affect the total socio-technical organization and provide the basis for the design, analysis, and renewal of organizations by giving joint consideration to the technological, structural, social, personal, and ecological variables affecting them. By reliance upon engineering and mathematics in addition to the behavioral sciences, the organization student or practitioner can marshal conceptual and practical skills to deal with organizations in their whole complex environment. When the engineer or mathematician uses the "word system," we are helped to see the input-output variables. As one definition states it:

A system is something which accomplishes an operational process; that is, something is operated on in some way to produce something. That which is operated upon is usually called input; that which is produced is called output; and the operating entity is called the system.[2]

In organizations we usually think of *inputs* as money, goods, services, and people. The *output* of the system is the product or service which the organization provides to society. The *state* of the organization's system, of course, is the sum of the functions necessary for the organization to operate—such as policy, division of tasks, assigning tasks, motivating people, task performance, information process, planning, coordination, and review process.

A major application of the systems concept has been in the information seeking, storage, retrieval, and utilization field. Most leaders in organizations find themselves surrounded by communication breakdowns. Executives, managers, and supervisors almost always mention "communication" as one of their major problem areas. Nearly all recognize that the vitality, productivity, and creativity of an organization depend upon the flow of ideas and information from person to person and from group to group.

In recent years social and management scientists have systematically studied this problem. Their research has pointed up the great complexity of organizational communication.

When organizations were small, a manager could communicate directly with all his employees. Even so, he often found that communication in face-to-face settings was cumbersome and difficult. While person-to-person communication skills are important to leaders, much of a manager's communication today is dependent upon other persons and partially or totally automated devices. As organizations increase in size, communication among the members and units becomes more difficult. As communication becomes more difficult, leaders find themselves increasingly dealing with problems of employee morale, efficiency, non-identification with organizational goals, public relations, and coordination of efforts. Many of these problems are rooted in faulty communication systems.

In recent years much attention has been directed to designing organizational information systems and work procedures that will minimize the necessity of certain kinds of personal communication and place emphasis on ways of organizing knowledge needed to accomplish work.

Other researchers are exploring the impact of automation and computers on communication systems. The primary value seems to be in the areas of reporting, information storage, retrieval, and timely availability of data. One of the great problems automation has created is the production of so much data and information that many leaders feel they are immobilized by the sheer volume. It is my feeling, however, that one of the most important contributions of information theory is to enable the manager to see the "organizational system as a problem-solving organism."

A. M. McDonough [3] states these six propositions:

1. An enterprise is a collection of problems to be solved.
2. Organization is the process of assigning problems to the most qualified person.

3. The most qualified person is the one who will need the least information service to make the best decisions.
4. Information is the measure of the value of a message to a decision-maker in a specific situation.
5. The purpose of a system is to carry information to decision-makers.
6. Any system is a logical configuration of the significant elements in a selected problem area.

Now let us move to the way the behavioral sciences look at organizations as social systems.

A *social system* may be defined as a "stable pattern of interaction between interdependent social units." It is a set of parts which stand in definite relationship to one another. This concept can be applied to *individuals,* in which case there is an interaction between the different roles that the individual person performs. It can be applied to *organizations,* in which case there is an interaction between social institutions (e.g., economic system, political system). An organization, in common with individuals, groups, and communities, may be regarded as an open, organismic system. We see the organization as a set of dynamic elements that are in some way interconnected and interrelated and that continue to operate together according to certain laws and in such a way as to produce some characteristic total effect. This serves equally well in referring to individuals, groups, organizations, or communities. All four levels of systems have their boundaries which separate them from their environment; each is constantly exchanging material and energy with this environment; each has a number of sub-systems within it which have to be functioning together to form a dynamic unity.

Such a social system performs certain necessary functions:

1. To keep the random actions of its members within limits so that they behave in accordance with *role* definitions. Supervisors are expected to supervise, workers to work, managers to administer, custodians to maintain the building, and so forth.
2. To reduce randomness and uncertainty in the relationships among the individuals or groups that make up the system, i.e., to meet man's need for structure and predictability.
3. To satisfy the shared needs and fulfill the shared goals of its members, both the implicit (usually not talked about) and the explicit (talked about), as defined by the system.
4. To survive as a system by meeting new concerns of its members and new demands directed toward it from the outside.

The nature of such a social system, however, is not all that obscure. It can be simplified for the purpose of examination. Figure 3–1 illustrates the progression from the individual human being to a complex organization of many human beings. The basic, micro-organismic unit—the sub-system we know as the *individual*—is indisputably as complex as other parts of the system, a fact which explains one of the reasons why organizations have problems. Two individuals constitute a *dyad;* more than two individuals form a *group.* Both the dyad and the group are subsystems. The *intergroup* is created when two or more groups establish a relationship. An *organization* usually is comprised of two or more groups having a more or less common reason for working together, although an organization can at any time consist of only a single group. A *community,* which in this scale is macro-organistic, is made up of individuals, groups and organizations in various intermixtures and associations. Schematically, as well as practically, all this forms a never-ended circle, and the whole of a society is made up of countless such circles interlocked like chainmail.

If we consider an organization to be a socio-technical system comprised of subsystems—i.e., individuals, dyads, and groups—we find that the sub-systems are influenced by certain behavioral elements regardless

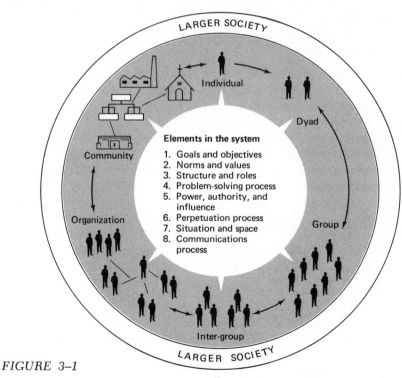

FIGURE 3–1

Behavioral Factors in Social Systems

of their size or complexity. Prior to examining these elements, however, it will be helpful to realize that they are manifested in both *formal* and *informal* contexts, or as *closed* or *open* states of the organization. Subsystems and the total organization manifest both open and closed aspects of their nature. One of the social scientists who has contributed a great deal to our understanding of this field is Milton Rokeach.[4] He took as a point of departure the writings of Eric Fromm on authoritarian character structure (in *Escape From Freedom*), Abraham Maslow (on the structure of authoritarian personality), and, of course, the massive work, *Authoritarian Personality*, by T. W. Adorno, E. Frenkel-Brunswik, D. J. Levinson, and R. N. Sanford. Rokeach proposes that every person and organization has a belief system which represents the total beliefs, opinions, sets, and expectancies—conscious or unconscious—that are accepted as being true; at the same time, he has a system of disbeliefs, which are defined as a *series of sub-systems* related to and not in agreement with the belief system.[5] Thus, for example, a person may accept a system of thought concerning a social organizational structure as being "true for a particular situation." If this is taken as a belief system, he simultaneously rejects, to a greater or lesser degree, all other organizational value systems.

If we applied Rokeach's characteristics of open-closed systems to organizations we could observe the following:

> An organization system is open to the extent that the *specific content* of beliefs by people in the organization is to the effect that the organizational work life *environment is primarily friendly;* it is closed when the work world is seen as a threat.
>
> Open organization systems hold to a scheme of values founded on the belief that *authority is rational and tentative,* and that persons are not to be judged according to their agreement or disagreement with authority. In closed systems the value is that authority is considered absolute, and that persons are to be accepted or rejected in accordance with their relation to such authority.
>
> Open organization systems will value and practice a relative *open communication* pattern among persons, and in a closed system the converse will apply.

The closed organization tends toward formal and inflexible structure, communications, and relations. An open organization is more flexible in its structure, informal in its human relationships, and leveling in communication. The formal aspect puts the individual at the summons of external demands—forces which originate outside his personality and are only indirectly fashioned out of his needs. The necessary submission brings its cost to the human personality; it causes fatigue, drains nervous energy, and produces anxiety. Formal relations need not, however, impair or destroy personality because the individual usually is revitalized and refreshed through the informal. It is a mixing of the formal with the informal that makes social systems bearable. Both are necessary; they are in dynamic relationship to each other. For each of the following elements, therefore, it is necessary to recognize the potential for reciprocal modification of the informal by the formal, and vice versa: [6]

GOALS AND OBJECTIVES. Each sub-system has certain goals toward which its behavior is directed. The conscious or unconscious perception of these goals may range from clear to vague. They may be short range or long range, fixed or flexible, explicit or implicit. Although not necessarily with absolute certainty or unanimously, goals reflect what the sub-system "wants to do." In small, informal, face-to-face groups the relevant goals are those which involve the interaction of the members of the group. In formal organizations, goals are the rationally contrived purposes of the organizational entity.[7] The goals set up by organizational sub-systems may be sought in different degrees as a result of the clarity with which they are conceived, their consistency with other goals, and the extent to which such goals are integrated with the next larger unit in the social system.

The functioning of an organization is often strongly affected by the nature of both its formal and informal goals and the extent to which those goals are understood and accepted by all members of the system. Vague or mixed goals tend to produce apathy and internal competitiveness; clear, accepted goals tend to produce greater commitment and interdependence.

NORMS AND VALUES. As it interacts with the environment, an organizational system will develop expected and prescribed ways of acting in relationship to its goals and objectives. These standards of behavior will be influenced by what has happened in the past as well as new experiences and requirements. These norms will include how people dress, whether personal relations are stiff or relaxed, how much "enthusiasm" about one's work is appropriate—and dozens of similar unspoken but powerful dictums. To act contrary to the norms may bring severe censorship or even total rejection by the group. Some norms are functional in getting the organization's task done; others may be incidental and nonproductive. Standards may rest on tradition as well as on changes produced by new experiences and requirements. Because norms and values sometime persist beyond the point where they are functional, some groups and organizations find it useful in the renewal process to periodically make their operative norms explicit. They ask, "Is this the way we really want to behave? What purpose is served by this norm?"

Norms and values form the culture in which people work.

. . . a social system is a function of the common culture, which not only forms the basis of the intercommunication of its members, but which defines, and so in one sense determines, the relative statuses of its members. There is, within surprisingly broad limits, no intrinsic significance of persons to each other independent of their actual interaction. Insofar as these relative statuses are defined and regulated in terms of a common culture, the following apparently paradoxical statement holds true: what persons *are* can only be understood in terms of a set of beliefs and sentiments which define what they *ought to be*. This proposition is true only in a very broad way, but is none the less crucial to the understanding of social systems.[8]

STRUCTURE AND ROLES.   A social system develops a pattern of expected behavior that determines the interrelationships of individuals and groups and, thereby, the structure of the organization. In the small group, organization for work is flexible, and can meet both group goals and member needs. The positions in the group are interchangeable and usually there is no stable, sharp role differentiation. Occupants of a position (e.g., group member, chairman) can move in and out of it with relative ease. The behavior of members is highly visible to all. Finally, the sequence of work operations can be relatively casual and circuitous without serious difficulty.

In the formal organization, on the other hand, we have closely defined positions in a network. These positions have *continuity*—they are maintained by the expectations of occupants of other positions. All this makes for more stability, but less flexibility. The positions usually are *not* easily interchangeable (e.g., the sales manager may not understand and therefore could not perform the chief engineer's job). Positions are clearly differentiated for an effective division of labor. Position occupants accordingly cannot easily move in and out of positions other than their own. Job behavior is not highly visible (e.g., most members do not know very much about what other members *do*) and sequence becomes very important (e.g., order slips have to be routed *this* way or we'll have confusion).

This behavioral element will both raise and answer many questions. How much social distance should exist between a boss and his subordinates? What sphere of influence does the controller have—and what data can he ask for without being accused of invading the privacy of some person or department? These role expectations, like norms, become powerful determinants of behavior within the organization.

PROBLEM-SOLVING PROCESS.   Each sub-system adopts a way to resolve its internal and external conflicts, and to eliminate threat or ambiguity. These processes may result in such behavior as flight, fight, or dependency; or they may involve behavior which copes with the situation *as it is* through analysis, progression, and evaluation.

Members of the organization develop a general feeling that "We're pretty realistic here" or "We really don't know how to come to grips with problems." In some systems, problem-solving is viewed as primarily an individual responsibility; in others it is viewed as group effort.

Again, basically, organization renewal is the process of realistically confronting situations so that problems are resolved in such a manner as to produce growth of individuals, groups, and the organization, as well as mature the process of problem-solving itself.

POWER, AUTHORITY, AND INFLUENCE. This element reflects the ability of a sub-system to exert change on other sub-systems within the same organization, and the ability of that organization to effect change within its sub-systems or to influence change in other organizations. Some of the factors affecting the results of power and authority are the sub-system's place in the hierarchy of the organization, the sanctions imposed upon it, the expertise it possesses, the capacity of one sub-system to reward or punish another, and the interpersonal skills which are brought into play. Power, in the sense of capacity to influence behavior, becomes more and more central as positions become more differentiated. Authority is here used to mean "legitimized" power (who has the right to make this particular decision), but it is clear that much "illegitimate" power is exerted in keeping any organization going.

Influence by participation in small, work group decision-making can be full and complete. Non-face-to-faceness, however, unavoidable in the large, formal organization, means that participation in *all* decisions by *all* persons is an impossibility and would be highly disruptive and ineffective. Trust or mistrust of those with greater power and efficiency becomes a pattern in organizations. As members of an organization gain sophistication, skill, and self-confidence, they increasingly resist direct commands and respond to the more sophisticated and sometimes informal influence of involvement and recognition.

PERPETUATION PROCESS. Every sub-system in an organization wishes to maintain its existence. The need felt by each sub-system to continue functioning is a dynamic factor in the development and growth of an organization, either positively or negatively. This need is a dynamic factor behind attempts to reorganize a personality or an organization. To demonstrate the power of this behavioral element, one needs only to note the number of committees, agencies, and organizations that continue to exist long after their stated mission has been accomplished.

SITUATION AND SPACE. Every system and sub-system exists within the sphere of influence of an even larger system, and the limits constraining each system or sub-system are determined by its particular circumstances with respect to situation and space. Studies in the field of socio-technical systems underscore the impact of physical arrangements on the operation of an organization. The location of one's office inevitably affects who he talks to most frequently and what persons enter his sphere of influence. The recognition of this fact—that physical arrangements can strongly influence interpersonal relations—has led some to complain that too often architects and engineers determine the climate of the organization without fully realizing the nature of their impact.

COMMUNICATION. A social system must communicate to survive and grow. Communication is the means for providing information which permits the system or subsystem to change, grow, and achieve its goals. In the small group, the communication net usually is fully interconnected—all persons can talk to all other persons, either singly or as a group. Under these circumstances, few rules are necessary to channel communications, and members follow these rules because they are clearly functional (e.g., one person should talk at a time). Since people are face-to-face, information is transmitted with less distortion. Small group information-handling is as good as possible because errors can be checked and corrected immediately ("Joe, do I hear you saying that . . . ?").

In a formal organization, on the other hand, the communication net limits and channels communication. Much information must travel through a number of persons in sequence; distortion increases sharply as data are abstracted and simplified, as some information is blocked, or some is added deliberately or via projection. Rules for communication become important (X reports to Y and sends carbons to Z, *only*). As work and authority problems mount, occupants of positions almost inevitably find that the formal communications channels are providing data of poor quality or insufficient quantity. Therefore, the rules are circumvented, persons are "gone around," coffee-break chats become essential, and an informal communication network appears. Finally, correcting information in an organization is a difficult and lengthy process (phone calls, memos, special meetings). Many problems can be attributed to "break-downs in communication." This process has been studied extensively and much is now known about the conditions which facilitate effective communications.[9]

Understanding and examining these behavioral elements is essential to real organization renewal. The sub-systems of the organization are complicated. One feature which makes organizations of particular interest as larger social systems is that they are composed of parts which are themselves more or less complete social systems. These sub-systems develop their own structures in each of the above areas and, especially, their own norms.

The degree to which the organization is integrated as a social system depends on the degree to which the sub-systems, with their own norms and procedures, work congruently with each other toward organizational goals. One of the major problems of organizations arises when sub-systems work at cross purposes with each other. The following typical kinds of special problems result:

Inter-group competition, possibly leading to collusion.
Restriction of output.
Bureaucratization, formalization, and professionalization.
Split loyalty for the individual.
Communication difficulties, especially for smaller sub-systems.
Decision-making difficulties, such as integrating the separate goals of different individuals or groups.

These problems put a special demand on the need for teamwork throughout the modern organization. Such teamwork in the varied, inter-facing human experiences and sub-systems of an organization will be required in light of complex problems, specialized knowledge, human relationship needs, and the increased size of modern organizations. Such team development will be particularly relevant for the temporary and permanent face-to-face groups that function in the organization. Achieving such group teamness will be elaborated in Chapter 6. The elements of a social system will be evident in all such team situations.

The "behavioral elements" of social systems, and their formal and informal manifestations, can be related to mathematical or engineering concepts so as to show us a social system in action:

INPUTS AND OUTPUTS. One of the characteristics of individuals, groups, organizations, and communities is that there is a continual input into the system and output from it. Things go into the system, something happens to them inside, and they come out in an altered form.

FLUCTUATION OF BEING OPEN AND CLOSED. Systems such as individuals, groups, organizations, or communities are neither completely open nor completely closed. They are some of both. Sometimes they tend to be more open; sometimes they tend to be more closed. Systems seem to go through a continuous cycle of alternate opening and closing. Sometimes one part of the system may be open while another is closed.

MAINTENANCE OF A STEADY STATE. They strive to maintain a particular kind of equilibrium which may be called a *steady state*. The maintenance by a human being of a fairly constant body temperature during changing hot and cold environmental conditions is a good example. The financial resources available to an organization, such as a voluntary agency, will fluctuate, but through a complicated process of self-regulation the organization is able to maintain itself in a more or less steady financial state, unless, of course, resources decrease beyond some critical point.

DEFENSE AGAINST INJURY AND REPAIR OF DAMAGE. It is a character-istic of organizational sub-systems that they will attempt to defend themselves against injury and will try to repair any damage they incur. This is why I feel that most organizations have a built-in potential for organization renewal.

MAINTENANCE OF BOUNDARIES. All social systems and their sub-systems appear to have a need for a clear sense of identity. There is, for example, a need for an organizational sub-system to know where its jurisdiction begins and ends; thus, it strives for a clear definition of its boundaries and tends to resist any external effort to change it. This boundary maintenance phenomenon might account for the con-tention that often exists between organizations or organizational sub-systems that operate close to one another. It is also one of the com-plications that emerges in this age of acquisitions and mergers.

Another complication is the effect that *external* factors have on the system's existence and *internal* processes. External factors will tend to affect mostly the input part of the system, but the data and output can also be affected. As stated by a leading sociologist: [10]

We call it external because it is conditioned by the environment; we call it a system because in it the elements of behavior are mutually dependent. The external system, plus another set of relations which we shall call the *internal system*, make up the total social system.

To fully understand a socio-technical system, it is necessary to appreci-ate both the external and internal forces at work; the formal and in-formal nature of the behavioral elements affecting the sub-systems; and the input-output process of the system itself.

What does all this imply for organization renewal? It implies that we must envision the renewal process within a total frame of reference: the human and nonhuman resources and the relationships between people, the situation, growth stage of the organization, and the external forces affecting the organization.

We must not overlook the multiple aspects of organizational life as outlined by E. Wight Bakke [11] in his paper entitled "Concept of the Social Organization." In his presentation of the present system concept of organizational life, he feels that the following must be involved:

1. *The Organizational Charter* or the image of the organization's unique wholeness.
2. *The Basic Resources,* human, material, capital, ideational, and natural, utilized in organizational activities.

3. *The Activity Processes,* essential to the acquisition, maintenance and utilization of these basic resources for the performance of the organization's function.

4. *The Bonds of Organization* integrating into operating systems (a) each of the activity processes, (b) the objective provided for by the organizational charter, and (c) the contributions to its operation of elements of the basic resources and the other essential processes. Each system or bond functions to develop and actualize the image of the organization's unique wholeness and to relate the organization and its parts to the external environment.

In my frame of reference, the environmental forces interacting with the stages of growth of the organization give the larger frame of reference for what Bakke refers to as the Organizational Charter. The subsystems are the basic human resources which, when combined with the material and capital resources of the organization, form the "critical mass" of resources of the organization. His Activity Process is illustrated in my discussion of the process of interfacing which involves the confrontation, search, and coping phases. Planned or unplanned situational responses, with continuing renewal stimulus, provides his Bonds of Organization. These ways of conceptualizing the organization place emphasis on the problem-solving nature of organizational functioning. They also point out the many factors that affect and contribute to this problem-solving. The quality and manner of problem-solving is being examined today in many organizations. As predicted by Bennis: [12]

> I suspect that we will see an increase in the number of planned-change programs . . . toward less bureaucratic and more participative, "open system" and adaptive structures. Given the present pronounced rate of change, the growing reliance on science for the success of the industrial enterprises, and the "turbulent contextual environment" facing the firm, we can expect increasing demand for social inventions to revise traditional notions of organized effort.

The need, therefore, for understanding the organization as a socio-technical system is apparent to those contemplating or involved in planned organizational change.

In addition, the organizational system of the future will utilize more and more the *matrix type* of organizational functioning. The old way of looking at individual departments as autonomous, line and staff as separate, and no interfacing between research and development and production is past. Development of the need for project groups, problem-solving task forces, quick responses to product specialization, and similar reality situations in the fast-changing organizational environment makes it necessary for an organization to identify its resources and reach out and utilize *any of its resources at any time* when they can help meet a need or solve a problem. It is frequently found that organizational problems are no longer the province of just one group, but that they cut across the multiple human, structural, and technological resources of an organization. The need for a *matrix organization* concept in practice is a trend in making modern organizational systems viable.

The development and utilization of special groups and sub-systems in organizations to solve problems is an example of the temporary societies concept of Bennis.[13] He points out that the characteristics of temporary systems are as follows:

> Time Boundary (either chronologically or in terms of a task completion).
> Insulation between the system and "outside" influences.
> Intense Involvement (in most cases).

To cope with these characteristics, people in the organization will need to be able to be many things and to take various roles, to identify with the adaption and change process, and to develop an ability to modify their commitments as needs arise.

Every responsible organization reviews its financial status at least once a year. But what about the social system status of the organization? This can easily go unreviewed because it is often subtle and hard to qualify. However, the renewal-oriented organization will find it useful to audit its *total* organization regularly and systematically. The purpose of such an audit is to identify symptomatic problems so that corrective action can be taken and, more importantly, to reinforce those processes that insure solid organization renewal and growth.

NOTES

1. Chris Argyris, *Integrating the Individual and the Organization* (New York: John Wiley & Sons, 1964), p. 11.
2. David Ellis and Fred J. Ludwig, *Systems Philosophy* (Englewood Cliffs, N.J.: Prentice-Hall, Inc., 1962), p. 3.
3. A. M. McDonough, *Information Economics and Management Systems* (New York: McGraw-Hill Book Co., Inc., 1963), p. 144.
4. Milton Rokeach, *The Open and Closed Mind* (New York: Basic Books, Inc., 1960).
5. *Ibid.*, p. 33.
6. The list of elements of a social system is a revised version of pp. 14–17 in the author's monograph written with Warren Schmidt, *Managing the Changing Organization* (Washington, D.C.: Leadership Resources, Inc., 1968). Used by permission.
7. Robert Tannenbaum, Irving R. Weschler, and Fred Massarik, *Leadership and Organization* (New York: McGraw-Hill Book Co., Inc., 1961), pp. 28–29.
8. Talcott Parsons, *Social Structure and Personality* (New York: The Free Press, 1964), p. 22.

9. William V. Haney, *Communication and Organizational Behavior* (Homewood, Ill.: Richard D. Irwin, Inc., 1967).

10. George C. Homans "Social Systems," in Joseph Litterer, ed., *Organizations: Structure and Behavior* (New York: John Wiley & Sons, Inc., 1963), pp. 4 and 187.

11. E. Wight Bakke, "Concept of the Social Organization," in Mason Haire, ed., *Modern Organization Theory* (New York: John Wiley & Sons, Inc., 1959), p. 37.

12. Warren G. Bennis, "Theory and Method in Applying Behavioral Sciences to Planned Organizational Change," *Journal of Applied Behavioral Science,* Vol. I, No. 4, 1965, p. 357.

13. Bennis and Philip E. Slater, *The Temporary Society* (New York: Harper & Row, Publishers, 1968), p. 127.

PART TWO

Organizations As People At Work

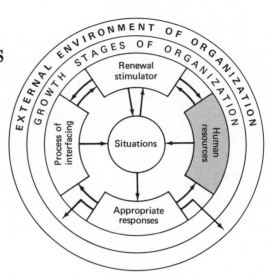

The key element in organization renewal is the effective functioning of the human resources. The human sub-systems of an organization include individuals, dyads, groups, and inter-groups.

In Chapter 4 the personality, motivation, and relationships of the individual are presented in terms of the role of the individual in the work situation, dyadic relationships, and work climate. Chapter 5 reviews the research in leadership and proposes an existential way of looking at organizational leadership behavior. Chapter 6 explores the dynamics of group and inter-group functioning as a particular point of focus in organization renewal.

4 INDIVIDUAL MOTIVATION, PERSONALITY, AND RELATIONSHIPS

Every science begins with individuals. From sensation, which gives only singular things, arises memory, from memory experience, and through experience, we obtain the universal which is the basis of art and science.
WILLIAM OF OCKHAM, *d. ca.* 1349

In addition to those economic factors that are considered time-honored and traditional, management is affected by a host of somewhat newly recognized, noneconomic factors. For example, the complexity of human resource development and utilization is seen as the key to achieving the objectives of organizations. The twentieth century has given society, through recognition of the importance of people, new insights about human behavior. More and more research is opening up insights about man's behavior. Organization renewal is based upon the release of the human resources of an organization. It requires, therefore, the renewal stimulator to become knowledgeable about the ways in which the personality and motivation of individuals will relate to the renewal process. In first looking at personality growth of the human being, we are brought face-to-face with the reality that organizational leaders must cope with adult human resources that have been mainly molded by past experiences. Any renewal process will need to be cognizant of this fact. The goal is not to change personality (this will be most improbable), but to understand the personality growth patterns that influence the functioning adult in the organization and to develop ways for people to continue their personal growth in the modern social system in which they work. Allport[1] defines personality as ". . . the dynamic organization within the individual of those psychophysical systems that determined his unique adjustments to his environment." A later modification of this definition by White[2] states that "personality is the organization of an individual's personal pattern of tendencies."

Many scholars have worked at describing personality and the factors contributing to its existence. The false dichotomy between those who choose either heredity or environment as the major influence on personality has flooded lecture halls and filled books with evidence on each side. The early attempts to identify traits were succeeded by the pioneer work of Freud and his systems of psychoanalysis. Freud stressed the importance of early childhood experiences in the development of the adult personality. He also assumed a basic and dynamic personality structure involving outside reality (mainly other people) and three aspects of the individual: the *ego*, the *superego*, and the *id*. He defined the ego as the aspect of personality that strives to be logical and reasonable and to cope with the world of reality; the id as the composite of pleasure-seeking instincts, illogical and infantile in its seeking of immediate satisfactions, and completely out of touch with reality; and the superego as an infantile combination of conscience and ego ideal (the person one wishes to become). Since the work of Freud a number of personality theorists such as Karen Horney, Erich Fromm, and Harry Stack Sullivan have built on the contributions of Freud and placed a greater emphasis on social motives.

Erik Erikson [3] took the basic stages of physical growth, related them to the environmental forces at work at each stage of life, and developed a very dynamic theory of personality development. In developing his theory he maintained that the *ego qualities* emerge from critical periods (the eight ages) of development in which the ego attempts to integrate the timetable of the organism with the structure of social institutions in the environment. Upon entering each period, the organism and environment interrelate to present a "crucial conflict" in the growth of the person. The aspects of conflict in the eight ages (such as trust vs. mistrust) are at the same time (a) ways of experiencing for the individual, (b) ways of behaving, and (c) unconscious inner stages. This approach has been properly referred to as the "crucial conflict" concept of personality growth. My rationale for elaborating on this approach to personality is two-fold: first, it integrates the Freudian and environmental schools of thinking; and second, it highlights the considerable experience the individual has had in confronting life situations.

The major thesis underlying my concept of organization renewal is the need for the people in an organization to confront realistically the situations with which they must cope. In Chapter 7, the interfacing process of dialogue, confrontation, search, and coping is described at greater length. Many managers and leaders tend to avoid conflict, to play "games," or to cover up problems with pseudo human relations. This is neither necessary nor desirable. Most normal adults have learned to confront life situations. They may not always have made the best reconciliation, but they have experienced confrontation.

In light of the compatibility between Erik Erikson's approach to personality and my view of organization renewal, it is appropriate to examine our common ground in some detail. Table 4–1 is a chart derived

Stages of Growth in Personality Development

Stages (with approximate ages)	Psychosocial crises	Radius of significant relations	Psychosocial modalities	Favorable outcome
1. Birth through first year	Trust vs. mistrust	Maternal person	To get / To give in return	Drive and hope
2. Through second year	Autonomy vs. shame, doubt	Parental persons	To hold (on) / To let (go)	Self-control and willpower
3. Third year through fifth year	Initiative vs. guilt	Basic family	To make (going after) / To make like (playing)	Direction and purpose
4. Sixth to onset of puberty	Industry vs. inferiority	"Neighborhood"; school	To make things (competing) / To make things together	Method and competence
5. Adolescence	Identity and repudiation vs. identity diffusion	Peer groups and out-groups; models of leadership	To be oneself (or not to be) / To share being oneself	Devotion and fidelity
6. Early adult	Intimacy and solidarity vs. isolation	Partners in friendship, sex, competition, cooperation	To lose and find oneself in another	Affiliation and love
7. Young and middle adult	Generativity vs. self-absorption	Divided labor and shared household	To make be / To take care of	Production and care
8. Later adult	Integrity vs. despair	"Mankind" "My Kind"	To be, through having been / To face not being	Renunciation and wisdom

SOURCE: Ernest R. Hilgard and Richard C. Atkinson, *Introduction to Psychology*, 4th ed. (New York: Harcourt, Brace & World, Inc., 1967), p. 74. Adapted from *Childhood and Society*, 2nd ed., rev. and enlarged, by Erik H. Erikson. Copyright 1950. © 1963 by W. W. Norton & Co., Inc.

from the Fact Finding Committee for the Mid-Century White House Conference on Children and Youth. In the first column will be found the stages of physical growth. In the third column are those environmental forces that are key influences on that particular growth stage of the individual. In the fourth row is how this crucial confrontation is expressed. In the final column there is a projection of the alternative consequence in one's adult life, depending on whether the crucial conflict is resolved in a healthy manner. Erikson [4] explains it this way:

> Each comes to its ascendance, meets its crisis and finds its lasting solution toward the end of the stages mentioned. However, this does not mean that they begin there nor that they end there. All of them begin with the beginning, in some form, although we do not make a point of this fact, and we shall not confuse things by calling these components different names at earlier or later stages. A baby may show something like "autonomy" from the beginning, for example, in the particular way in which he angrily tries to wriggle his head free when tightly held. However, under normal circumstances, it is not until the second year that he begins to experience the whole conflict between an autonomous creature and being a dependent one; and it is not until then that he is ready for a *decisive encounter with his environment,* an environment which, in turn, feels called upon to convey to him its particular ideas and concepts of autonomy and coercion in ways decisively contributing to the character, the efficiency, and the health of his personality in his culture. It is this *encounter,* together with the resulting *conflict,* which is to be described for each stage. Each stage becomes a *crisis* because incipient growth in a particular part makes an individual particularly vulnerable in that part.

Let us briefly examine these social conflicts in personality growth in the order they almost always occur:

TRUST VS. MISTRUST. In the beginning an infant slowly becomes familiar with his own senses, and thereafter is aware of comfort and discomfort as a result of experience with people and physical conditions. One of his first social achievements is that of being alone without suffering anxiety or rage. He is constantly testing (and tasting) his environment, developing trust as a form of confidence in uncertain surroundings. He has much to learn in developing trust or mistrust— about people, about the effects of his own actions, about the functions of his own body. Normally, his trust grows out of the quality of parental care, not the quantity, and his parents reinforce or destroy each incremental gain he achieves. Here is the beginning of social interaction.

AUTONOMY VS. SHAME AND DOUBT. As the child grows physically, his muscular maturation allows two social modalities: the first is *holding on* and the second is *letting go.* Both actions are, or can be, either benign or hostile. His environment eventually encourages him to "stand on his own feet," but it may or may not protect him from anarchic discrimination in holding on or letting go, or from meaningless and arbitrary feelings of shame and doubt. Too much shame—a crucial emotion at this stage of personality development—creates a desire to "get away" with things.

The child that endures too much shame starts to see malice in those who shame him and evil in the action that caused the shame. Mistrust and doubt tend to develop a precocious conscience, resulting in failure to test elements of the environment properly and purposefully. Seeking autonomy, he may become obsessed with a desire to control his environment in the face of uncertainty and to gain power through sheer stubbornness. Here the child's personal ratio of love to hate, and of cooperation to willfulness, is formed. The first vestiges of pride sprout. Self-control and effectiveness, without concomitant loss of pride, lead to self-confidence; loss of control and a lack of effectiveness, with concomitant loss of pride, lead to shame and doubt—and to insecurity.

INITIATIVE VS. GUILT.   For a child to practice initiative is tantamount to a blossoming of hope and a realization of responsibility. This stage is exhibited in several ways: he overcomes fumbling and fears, there is a more accurate approach to desired objectives, and more "self" emerges as personality develops. Failures are quickly forgotten in an outburst of surplus energy, and pleasure accrues from the "attack and conquest" of people and things. There is more and more responsible participation in his surrounding world, more comfort in the midst of taboos; but these things usually occur only when regulation is reciprocally balanced between the parent and the child. Moral responsibility, and the learning of mutual role relationships as well as responsibility to others, is gradually developed. Early goals are established under the restriction or lack of restriction imposed by a learned moral code. If adult guidance expects too much too soon, the child will feel a need to control himself excessively. The latter often breeds resentment, especially when the same adults do not live up to the great expectations demanded of the child.

Depressing and dangerous guilt, on the other hand, is born of conflict and often springs from overly aggressive acts of manipulation or coercion. These are typically manifested by fights with other children, rage over any encroachment on self-autonomy, and rivalry over things. Another form of guilt-producing conflict lies in a child's need to compete for the attention of one or the other of its parents. Later in life, these conflicts, and their resultant guilt, may be expressed in the form of self-denial, inhibitions, compensatory exhibitionism, or moralistic judgments.

INDUSTRY VS. INFERIORITY. Now the child is set for entrance into life. The process of socialization which occurs in school involves harnessing and channeling exuberance into activities which gain him recognition because he produces *things*—the result of manipulating tools and ideas, and of testing his skills, as contrasted to an earlier manipulation only of people. The fundamentals of technology are gradually developed, the pleasure of work and accomplishment becomes known and felt, his industry is rewarded. These things are socially decisive because the child is doing things with others and, as compatible with the culture in which he lives, developing a technological ethos.

But the further he advances into the social world, the greater becomes the possibility of experiencing inadequacy and inferiority. His failures affect, more or less, his identification with other children and the tools he is learning to use. Failures can pull the child back into oedipal rivalries. His drives are frustrated by both inner and outer hindrances; but these frustrations usually lie dormant, a lull before the storms of puberty.

IDENTITY VS. ROLE DIFFUSION. If a good relationship has been established with the world of skills and tools, childhood comes to an end and youth begins. Bodily changes cause questioning the sameness and continuity relied upon in earlier stages, and there is to some degree a loss of some of the security that had been attained earlier. The youth becomes concerned with how he appears in the eyes of others, and how they feel about him. A new search for identity and continuity commences; a career, relative to those with whom he associates, is sought.

Concurrently, he is apt to be confused about his role in life, unable to settle on an occupational identity. This often causes overidentification with cliques and premature "loves" in which his ego image is projected onto others in order to obtain clarification. "In-groups" and "out-groups" are conceived that provide a defense against identity confusion, with identity being attained in association with the former and intolerance of the latter. The cliques and "loves" tend to become stereotyped and, to reinforce the ego image, they demand ever greater fidelity. Here the youth emerges into a moratorium stage that lies between childhood morality and adult ethics, and his ideological outlook helps to confirm his identity.

INTIMACY VS. ISOLATION. Using strengths acquired in the previous stage, the near-adult is now willing to take more chances with people, to fuse his identity with that of others. A readiness for intimacy occurs, but the body and ego of the near-adult must master new conflicts as well as face a loss of ego as a result of personal intimacy. The latter is typified by fear of such associations as sexual union, close friendships, or physical combat. Here the near-adult sometimes attempts to isolate himself from such fear, trying to destroy or offset those forces which tend to push him toward intimacy or which threaten his ego. Confusion is created because intimate and combative relations occur with the same people. If a sense of adult ethics is to evolve, if satisfying interpersonal relationships are ever to emerge, the near-adult must learn to differentiate between the intimate and the combative. It is important that associations do not become so obsessive as to interfere with accomplishment, or that the search for accomplishment does not become so paramount in importance that it blocks a capacity for association.

GENERATIVITY VS. STAGNATION.   After the crises of personality development in childhood, man becomes a learning and teaching animal with a desire to establish and guide a succeeding generation. He exhibits this desire basically in generativity. His ego interests and libidinal investments are recast as that which he generates. In the absence of generativity, stagnation and personal impoverishment occurs, but the mere fact of wanting or having children does not assure generativity. Too much self-love, self-indulgence, self-concern, and pseudo-intimacy can result in lack of faith in the species and in the community. Generativity is produced by the relationship between child and parent, and its quality is a measure of the parent's ego.

INTEGRITY VS. DESPAIR.   Ego identity involves the adult's adaptation to triumphs and disappointments, and his assurance of order and meaning. It requires his acceptance of the life cycle as inevitable. It produces in him a sense of an alliance with time and history, permitting dignity to life itself and reflecting an appreciation for human striving in which life is a single coincidence among many lives. With ego identity, death loses its sting; without ego identity, death is feared and despair mounts with the realization that there is too little time to start a new life. Disgust is often used to hide such despair. There is a relationship between infantile trust and adult integrity.

It is important to realize that these social conflicts are being "worked" on by the individual prior to and after the crucial stages of their optimum confrontations. It is important for those of us involved in the renewal process to realize that adults can still change, but that some strong forces have forged the personality of those with whom we work and solve problems. The interrelationship between our social goals and concepts of healthy personality development are well defined by this comment: [5]

We are now working toward, and fighting for, a world in which the harvest of democracy may be reaped. In order to make the world safe for democracy we must make democracy safe for the healthy child. In order to ban autocracy, exploitation, and inequality in the world we must first realize that the first inequality in life is that of child and adult. Human childhood is long, so that parents and schools may have time to accept the child's personality in trust and to help it to be human in the best sense known to us.

What is the implication of a theory of personality for the everyday managing of people? Certainly it is not intended to help the management of an organization to deal with the more extreme psychological aberrations frequently found among employees, those termed by Harry Levinson,[6] director of Menninger's Industrial Mental Health Division, as "people problems." This includes those who are suffering from undetected mental illness; those who exhibit various symptoms of hostility, such as the authoritarian who pushes people around, the irritable individual who "loses his cool" too often; the aggressive egocentric, and the psychological casualty; those whose job has grown too big; and those who are too impulsive or too unflexible. It also includes people who become despondent when pressed too hard for performance or who have a morbid fear of change.

On the other hand, some of the behavior manifestations of personality which are commonly encountered by those involved in organization renewal are:

FIGHTING WITH OTHERS. Disagreeing, making snide remarks, humorous undercuts, debate and argument, semantic quibbling, withholding support deliberately, "yes-but" reactions, abuse of parliamentary procedures.

WITHDRAWING FROM OTHERS. Daydreaming, staying out of the discussion, withholding involvement, becoming the group observer or an umpire, listening, sulking.

CONTROLLING OTHERS. Making suggestions, asking others to do things, making and enforcing rules.

BEING DEPENDENT ON OTHERS. Making demands on others, asking for clarification of task, looking to others to initiate, leaning on the leader to tell the group what to do.

PUNISHING OTHERS. Not paying attention, ignoring others, derogatory comments, criticism, interrupting, embarrassing others, embarrassing self, mobilizing support against others.

HELPING OTHERS. Expressing affection, cooperation, being friendly, agreeing, supporting others actively.

These behavior manifestations are the combined result of personality, one's role in the organization, and the motivational needs of the individual.

Argyris [7] points out some significant incompatabilities between individual personality growth and the organizational system:

If the principles of formal organization are used as ideally defined, then the employees will tend to work in an environment where (1) they are provided minimal control over their work-a-day world, (2) they are expected to be passive, dependent, subordinate, (3) they are expected to have a short-time perspective, (4) they are induced to perfect and value the frequent use of a few superficial abilities, and (5) they are expected to produce under conditions leading to psychological failure.

In describing maturation of personality, Argyris refers to the fact that as an individual grows from childhood to adulthood he moves from passivity to a more active social role, from dependence on his environment to independence, from specialized functioning to flexibility, and from a subordinate to a supraordinate position in life.

The concept and practices in many organizations are such as to delimit the opportunities for individual growth. Even organizations with lofty ideas and purposes—such as church, health, welfare, and educational institutions—while giving "lip service" to the practice of something they refer to as "democratic administration," actually execute only the rather obvious, good-intentioned kind of concern for others that may develop dependency and warmth but limits the individual's growth to achieve his highest needs.

This brings us to consideration of the ways in which the motivation of adults is blocked, manipulated, or released by the behavior of managers and the climate of the organization. As in the field of personality, there are several "schools of thought" in the field of motivation theory, research, and practice. It is my desire to present some of the commonly held beliefs about motivation at work that have resulted from behavioral science research in organizations since the famous Hawthorne plant studies by Elton Mayo and Fritz Roethlisberger.

Those responsible for initiating organization renewal cannot afford to approach their responsibility with outmoded assumptions about motivation. As examples, once-honored concepts of motivation that held that men inherit most of their capability to perform well and that they can be influenced only by reward and punishment are no longer valid. We know now that employees and voluntary workers, and managers themselves, harbor expectations and needs that yearn for satisfaction. We know that man is often motivated by social needs and obtains many of his basic satisfactions through relationships with others. In these relationships, man desires ego satisfactions as well as a feeling of accomplishment; self-identification and self-realization become increasingly important at various levels of his hierarchy of needs.

Most theorists have accepted the existence of a *psychological contract* between individuals and their organization. Harry Levinson, of the Menninger Foundation, refers to this as "reciprocation." In other words, the managers enforce their expectations through the use of authority and power, while the individual enforces his expectations by attempting to influence the organization or by withdrawing all or part of his participation and involvement. Both parties to this psychological contract are guided by their assumptions as to what is equitable and justified. In reporting on the man-organization relationship, the Menninger Foundation study [8] pointed out that the process of fulfilling a contractual relationship focuses upon the following concerns:

> The problem of dependency, and the balance between the necessary reliance on the environment for psychological support and structure versus the need to achieve some degree of autonomy and independence as an adult;
>
> The achievement of appropriate and psychologically rewarding relationships with other people, thus avoiding both inappropriate intimacy and chronic isolation;
>
> Coping with stressful aspects of the inevitable changes which occur within oneself and in the environment with the passage of time.

If we are to understand fully the implication of this psychological contract in the process of organization renewal, we need to explore the relationship between the job role, expectations, and performance, on the one hand, and individual personality and needs, on the other, as shown in Figure 4–1. Life in an organization requires a constant transaction between two sets of demands—those emanating from the requirements of organized work, and those coming from persons as persons.

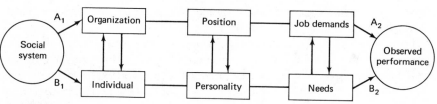

FIGURE 4–1

Individual Interacts With Work Situation

Any larger social system is inhabited both by individuals and by sub-systems of organizations. Organizations contain positions which in themselves have particular demands for particular behavior (e.g., the controller has to be concerned with where the money's going). If people were automata, the resultant behavior would be totally predictable, and totally "rationalized" in the sense of the early management theorists. But individuals have personality structures, which imply certain needs. If there were no additional work and family environment making demands on the individual, we might be able to predict his behavior from his needs.

If we emphasize organizational demands, the emphasis along the line A_1–A_2 will be uppermost, and "effectiveness" will be high. But this says nothing about needs. Productivity can be high and morale low. If we emphasize need-meeting, the line B_1–B_2 will be most important; but this suggests a happy organization that is not doing very much. If we can create conditions such that position demands are congruent with personality needs (e.g., the controller is a person with strong needs to keep things neat), then satisfaction is likely to be high. This may or may not lead, however, to either organizational goal-achievement or individual need-meeting.

The antithesis suggested here is by no means this simple; nor must organizational and individual forces necessarily be opposed. When individuals really accept organizational goals, the suggested opposition decreases sharply. The significance of the interrelationships in Figure 4–2 may be that it offers a concrete image of how organizational goal-seeking can encompass or even enhance individual need-meeting if such an integration begins to take place. But the fact remains that people get frustrated in organizations, and the working procedures inherent in "an organization" often prove unsuccessful in reaching the goals men hope to reach by using them.

One of the consequences of the greatly increased emphasis on large organizations in modern society is the sharpness of the distinction we make between *person* and *role*. This separation is reflected in many of our institutions. The company lawyer gives legal advice, but is not a regular member of the management team. In organizational training, and education generally, the aim is to teach individuals how to perform specialized roles in complex organizations. The training is oriented to the needs of the organization rather than to the needs of the individual. In many organizations the interest is in integrating various roles in the organization, rather than organizing these roles to fit the persons in the organization. Even human relations training often aims only to teach the person to perform the social or interpersonal operations that are part of an occupational role. In fact, education is not supposed to be concerned with the organization of the person. The functions of individual therapy and of education are usually understood to be distinct and separate undertakings.

One of the unfortunate consequences of this distinction is the relative ineffectiveness of such training. We might say that "personality shows through" the role, meaning that the role has not been integrated into the personality, and so we find that the person communicates one set of attitudes with the words he uses, and quite another set by "the way he says it" and "what he does." So when it is said that a role is like dress—wearing the appropriate clothes for some given activity—there is still a problem of how well the clothes fit the person.

As a mechanistic ideal, an organization can be described as an integrated set of roles, and each person has the task of living according to a set of rules which have been designed with the organization's goals in mind. In such a situation, there is theoretically no room for role conflict or ambiguity, or need for role flexibility. That is to say, the role expectations of the individuals are synchronous with those of the organization and the way an individual expects another to act in a given situation is the way that individual does act. The intentions of an individual—his perception of his own role—will be perceived by other members as they are by him. Such "ideal" conditions are rarely encountered. In the first place, job descriptions usually leave some room for the personality of the job holder to express itself—he has his own style. Depending on the amount of detail with which a job can be described in advance, the employee has more or less freedom, or the opportunity to structure it, according to his own and the organization's needs. In the research laboratory, therefore, there may be tolerance of a wide variety of role behavior.

Where much of the role definition is left to the individual, role expectations and perceptions may not have the synchronous character referred to above. This can lead to interpersonal conflict, and to role conflict wherever the situation is ambiguously defined. If two roles call for different behavior, a supervisor may sometimes be undecided whether he should act as the "friend" or the "boss" of one of his subordinates. A problem of organizational life becomes, therefore, how can we get the job done in a way that meets people's needs, role expectations, and organizational needs? This problem is one which challenges theorists, researchers, and practitioners alike.

Man's needs [9] differ, collectively or individually, at any particular time. Nevertheless, certain levels of needs have been determined as common to man's life experience. Maslow [10] organizes these into a hierarchy of needs as shown in Figure 4–2. At the fundamental level of man's existence one finds the *physical needs*. Food, water, and air form the basic elements of life itself. One does not search for much else in life when these elements are not provided. Historically, even the earliest examples of coercive, industrialized civilization helped man to meet some of these basic life needs.

With the basic physiological needs met, man becomes interested in his *safety* and *security*. The desire to be safe at work and to have a guaranteed wage with retirement benefits is important to most employees.

At the next level, however, we have the basic *social needs* for affection, belonging, achievement, and recognition. These are part of the motivational system of each individual. The historical shift in influence

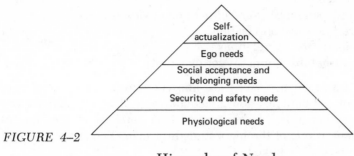

FIGURE 4–2

Hierarchy of Needs

patterns from autocratic to benevolent systems (through organizations) was brought to the fore by an increasing standard of living in which man's physical needs were being met, and by the aura in which he commenced wanting and expecting much more than mere subsistence. In the nineteen-forties we began to see the management of organizations provide bowling leagues, retirement benefits, awards, annual picnics, and similar activities initiated by organizations to meet these "social needs." Such endeavors were motivated by multiple causes—desire by management to increase production, to combat increased unionization, to help the workers enjoy life more adequately, to meet the requirements of government regulations, and to help offset the increasing impersonalization of large organizations.

These endeavors to meet some of the social needs of individuals through benevolent patterns of activity and leadership have been partially successful. Certain improved working conditions, closer relationships with the worker, less stringent controls, and less frustration have resulted from the benevolent system. On the other hand, the paternalism implicit in this approach to relations with others creates dependence, does not account for man's change and growth, and creates a tension between the highest level of man's needs and the organization at work.

As we view the higher level of needs we find man's *ego needs* seeking satisfaction. Man's need for identity and ego satisfaction is well annotated, and frequently reacted to by organizational management through office size, parking spaces, and other responses to the level of man's needs-actualization.

Maslow [11] in his interviews of selected subjects found self-actualizing persons to be characterized by the following:

Efficient perception of and comfort with reality.
Acceptance of self, others, and nature.
Spontaneity.[12]
Problem-centered.

Quality of detachment.
Autonomy, independence from culture and environment.
Continual freshness of appreciation.
Effective in interpersonal relations.
"Gemeinschaftsgefühl" (empathy for mankind).

As Maslow states, such persons are idiosyncratic in the expression of themselves, "for self-actualization is actualization of a self, and no two selves are altogether alike." Other writers have referred to the concept of self-fulfillment as one of the highest goals of man. These two concepts would seem to be closely linked.

A second aspect of man's highest needs is the expansion of the creative ability of man. In today's organization we need persons who will create new methods, new products, new ideas, and new solutions. Studies of originality undertaken in the past few years show that originality results from divergent thinking; it means getting out of a mental rut and looking at things in a new and different way. This kind of creative thinking occurs at three distinct stages: the discovery phase, the insight phase, the inventive phase.[13] Such creativity is essential for organization renewal with effective problem-solving. Most organizations have more creative talent than they use effectively. The need and ability for creativity are stifled by the size of the organization, its control factors, and its patterns of leadership.

The third part of man's highest needs is his sense of values. The need for man to find meaning in existence, to develop a philosophy of life, to see the world as something of and beyond himself, and to give an expression of faith in something meaningful, is one of the great human potentials.

If an individual is primarily concerned with his physical needs, it is difficult for him to reach out for this "higher" man. It would seem that in most organizations, however, the challenge of a changing society will require functioning in such a way as to encourage the individual to achieve his highest goals and, in so doing, to contribute to the goals of the organization.

This does not mean that individuals shall function in a completely "free" way, unfrustrated and nonconforming. All of life requires mutual adjustment amongst law, order, and freedom. The concept of an organizational climate to provide growth opportunities for the individual does not imply that all of man's needs shall or can be met. It does imply, however, that organizational leaders and members need to search and work diligently for those kinds of human relationships that will provide the best possible opportunities for an individual to reach his full potential:

> This dilemma between individual needs and organization demands is a basic, continual problem posing an eternal challenge to the leader. How is it

possible to create an organization in which the individuals may obtain optimum expression and, simultaneously, in which the organization itself may obtain optimum satisfaction of its demands.[14]

In operational terms the hierarchy of needs functions as follows:

Needs at one level tend not to become activated until those at the next lower level have become satisfied.

Once a level of need has been satisfied and remains satisfied, it tends to cease to be a source of motivation.

As lower-level needs become satisfied, needs at a higher level merge into operation: the individual is never completely satisfied.

If organizations are to meet the needs of people, however, it will be necessary to find what merely gives people satisfaction and what "turns them on." This fine delineation has come about in the studies of Frederick Herzberg [15] who differentiates between *hygiene* factors and *motivation*. Hygiene factors are those that people expect at work, which if not provided will cause dissatisfaction. They are closely aligned with Maslow's first three levels of needs, and most of them are related to the job environment such as work conditions, salary, company policy and administration, security, relationship with supervisors, and one's status. The motivations are growth factors that really "turn you on." These tend to be related to the job content and are such things as advancement, growth, responsibility, recognition, achievement, and the work itself. Herzberg feels that the challenge to leading organizations is to emphasize the motivations or growth factors while making sure the hygiene factors are provided as a basis for the *psychological contract*. The method he suggests is what he refers to as *job enrichment*.[16]

Job enrichment will not be a one time proposition, but a continuous management function. The initial changes, however, should last for a very long period of time. There are a number of reasons for this:

The changes should bring the job up to the level of challenge commensurate with the skill that was hired.

Those who have still more ability eventually will be able to demonstrate it better and win promotion to higher-level jobs.

The very nature of motivators, as opposed to hygiene factors, is that they have a much longer-term effect on employees' attitudes. Perhaps the job will have to be enriched again, but this will not occur as frequently as the need for hygiene.

Organization renewal must take into account the complex motivation forces in the work environment. No easy formula is applicable. A renewal stimulator will need to examine his own motivation as well as that of others, to see if the conditions block or contribute to the potentiality of renewal.

To state the obvious, perhaps all of the relations within an organization consist of social interaction between two or more individuals, and
the interrelationships of a dyad constitute the smallest group affecting
organization renewal. It has been stated that such a paired relationship
represents man's most natural attempt at socialization.[17] In the dyadic
working relationship, whether it involves influencing by the individual
of a peer, subordinate, or a superior, it is obvious that the two-person
relationship is an important factor in organizational growth because distribution of power, and how it is used or abused, directly affects communication, as well as morale, productivity, and human satisfactions. The
more reciprocal the attempts of two individuals to influence one another,
the more effective all the kinds of relationships essential to organization
renewal. This is true even though the degree of reciprocity may vary
considerably with the nature of the work situation and the relative positions of the individuals within the organization. Two other factors are
equally important: the amount of mutual trust which exists between
individuals and the manner in which "feedback" is conducted from one
to another.

George Homans [18] sets up a series of hypotheses about person-to-
person relationships. First, he says, people have relationships because of
the things they do, that is, they work in a physical environment, with
implements, and with other persons. He calls this element *activity*. Secondly, he says, a unit of activity of one person may be stimulated by
some unit of activity of another. He calls this element *interaction*. Thirdly,
as people engage in activities and as they interact with one another, they
have emotions, feelings, and attitudes. He calls this element *sentiment*.

The smallest work group, two persons, has all of these elements. They
have some common need (sentiment) which draws them together, they
have some work to do in common (activity), and they communicate with
each other (interaction). He found a mutual dependence of sentiment
and activity. For example, if two men like each other very much, they
may seek to increase those activities which throw them together. On the
other hand, if their work (activity) regularly brings them together, it
may increase or intensify their feelings about each other (sentiments).

He found a similar mutual dependence between activity and interaction. In general, if the pattern of activities is changed, the pattern of interaction will also change, and vice versa. Logically, he found a mutual
dependence between interaction and sentiment. Persons who interact
frequently and positively with one another, tend to like one another.
If the frequency of interaction between two persons increases, the degree of their liking for one another increases, and vice versa. The interaction need not be one of compatibility.

Robert Dubin [19] points out that two kinds of pair relationships seem
to exist. In one we see an identity of personality, ideas, feelings, and

emotions. To an observer, they appear to be sharing a number of common characteristics. They tend to behave and act alike. On the other hand, we see a paired relationship in which the members have unlike characteristics. For example, a competent worker may have a much less competent worker as an associate. The less competent gives his gifted associate admiration; the associate reciprocates with recognition and association. The pair, says Dubin, is a highly cohesive social unit. For example, a supervisor may observe that one member of a pair is discontented because of some adverse circumstances affecting the other member of the pair.

The pair seems to differ markedly from a triad or a larger group. In a triad, one can note the beginnings of division of labor, including the emergence of a leadership role; whereas in the pair unified action is more nearly the consequence of a feeling of identification and sensing of agreement. In a triad the grounds for agreement are more likely to be explicit.

The superior-subordinate paired relationship and the peer-pair relationship are among the relationships that can supplement in a meaningful way the role of the face-to-face work group in strengthening the *psychological contract* which is discussed in detail in Chapter 6 and referred to above in this chapter.

In all the relationships the individual has in the organization, a key element is the socio-psychological atmosphere or climate which exists. Does the behavior of the leader suggest creativity? Is difference of opinion encouraged? Do we solve problems or subtly "attack" each other? These and other questions will answer the question as to whether a group or an organization has developed the kind of climate that encourages mature behavior.

In this sense, maturity connotes a permissive and informal atmosphere, for this determines whether the individual feels free to behave honestly and speak frankly. It not only encourages him to participate when he is ready to do so, but actually makes it seem natural and easy for him to express his ideas. By contrast, rigid and formal situations cause feelings and differences to remain unspoken and this serves to disrupt and delay the problem-solving process.

Rather than a climate which induces defensiveness, there needs to be developed a climate of supportive communications:

> Defensive behavior is defined as that behavior which occurs when an individual perceives threats or anticipates threats in the group. The person who behaves defensively, even though he also gives some attention to the common task, devotes an appreciable portion of his energy to defending himself. Besides talking about the topic, he thinks about how he appears to others, how he may be seen more favorably, how he may win, dominate, impress, or escape punishment, and/or how he may avoid or mitigate a

perceived or anticipated attack. . . . The more "supportive" or defense reductive the climate the less the receiver reads into the communication distorted loadings which arise from projections of his own anxieties, motives, and concerns. As defenses are reduced, the receivers become better able to concentrate on the structure, the content, and the cognitive meaning of the message.[20]

One important aspect of such a supportive climate is an opportunity for two-way communication in which the individual may relate his achievements to group and organizational goals—a "feedback" communications system:

Each individual needs to get accurate information about the difference between what he is trying to do and how well he is doing it. He needs to be able to use this information to correct or change his actions. Then, basically, he is steering himself.[21]

As individuals are involved both in making and carrying out decisions, thus providing them with a real feeling of influencing the direction and manner in which organizational objectives are achieved, more aspects of their abilities are uncovered and more opportunities for personal growth are made evident. This is vital inasmuch as organization renewal always must be founded on individual growth; and, collaterally, in his face-to-face task group, the individual can be an important force in setting the norms of behavior and work output that affect goal achievement.

In autocratic situations, the individual usually has little if anything to say about the goals, purposes, or methods of his own activities and work. In a relationship directed toward organization renewal, however, he is asked to share in goal-setting and to make suggestions as to how the goal can be reached. Conversely, it is only through the individual's being permitted to participate in the setting of goals that such goals have value for him. It cannot be stressed too often that people tend to support what they create; when they have an opportunity to set their own standards, it is revealing to see the high level of achievement they will usually establish.

Many factors in the traditional organizational pattern cause many individuals to be seen as only "the doers of work." Their accomplishment of their task is the major concern of the manager or management. If inept or untrained as a leader, the manager is frequently so intent upon applying rules and maintaining his own leadership position that he is unaware of the many individual resources within the work force. He is insensitive to the feelings and needs of those whom he supervises, and this in turn produces counter-productive frustration among them. Even when the manager has no intention to be autocratic, his rigid adherence to procedural rules and his lack of sensitivity blocks individuals from contributing to individual, dyadic, or group action.

The effective manager, the one who is contributing to organizational growth, recognizes that in the process of achieving organizational goals one of his major responsibilities is to develop in others certain adult patterns of self-control and expression. Therefore, he focuses on "person-centered" needs in order to release their individual potentials. This kind of management fits the job to the person, rather than expecting the person to mold himself to a standardized job description. It recognizes that individual and group performance improves when members of the group are allowed to set their own "targets" for work achievement, work standards, and personal growth and, through such "target-setting," each individual in the group is able to meet his own task goals in terms of his own drives, standards, and needs.

If this is not taking place, it may well be that the process of problem-solving is inadequate, that there is an absence of dialogue, inadequate confrontation, or a lack of awareness on the part of management as to the true state of affairs. In some cases all of these factors may exist and one can see an organization that is incapable of renewing itself.

An essential factor in organizational growth—in the dyad as well as larger groups—is the confidence the members and leaders have in one another's integrity, goal orientation, and commitment to a problem-solving process. This confidence—or call it trust, if you wish—is not dependent upon individual authority or status. As task relationships within an organization grow in effectiveness, a common trust can develop among the members and group standards allowing for individual differences can be established. On the other hand, ineffective task relationship experience, for whatever other reason, tends to take the opposite tack, with corresponding damage to organizational growth. The ideal task group develops the individual member's sense of security in his own interpersonal relationships, and helps him to understand his own and other's functions and contributions. Thus, as an individual gains the group's respect for his contributions, he is usually given more freedom for creative participation which, in turn, contributes proportionately to organization renewal. Respect is conceptually basic here, because contrary to widely held but erroneous belief, group cohesion [22] is not created or maintained only on the basis of all the members "liking" one another. A mutual admiration society can be and frequently is dogged with failure in a problem-solving situation. Respect is a deeper, more solid emotion than "liking," and numerous studies of effective task groups have demonstrated that group maturity normally develops at this deeper level of interpersonal relationship.[23]

Groups in the organization need to be flexible in setting goals and establishing procedures so that they meet the requirements of individual members as well as the requirements established by the organization. Such work group goals can be immediate, short-range or long-range, but they must be clearly communicated to the individual. Sometimes group goals are derived from individual members, more often they are imposed by the organization; an effective task group must be able to accomplish both. It is important, therefore, that these goals be realistic in terms of attainability and the human resources in the situation.

Many management experts have taken a pessimistic view of the utilization of the individual in today's large organization. One leading management consultant and writer has pointed out the damages that the large corporation suffers through the suppression of individualism, because the "employee society," perhaps more than any other society, demands the maximum utilization of all the human resources at its command:

> We have not acquired the knowledge to make man better. We have not learned very much, if anything, to enable man to control himself. But we have learned how to make man worse. We have acquired knowledge how to control others—how to enslave them, destroy them, dehumanize them. We have acquired the knowledge to destroy man psychologically and morally by destroying his personality. And we are fast approaching the point where this too will become absolute knowledge capable of the total destruction of man as a moral being, as a responsible will, as a person.[24]

I share this concern for the problem of diminishing individualism, but I am inclined to feel that knowledge being acquired about man's behavior is steadily providing more and better corrective guidelines. Nevertheless, a very practical on-the-line executive of a major industrial firm [25] feels we have not yet been able to practice what we sometimes preach:

> I am convinced that a majority of employees work to please the man who is their superior—not to accomplish what they understand to be their particular piece of the common objective of the entire organization.

The key is to develop management understanding and leadership skills, together with a suitable organizational climate, so that the individual may thrive. It has been aptly pointed out that *all* organizations share a responsibility in this respect: ". . . society as a whole must come to the aid of the individual—finding ways to identify him as a unique person and to place him alongside his fellow men in ways that will not inhibit or destroy his individuality." [26]

In this chapter it has been our goal to examine the complexities of the individual in relationship to the organization, his personality, role, and needs. In addition, we must see the multiple sub-system relationship that the individual is involved with in trying to achieve a meaningful relationship.

It is only fitting, I think, to let the usually cogent Peter Drucker [27] respond to my use of his earlier note of pessimism with this challenge for tomorrow's manager:

For the new organization . . . authority and responsibility may well be the wrong principles of organization. It may well be that we will have to learn to organize not a system of authority and responsibility—a system of command—but an information and decision system—a system of judgment, knowledge, and expectations. . . . We may even have to learn to consider authority, responsibility, rank, and reward as four separate and distinct variables to be merged in a configuration, rather than as synonyms for the same thing. We may have to learn to look at an organization as a process . . . rather than as merely a mechanism; in other words, as something in which there is no "higher" or "lower" but only a "different."

It is this unique and "different" response that each organization needs to discover for itself in renewal process. We do not know all there is to know about the human being. The multiple ideas about personality and motivation are a testimonial to this reality. We are quite sure, however, that meaningful human relationships are found in the interfacing process. Such a process, as it involves dialogue, confrontation, search, and coping, is not alien to the individuals in organizations. As pointed up by Erik Erikson's monumental work, each person is experienced in confronting crucial conflict as he grows and develops. In a very real sense, therefore, an organization renewal process that encourages the confrontation of real organizational problems, will find people ready to engage in such a process if conditions and skills are properly created and developed to release the problem-solving potential of man.

NOTES

1. Gordon W. Allport, *Personality: A Psychological Interpretation* (New York: Holt, Rinehart and Winston, Inc., 1937), p. 48.
2. Ralph W. White, *The Abnormal Personality* (New York: The Ronald Press Co., 1948), p. 106.
3. Erik H. Erikson, *Childhood and Society*, 2nd ed. (New York: W. W. Norton & Co., Inc., 1963), p. 166.
4. *Ibid.*, pp. 11–12.
5. *Ibid.*, p. 57.
6. Harry Levinson, Charlton R. Price, and others, *Men, Management, and Mental Health* (Cambridge: Harvard University Press, 1963), pp. 23–37.
7. Chris Argyris, "The Individual and Organization: Some Problems of Mutual Adjustment," *Administrative Science Quarterly*, Vol. 2, No. 1, 1957, p. 10.
8. Levinson and others, *op. cit.*, p. 38.
9. The rest of this chapter contains portions of the author's previous article, "Organizational Climate and Individual Growth—The Consultative Process at Work," reprinted by permission from the September–October, 1960 issue of *Personnel Administration*, copyright 1960, Society for Personnel Administration, 1221 Connecticut Avenue, N.W., Washington, D.C. 20036.

10. Abraham H. Maslow, *Motivation and Personality* (New York: Harper & Row, Publishers, 1954).
11. Maslow, "Self-actualizing People—A Study of Psychological Health," *Personality Symposium No. 1,* 1950.
12. Referred to as *spontaneous competence* by Gordon L. Lippitt and Ross Snyder in an unpublished manuscript written for the National Training Laboratories Church Leadership Laboratory, 1956.
13. *Creativity and Conformity: A Problem for Organizations* (Ann Arbor, Mich.: The Foundation for Research on Human Behavior, 1958), p. 11.
14. Argyris, *op. cit.,* p. 24.
15. Frederick Herzberg, *Work and the Nature of Man* (Cleveland: The World Publishing Co., 1966).
16. Herzberg, "One More Time: How Do You Motivate Employees?" *Harvard Business Review,* January–February, 1968, p. 62.
17. George C. Homans, *The Human Group* (New York: Harcourt, Brace & World, Inc., 1950), p. 36.
18. *Ibid.,* p. 18.
19. Robert Dubin, *The World Of Work* (Englewood Cliffs, N.J.: Prentice-Hall, Inc., 1958), Chapter IV.
20. Jack R. Gibb, "Defensive Communication," *Journal of Communications,* September, 1961, p. 144.
21. Leland P. Bradford, "A Fundamental of Education," *Adult Education,* April, 1952, p. 85.
22. Dorwin P. Cartwright and Alvin Zander, eds., *Group Dynamics, Research and Theory* (New York: Harper & Row, Publishers, 1960), Chapter IV.
23. Bernard M. Bass, *Leadership, Psychology, and Organizational Behavior* (New York: Harper & Row, Publishers, 1960), Chapter III.
24. Peter F. Drucker, *Landmarks of Tomorrow* (New York: Harper & Row, Publishers, 1959), p. 258.
25. Benjamin D. Mills, Vice President, Ford Motor Company, "Management Without Meddling," *Think,* October, 1958, p. 9.
26. "Prospect for America," *The Rockefeller Panel Reports* (Garden City, N.Y.: Doubleday & Co., Inc., 1961), p. 102.
27. Drucker, in D. H. Fenn, Jr., *Management's Mission in a New Society* (New York: McGraw-Hill Book Co., Inc., 1959), pp. 174–175.

5 LEADERSHIP IN ORGANIZATION RENEWAL

> There is nothing more difficult to take in hand, more perilous to conduct, or more uncertain in its success, than to take the lead in the introduction of a new order of things.
>
> NICCOLÒ MACHIAVELLI, 1469–1527

"Leadership" is a term that has been bandied about quite a bit during the past several decades. It is a human activity which has been studied with ever increasing intensity. Mostly, we have learned it is easy to pontificate that a viable and self-renewing organization must have capable leadership, but that it is not so easy to prescribe a formula for leadership, or to describe a leader in absolute terms, or to develop leaders. The ingredients, prerequisites, and optimum styles of leadership have long eluded researchers even though they have thrown the spotlight of specific inquiry on it.

Early studies, which focused largely on personality traits, were generally disappointing, and resulted in little agreement about the importance of any particular set of traits. Fifteen years ago, an analysis of 106 studies of leadership revealed that only 5 percent of the total number of traits isolated appeared in four or more of the studies. In the late nineteen-thirties, several pioneering studies were made of autocratic, democratic, and laissez-faire styles of leadership. A style called "benevolently autocratic" was uncovered somewhere along the line of search. More recently, researchers have concentrated on the functions of leadership that are necessary to get a particular job done. Some of this research has dealt with leadership actions affecting group action, but in spite of all the ground that has been covered, neither the behavioral sciences nor successful leaders can provide simple, definitive answers.

There are indications that an effective leader is one who is flexible rather than rigid, one who is aware of the forces in himself and understands his own motivations, and one who builds trust relationships with those he leads. It seems that most leaders take into account both the short-range and long-range nature of the situation they face, and that they more or less involve those who are to implement a decision in making it.

So much has been so well written about leadership, and about the larger function in organizations to which it contributes—management—that I do not feel any real purpose will be served here by anything other than an overview discussion of those aspects of leadership, and the principles involved, which seem to have a pertinence to organization renewal. We have come to realize that leadership is dispersed in many groups and fragmented among many people. No one person is powerful in all ways. A leader in one field often does not know leaders in other fields. Thus, important organizational issues and problems are settled, not by one leader or one power group, but by a balance of power.[1]

In trying to identify leaders in various ways, to determine what makes a man a leader and not a follower, the behavioral scientists have identified at least four different concepts:

GREAT MAN THEORY.   We used to hold to the theory that a leader is a great man, that leadership qualities are inborn, that people naturally follow the individuals who have these qualities. In this theory the great man is responsible for history, rather than history responsible for the great man.

TRAIT APPROACH.   In this theory we try to identify the traits of a great leader that make him different from the rest of us. There do not seem to be any characteristic physical attributes, nor is the leader necessarily endowed with superior intelligence. Chromosomes and genes have not been positively related to leadership in terms of inheritance, nor has a particular personality or behavior pattern been identified. The only conclusion so far reached is that there is nothing conclusive about leadership traits.

FUNCTIONS APPROACH.   It has been learned that most leaders, to one extent or another, perform four major leadership functions. One may be essentially decision-making, with implementation to be carried out by others. Another may be that of providing information and advice. A third, and probably the most common, is that of planning. The fourth is largely symbolic, such as that Queen Elizabeth II serves.

SITUATIONAL APPROACH.   Here it is assumed that there are certain traits and capacities that are crucial for effective leadership in one situation and not in another. Studies in this area indicate that there is a need for flexibility in the selection and training of leaders for different situations.

The functional approach deserves a bit more explanation. Here the leader seeks to discover what actions are required by groups, under various conditions, if they are to achieve their objectives, and how different members take part in these actions. Leadership is viewed as the performance by the leader of those acts which are required by the group. This is diagrammed in Figure 5–1.

The group-function approach to leadership may incorporate the other approaches. Groups differ in a variety of ways, actions vary from one group to another, and the nature of the leader's acts will vary from group to group. Situational aspects (e.g., nature of the group's goals, structure of group, attitudes of members) will determine what functions are needed and who will perform them. There appear to be two main leadership needs in groups: the achievement of the group goal and the maintenance or strengthening of the group itself. A specific function may be helpful to both or favor one at the expense of the other. For example, a group and its leader may be so intent upon maintaining good relations that they avoid interpersonal friction at all costs, thereby retarding the problem-solving process. On the other hand, wise solution of a problem forged in conflict may help the solidarity of the group.

The distribution of leadership functions in a group occurs in several ways. Usually, in a mature group, members will assume responsibility for group roles necessary for effective functioning. Studies and experi-

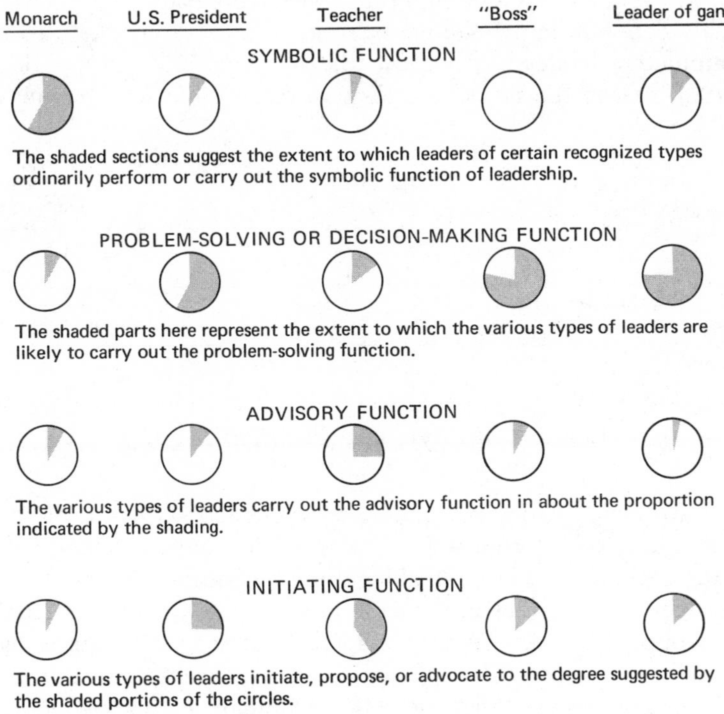

Monarch   U.S. President   Teacher   "Boss"   Leader of gang

SYMBOLIC FUNCTION

The shaded sections suggest the extent to which leaders of certain recognized types ordinarily perform or carry out the symbolic function of leadership.

PROBLEM-SOLVING OR DECISION-MAKING FUNCTION

The shaded parts here represent the extent to which the various types of leaders are likely to carry out the problem-solving function.

ADVISORY FUNCTION

The various types of leaders carry out the advisory function in about the proportion indicated by the shading.

INITIATING FUNCTION

The various types of leaders initiate, propose, or advocate to the degree suggested by the shaded portions of the circles.

FIGURE 5–1

Functions of Leadership

ments indicate that groups which distribute leadership functions usually achieve greater productivity and morale.

Studies of the roles of group members show that there tend to be group-centered, task-centered, and self-centered member functions. Studies of the effects of these roles indicate that certain functions are required for a group to make a decision, come to a conclusion, or resolve a conflict.

Functional leadership means that group members have a shared responsibility to carry out the various tasks of leadership. The designated leader, however, has a responsibility for being sensitive to those functional needs and for seeing that they are accommodated.

One observation frequently made by leaders is: "Democratic or problem-solving leadership is all right, but it is too time-consuming, and I have a job to get done." It is true that when reaching a decision is the sole objective, problem-solving leadership usually takes longer than manipulative or autocratic leadership. However, studies show that problem-solving leadership can be more effective even from the point of view of time consumed if we consider the total time elapsed from the emergence of a problem to the implementation of a solution.

Figure 5–2 shows that although problem-solving leadership takes longer to reach a decision, implementation is much more rapid than in the case of manipulative leadership because the members of a group that participate in making the decision feel more responsible for carrying it out.

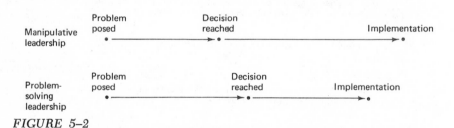

FIGURE 5–2

Leadership Style and Problem-Solving

There are at least four reasonably well defined styles of leadership—autocratic, benevolently autocratic, laissez-faire, and democratic. In the autocratic style, the decision-making function resides in the leader; in the laissez-faire, it resides in the individual; in the democratic, it resides in the group. The benevolently autocratic style, while quite distinct, seems to be most like the democratic style, except that this kind of leader does not possess the basic skills in human relations which permit a really shared problem-solving approach in his relationships with others.

Which of these styles is best? In some situations, autocratic leadership

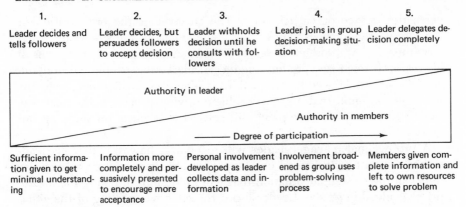

1.	2.	3.	4.	5.
Leader decides and tells followers	Leader decides, but persuades followers to accept decision	Leader withholds decision until he consults with followers	Leader joins in group decision-making situation	Leader delegates decision completely

Authority in leader

Authority in members

——— Degree of participation ———>

| Sufficient information given to get minimal understanding | Information more completely and persuasively presented to encourage more acceptance | Personal involvement developed as leader collects data and information | Involvement broadened as group uses problem-solving process | Members given complete information and left to own resources to solve problem |

FIGURE 5–3

Degrees of Participation Related to Leadership Response

is best. In some, democratic leadership is more effective. And in some situations the laissez-faire style does the best job. There can be no one set style of leadership which we can develop in ourselves or teach to others. Leadership must be flexible in style to meet the need of a particular situation which involves an individual, a group, an organization, or a nation.

In this context I would like to further develop the concept of a leadership continuum that has been produced by the works of Tannenbaum [2] and Schmidt,[3] who point out that forces in the leader, forces in the group members, and forces in the situation apparently combine to make it necessary for a leader to respond at any given moment with a style of leadership appropriate to that particular situation.

This concept is in keeping with my contention in Chapter 1 that a renewal stimulator in an organization should respond to situations as a professional *existential pragmatist.* In a very real sense I feel that it is not appropriate to classify leaders by the stereotypes of autocratic, benevolently autocratic, democratic, and laissez-faire. In similar fashion I feel that classifying organizations as authoritative or participative [4] may do a disservice to the reality of situational needs and demands.

In whatever manner a leader or management responds, there will always be a *degree* of participation as indicated in Figure 5–3. The amount of appropriate participation, involvement, and delegation is not only related to the skills of the leader and the ability of the group members, but also to the nature of the existential situation as it is influenced by organizational needs, response to the environment, and the interfacing process in the human sub-systems of the organization. It may very well be appropriate in the case of a company policy, safety regulation, or the announcement of a budget cut for a manager to permit only a "tell or persuade" degree of participation. The survival of the organization or the safety of employees may be the key element in the situation. In determining a new product or service, the manager may want to consult his research scientists, product engineers, marketing people, accountant, and his patent lawyer before making a decision. In another case, the manager may find that a group problem-solving process is the best way to decide on how the company will solve a bottleneck on shipping out orders.

A professional manager-leader will recognize, however, that his leadership response will depend on a sophisticated diagnosis of the complex forces in the existential situation that will guide him in taking the appropriate leadership stance. Leadership is the effective meeting of the situation—whatever the situation is. And this effective meeting comes through confrontation, search, and coping.[5]

CONFRONTATION.   The effective leader does not run away from involvement. He confronts people and situations. He takes the initiative, does not pussyfoot, does not play games. He does not just react to a situation, he acts, facing up to issues and problems.

The effective leader understands himself, and the person who understands himself is best able to confront situations and lead others. Further, in growing into leadership, a man needs to be himself, not try to be a copy of someone else. He does not put on a role or mantle of leadership.

The effective leader must confront the needs of people in each situation, with a solid understanding of his follower's goals, his own goals, and the organization's goals. Without confrontation and the adequate communication confrontation involves, a man cannot be an effective leader.

SEARCH.   Here the leader searches for understanding of the people, the situation, and the causes involved and treats shadows cast by deep-seated causes. Using the delicate radar of his five senses, he tunes in on his followers and develops mutual empathy by placing himself in their situation. Similarly, he searches for facts, for data which will help him to make sound decisions and to obtain the confidence of those he leads.

COPING.   The best kind of coping with problems and situations involves a minimum attempt to control other people, a minimum pulling of strings, because while people like to be told honestly what to do, they do not like to be controlled, clobbered, or manipulated.

An effective leader uses a problem-solving approach to situations, knowing there are frictions and disagreements which can often be eliminated if they are brought out, looked at, and played out in an atmosphere of experimentation, flexibility, and adaptability to change. He is willing to take risks, is not afraid to rock the boat, does not fear failure. Attitudes and values condition personal leadership, contributing to a relationship between the leader's philosophy of life and his philosophy of leadership. If the latter is based on something akin to Douglas Mc-Gregor's Theory "Y"—an assurance that people really want to do a good job, want to better themselves, and are willing to change as change becomes necessary to the organization—the results are more often than not favorable. Insofar as leadership is related to accomplishment, this philosophy expects much and obtains much, because the leader is trading on his follower's worth and potential.

Many a leader has learned that in certain situations his ability to confront, search, and cope depends on a trust *relationship* being established between himself and the other members of the group or organization. All too often a cause of misunderstanding, and of damaged job performance and personal relations, is created when communications between the leader and the members of the group are merely superficial facades behind which those involved, on both sides, conceal their real feelings. A frequent reason for such a lack of real dialogue is a lack of trust.

What constitutes trust varies from person to person, largely depending upon the individual's situation. Trust can be unilateral, wherein one member of a dyad experiences certainty in his relations with the other, without reciprocity. Trust can be mutual, wherein the two members of a dyad reciprocally experience certainty. Each of these two kinds of trust, not dissimilar to the nature of the group interaction itself, can be either task- or socially oriented, or a combination of both. Task-oriented, or working, trust is more or less impersonal and related solely to the trusted person's ability to perform his function as a member of a group. Social trust is limited to personal, informal relationships between people, as in friendships. Working trust seems to be largely subconscious.

A combination, a working-social trust, is the strongest form because it provides for the existence of anticipated, positive, reality-based response from the trusted person. In this sense, positive response is perceived as helpful in achieving a goal (working trust) and helpful in strengthening the relationship bond (social trust). Reality-based response involves more than only looking on the bright side of things. Carl Rogers [6] maintains that genuineness, acceptance, and empathetic understanding are the dynamic factors in a trusting relationship.

Mutual working-social trust is important to organizational renewal. Change of performance and the solving of problems will occur most effectively when a climate of trust is developed (see Figure 5–4). In developing trust, Dale Zand indicates that the cycle starts with reality communication. The support given by leaders and accepted by followers is an outgrowth of open communication and directly related to the amount of caring which members of a group give in mutual influence circumstances.

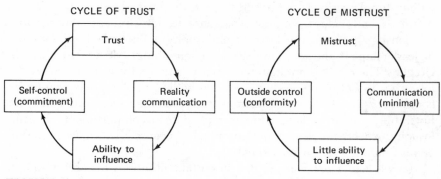

FIGURE 5–4

Cycles of Trust and Mistrust

The concept illustrated here is a further elaboration of the work of Dr. Dale Zand, Professor of Business Administration, New York University.

The latter, in turn, is directly related to the amount of cooperation and coordination exhibited between peers in the organizational hierarchy. Similarly, trust can be considered a factor in the forces affecting the attitude of each member of a group with respect to his wanting to remain in the group. It can be surmised, therefore, that trust also can be a major factor in each member's willingness to change and to communicate openly, both of which are essential to organization renewal.

The leader's ability to exercise influence is founded in trust—both his trust in others and their trust in him. Research [7] has indicated that the following basic characteristics promote trust:

Integrity: Sound and honest in character and moral principles.
Justice: Possessing a sense of right and equity.
Ability: Capable of performing well in the task or relationship involved.
Intention: Determined to achieve some desirable action or result.
Reliability: Dependable in carrying out a commitment.

Most people, in extending trust to a peer having work-status equality, require only that he have the qualities of integrity and reliability. In a leader, however, most followers pay more attention to ability and intention, in terms of "Does he know his job well?" and "Does he let me know why he takes certain actions, when these actions seem to concern me?" Integrity places third in a list of personal qualifications desired in a leader, but this does not necessarily include his having a good personal reputation. Too often, would-be leaders believe that a reputation as a "good fellow" is indispensable. Nothing could be farther from the truth.

The multiple forces affecting a trust relationship between a manager and employee highlight the reality that although they are not precisely the same thing and do not call for identical capabilities, most organizations tend to equate leadership with management. With this in mind, it seems appropriate to determine their place concurrently in a scheme of organization renewal. Certainly, both emphasize problem-solving, decision-making, and the successful implementation of decisions by and for the organization. Far too often, the ordinary concept of leadership or management stops with this relatively simple outline of functions—which has led to the *inadequate* definition: "Management is getting things done through people."

Actually, there are in almost all organizations of significant size, at all levels, six distinct roles to be played by a manager: [8]

IMPLEMENTER. A great premium on qualities of leadership; ability to communicate and to identify the best abilities in people; and to motivate people to exercise these abilities to the fullest; gregariousness; understanding of human motivation and behavior; and some degree of personal charisma.

ADMINISTRATOR. Basically a matter of control, calling for a thorough understanding of how the organization gets things done and of the things critical to its success; and an ability to pinpoint existing or impending troubles and the imagination to develop corrective courses of action; an awareness of human elements, but not so conscious of them as to permit personal loyalties and influences to obscure recognition of the substantive causes of problems; and willingness to face up to the personal conflicts precipitated by toughminded decisions.

EXTRAPOLATIVE PLANNER. Basically an organizer, inward-oriented toward internal problems; skilled in creating a structure of relationships between people and physical resources so as to assure the organization's greatest performance potential; ability to develop guidelines, programs, and budgets which assure smooth functioning of such a structure; an aptitude for designing such a structure as contrasted to operating it, which involves an ability to extrapolate the past into the future, to consolidate and schedule complex operations.

ENTREPRENEURIAL PLANNER. Basically a risk-taker, outward-oriented toward changing or enlarging the organization; more concerned with the future than the past or present, with opportunities outside rather than inside the organization; searches out and establishes new and challenging organizational goals.

SYSTEM ARCHITECT. Primarily concerned with management of the "information explosion," its volume, and substantive content relevant to the needs of management in decision-making; skilled in or knowledgeable about acquiring, disseminating, displaying, and interpreting information in proportion to the organizational investment in computers.

STATESMAN. Capable of seeing the organization in the broadest perspective, as a part of the total environment; cognizant of the growing importance of organizations as a social force, and society's concern with social welfare; able to compete or cooperate effectively with other organizations, including government agencies, universities, foundations and nonprofit institutes; able to cope with decision-making in complex economical-social-political-cultural interactions in widespread geographical locations throughout the world.

All of these six roles are not necessarily in the forefront simultaneously, but sooner or later most organizations will be faced with a serious need for the particular skills each involves, although perhaps not to the same extent as an international industrial giant. One peculiarity is that these roles are seldom interchangeable in the same person: [9]

> There is no reason to expect that a man who has acquired a fairly high level of personal skill in decision-making activity will have a correspondingly high skill in designing efficient decision-making systems. To imagine that there is such a connection is like supposing a man who is a good weight lifter can therefore design cranes. The skills of designing and maintaining the modern decision-making systems we call organizations are less intuitive skills. Hence they are even more susceptible to training than the skills of personal decision-making.

Thus, while organizational management usually requires an extraordinary measure of leadership, in the connotation of guiding, influencing, and directing the behavior of others, such leadership in and of itself does not constitute all the needed skills, learning, and abilities organizations require. And successful leaders—those we call executives in the marketplace—while not born with executive, leadership, or managerial talents, seem to have trod a somewhat similar upward path. Marvin D. Dunnette [10] summarizes some major studies of executive predictability as follows:

1. Intelligence seems uniformly to be important wherever it has been studied.
2. Effective executives tend to show personalities characterized by dominance, self-confidence, and manipulative sociability; they are interested in power, money, and political manipulation . . . a desire for independence emerges quite often.
3. It appears that effective executives are people who have shown a total life pattern of successful endeavor. They have been good in college, had high socio-economic aspirations; they have been forceful, dominant, assertive, confident kinds of people. Their habit patterns have been rather consistent day-to-day and year-to-year demonstrations of success. This extends certainly into the school situation, and some of the biographical data suggests that it extends also into the earlier background of the home situation.
4. We have information that effective executives, their wives, and their families are better educated.
5. We have evidence of open, less restrictive upbringing in the family situation, greater conscientiousness in school, and a more purposeful and more successful approach to college.

6. . . . it seems that higher-level executives are persons who seek achievement, autonomy, and recognition more than they seek strictly money or
interesting work. This is not to say that they do not appreciate the fact
that achievement usually leads to increased material advantage.

Dunnette goes on to say, however:

. . . I do find myself pessimistic, at this stage, about our ability to develop
in others, rather late in life, the kinds of traits that have shown up to be
predictive of executive success in these various studies. I would argue . . .
that perhaps we should be aiming at defining other kinds of industrial
[organizational] success, thereby changing the industrial [organizational]
milieu to allow the more innovative, more creative, more divergent and possibly less dominant, less forceful, non-joining types of persons to emerge as
"successes." [11]

On the other hand, Fred E. Fiedler [12] highlights one of the essential
reasons for organizational renewal when he discusses leadership failures:

When a valued executive [leader] performs poorly in his position, or when
the outstanding specialist, the expert in his field, or the particularly knowledgeable member of the organization is unable to deal with his leadership
responsibilities, the organization is faced with the dilemma of getting rid of
the man or shifting him to another job in the hope that he may improve in
time. It is essential that we realize that poor performance in a leadership
position is likely to be as much the function of the leadership situation as it
is the function of the individual's personality structure. An alternative to
discarding the poorly functioning leader is then to engineer the organizational dimensions of the leadership job so that the specialist can function
effectively not only as a technical expert but also as a manager and leader.
In view of the increasing scarcity of highly trained executive manpower, an
organizational engineering approach may well become the method of necessity as well as of choice.

Leadership is under the greatest pressure, and most often fails, when
certain recognizable, nonfinancial crises occur in the life cycle of the
socio-technical system. (See Chapter 2.) Management cannot control the
emergence of critical issues; it can only control how they are resolved.
Table 5–1 shows some of the knowledge, skills, and attitudes organizational leaders must bring into play in coping with each critical need, and
this may help explain why it is that one who is an effective leader in the
developmental stage may prove to be quite ineffective in another stage.
While it will be unlikely that an organization will change its type leadership as each new stage of growth and need arises, it can and will
develop a top level team that will combine the multiple skills and
abilities needed at different times and in varied situations. Does this
mean that there are no guidelines to help a person improve his potentiality for organizational leadership? No, some focus can be provided
out of the many studies in leadership in organizations.

Many variables enter into producing leaders. There are, however, only two forces which influence how a leader arrives at a leadership position. These are illustrated in Figure 5–5. Sometimes people are motivated by personal drives to become leaders; sometimes they find themselves in leadership positions as the result of external forces, of which they may or may not be aware. Usually both factors are at work.

FIGURE 5–5

Leadership Development

A more integrated concept of leadership relates the appropriate function of a leader to the kind of organization and the types of situations in which leaders find themselves. To me, however, it seems that regardless of the type of organization or situation, there is a need for some basic individual goals toward which the person who is attempting to develop leadership attempts to move. Some of these goals have become apparent in recent leadership-training and executive-development conferences: [13]

INSIGHT INTO SELF. Some research findings clearly indicate the factor of self-insight as paramount to the healthy personality and, therefore, to the effective leader. Inasmuch as a leader who, in the light of his power and influence in many situations, must understand his effect on others, it is essential that he understand his own feelings and motivations.

A MODICUM OF PERSONAL SECURITY. Research in the field of mental health indicates the importance of personal security in interpersonal relationships. Certainly, a leader needs to have a modicum of such security so as to be nonpunitive in his relationships with subordinates and with the groups to which he relates. He needs to be able to listen and work effectively with other people without the constant necessity for self-justification. The ability of a leader to keep his behavior consistent with his intentions is an outgrowth of personal security and interpersonal skills.

APPROPRIATE SENSITIVITY TO SITUATIONS. A leader must be sensitive, both emotionally and rationally, to the situations in which he finds himself, and sensitivity to interpersonal relationships—be it with an individual, a group, an organization, or a larger social system—is an important dimension in leadership action.

TABLE 5–1

Leadership Abilities at Stages of Organizational Development

Critical concern	Knowledge	Skills	Attitudes
To create a system	Clearly perceived short-range objective in mind of top man	Ability to transmit knowledge into action by self and into orders to others	Belief in own ability, product, and market
To survive	The short-range objectives that need to be communicated	Communications know-how; ability to adjust to changing conditions	Faith in future
To stabilize	How top man can predict relevant factors and make long-range plans	Ability to transmit planning knowledge into communicable objectives	Trust in other members of organization
To earn good reputation	Planning know-how and understanding of goals on part of whole executive team	Facility of allowing others a voice in decision-making, involving others in decision-making and obtaining commitments from them, and communicating objectives to customers	Interest in customers
To achieve uniqueness	Understanding on part of policy team of how others should set own objectives, and of how to manage sub-units of the organization	Ability to teach others to plan; proficiency in integrating plans of subunits into objectives and resources or organization	Self-confidence
To earn respect and appreciation	General management understanding of the larger objectives of organization and of society	Ability to apply own organization and resources to the problems of the larger community	Sense of responsibility to society and mankind

SOURCE: Gordon L. Lippitt and Warren H. Schmidt, "Crises in a Developing Organization," *Harvard Business Review*, Vol. 45, No. 6, November–December, 1967, p. 110. Copyright © 1967 by the President and Fellows of Harvard College.

DIAGNOSTIC ABILITY. Leadership is seldom adequate when performed on a "hunch" or "flying-by-the-seat-of-the-pants" basis. Too often, leaders treat symptoms of situations instead of making an adequate diagnosis of causes. The ability to diagnose a situation objectively is a prime "dimension" in any leader's self-development.

FLEXIBILITY IN ONE'S ROLE RELATIONSHIPS. The complexity of the situations in which a leader finds himself makes it necessary to be flexible to changing demands. Such flexibility is not to be confused with being unsure or ambivalent. The concept of role flexibility means the ability to function in the varied roles needed to resolve problems and secure action.

RATIONAL RELATIONSHIPS THROUGH APPLICATION OF SCIENTIFIC PROBLEM-SOLVING. To work effectively with others, the leader must practice the problem-solving approach used by scientists. To be sure, the web and fabric of man's life are emotional relations, but they are susceptible to the application of reason. The ability to understand and live through the application of the scientific process is an achievement toward which the leader must aspire.

SELF-ACTUALIZATION AND CONTINUOUS LEARNING. At the top of Maslow's hierarchy of needs, we find "self-actualization." This is the same as Karl Menninger's concept of "personal fulfillment." These terms denote both achievement and value. The way in which an individual discovers the larger world about him, and sees himself and the world in perspective, is a basic element of his self-actualization. This concept, as used in the field of mental health, is not to be confused with status or recognition. The internal-external dimension of this concept of self-actualization comes from the individual's ability to continue to learn from those associations, experiences, and awarenesses he encounters throughout his life span. One of the major achievements of any individual, particularly leaders, is learning how to learn. If leaders can learn from failures, frustrations, disappointments, achievements, and despair, they will have found major dimension of leadership.

These basic dimensions of leadership development are not mutually exclusive, nor are they a complete list. They do restore the dimension of personality to our understanding of leadership, and give some point of reference. In any development of leadership, the target will be the learning and growth of that individual in his ability to relate effectively to others in a variety of human situations. Working effectively with others requires many skills and insights; the search for these skills and insights is difficult, but the achievement is a discovery of self, a discovery of the mature person in action.

NOTES

1. Portions of the author's previous article, "What Do We Know About Leadership?" *NEA Journal*, December, 1965, are adapted in this section of Chapter 5.
2. Robert Tannenbaum, Irving R. Weschler, and Fred Massarik, *Leadership and*

Organization: A Behavioral Science Approach (New York: McGraw-Hill Book Co., Inc., 1961).

3. Warren H. Schmidt, *The Leader Looks at the Styles of Leadership*, Looking into Leadership Monographs (Washington, D.C.: Leadership Resources, Inc., 1961).

4. Rensis Likert, *The Human Organization* (New York: McGraw-Hill Book Co., Inc., 1967).

5. Portions of the author's previous articles on leadership are utilized in this section, namely, "Leadership—A Mix of Many Ingredients," *Nation's Cities* (the magazine of the National League of Cities), July, 1967; and "Changing Concepts of Managerial Leadership," *IMC Bulletin* (a publication of the National Council of Industrial Management Clubs of the YMCA), January, 1967.

6. Carl Rogers, *On Becoming a Person* (Boston: Houghton Mifflin Co., 1961).

7. Frank Ephraim, *Trust Formation in Work Groups in a Government Agency*, unpublished research paper, George Washington University, 1964.

8. H. Igor Ansoff and R. G. Brandenburn, *The General Manager of the Future*, mimeographed paper presented at 1968 Conference of the American Society for Training and Development, April, 1968.

9. Herbert A. Simon, *The New Science of Management Decision* (New York: Harper & Row, Publishers, 1960), p. 103.

10. Marvin D. Dunnette, in Frederick R. Wickert and Dalton E. McFarland, eds., *Measuring Executive Effectiveness* (New York: Appleton-Century-Crofts, 1967), p. 40. Copyright © 1967, Meredith Corporation. Reprinted by permission of Appleton-Century-Crofts.

11. *Ibid.*, p. 41.

12. Fred E. Fiedler, *A Theory of Leadership Effectiveness* (New York: McGraw-Hill Book Co., Inc., 1967), p. 260.

13. Lippitt, "Elements of Leadership Growth," *Leadership in Action*, NTL Reading Series (Washington, D.C.: National Education Assn., 1961).

6 WORK GROUPS IN ORGANIZATIONS

We need people of our environment in order . . . to give meaning and content to our lives. It is just the same with the encounters and events of our existence. All together they make up the mosaic of our life. They become meaningless only when we take them out of the picture one by one and examine them in isolation. Philosophy affirms relationships. It has to reject the idea of meaninglessness.

WILLI HEINRICH, 1920–

The organization renewal process is frequently centered on the social sub-system we call the *group*. Many experiences and research efforts have demonstrated the need for work unit teamwork to exist if organizational change and effective problem-solving are to exist. Whether they have produced action or inaction, groups are as old as mankind. In recent years, our society has come to place increasing emphasis on them, partly because we have become more interdependent in the complex organizations we have created; we necessarily must rely on and collaborate with others. Paradoxically, as our lives and occupations as individuals become more specialized and fractionated, we experience a greater need to meet and work with others. Our expectations in this regard are not always fulfilled; but in spite of the complaint that "a camel is an animal put together by a committee," groups can be and frequently are effective.

In organizations, the face-to-face work group is the place where the individual potentially can satisfy his needs, influence the organization, and attempt the integration of his goals with those of the group and the organization of which the group is a part. The "psychological contract" [1] that takes place between the individual and the organization helps us to see the importance of the work group. (See Figure 6–1.)

The concept of a psychological contract connotes the idea that the employee has certain expectations of the employing organization, and that the employing organization expects certain things from the employee. These expectations relate to work performance, quality of work, rights, rewards, roles, and the obligations of both parties. Only a portion

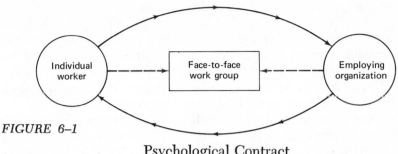

FIGURE 6–1

Psychological Contract

of these expectations are ever expressed in a formal way, such as by job descriptions and performance targets. Many times they are in the unwritten manifestations of behavior. As organizations become larger, more impersonal, more structured, the individual finds that the face-to-face situation is usually the most likely place to resolve his and the organization's expectations.

Another reason for the importance of the face-to-face group, according to recent research, is that these overlapping work groups enable group leaders to be a "link" between the various levels of organizational functioning. In the research work done at the Institute of Social Research at the University of Michigan it was indicated that one of the general patterns of high-producing and high-morale types of organizations revealed a tightly knit and effectively functioning social system. The major feature of this system was the interlocking work groups having a high degree of group loyalty, a climate of trust between leader and members, and effective patterns of interaction. Or, as Rensis Likert [2] comments:

> Management will make full use of the potential capabilities of its human resources only when each person in an organization is a member of one or more effectively functioning work groups that have a high degree of group loyalty, effective skills of interaction, and high performance goals.

In a very real sense, the organization is a system of overlapping groups as indicated in Figure 6–2.

An organization leader is a *member* of one group in the organization with his superiors, and a *leader* of his own work group, and serves thereby as a "linking pin" between the two groups. A supervisor, therefore, belongs to one group with his superior, to another group as the leader, and is usually a member of an informal group such as the "car pool" or "coffee-break" group. This way of looking at an organization is more prevalent today, and more concurrently relevant to the real operations of a socio-technical system. These groups "link" together the organization, and management personnel are the key linkers because of their multiple group responsibilities and involvements.

In light of these two factors, the group is a principal point of focus in initiating organization renewal. It is here that interfacing—the process of coping with situations through dialogue, confrontation, and search—can take place most effectively. It is not enough for an individual to want change, but rather an important group or a number of groups must desire change, to achieve renewal and growth of the organization.

During the years since World War II, social scientists have increasingly devoted their research efforts to group phenomena—the "how" and "why" of group behavior. In trying to discover what it is that makes some groups effective and others ineffective, they have particularly examined the forces which normally determine the behavior of the group and its members. These forces are called the "dynamics" of the group:

> "Group dynamics" is not something that occurs or disappears according to the wish of the leader or its members. *Every* group has its dynamics—its unique *pattern of forces*. These forces describe the interaction in the group —the interpersonal relationships, the communications problems, the way the members make decisions. Although these forces may exist in varying degrees, an examination of any group shows that they are always present.[3]

Most groups fall into two categories. Our concern here is with the task-oriented group, rather than the primarily social group. The task-oriented group performs two interrelated functions: first, the mainte-

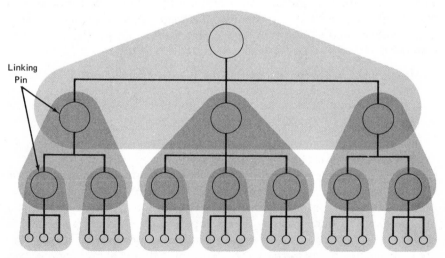

FIGURE 6–2

Overlapping Work Units in Organizations

nance function—achieving viable continuity—and second, the task function—achieving an assigned or chosen goal. An effective task group must perform both of these functions well if it is to achieve effective teamwork.

Research conducted on the characteristics of groups, their dimensions, the functions of their leadership, their decision-making processes, and other factors now makes it possible to analyze the dynamics of a group, and to prescribe ways it can better deal with its problems. It is from this research, also, that ideas regarding organization renewal have been developed. Generally speaking, these things are known about groups:

> Successful group productivity depends on the ability of the members to exchange ideas freely and clearly, and to feel involved in the decisions and the processes of the group.
> A collection of capable individuals does *not* always produce a capable group. Mature adults often form an immature working team. When people get together, they assume a character and existence all their own, growing into a mature working group or becoming infantile in their handling of problems. A number of investigators are now studying this area of group pathology, identifying reasons why some groups fail to be creative and productive.
> Groups may be helped to grow to maturity; they need not develop like Topsy. By using appropriate procedures, groups can become more productive, channel energies into effective work, and eliminate or replace internal conflicts that block group progress.
> The ability of a group to function properly is not necessarily dependent upon the leader. No group can become fully productive until its members are willing to assume responsibility for the way the group acts. Any group can benefit from a skilled leader, but to get creative group thinking, group decisions, and group actions, many different roles are required. The effective leader must realize (and help the members to realize) that each member must contribute to the total task of leadership.[4]

According to some studies, the average executive or manager spends as much as 70 percent of his workday in group relationships or conferences of one kind or another.[5] The investment of so much time with other people indicates the nature of procedures and tasks in today's organizations, but many managers consider much of this involvement in face-to-face groups to be a waste of time. Therefore, since organizational growth relies so much on the effectiveness of work group teams, we are challenged to learn more about how they can best be managed. Certainly the face-to-face work group is a key factor in the morale and productivity of any organization:

> Each of us seeks to satisfy his desire for sense of personal worth and importance primarily by the response we get from people we are close to, in whom we are interested, and whose approval and support we are eager

to have. The face-to-face groups with whom we spend the bulk of our time are, consequently, the most important to us. Our work group is one of the most important of our face-to-face groups and one from which we are particularly eager to derive a sense of personal growth.[6]

The manager should not impose his will on a group because his basic goal is to develop the potentiality of a group to work together as an effective team. The advantages of either individual or group action should not be described in absolute terms, because both can be appropriate. As a matter of fact, meaningful group action more often than not reinforces the role of the individual:

> Social science, by discovering what happens in group situations and what causes different individual behavior, and by contributing to the recent growing movement of leadership and membership training, has aided materially in freeing and developing the individual rather than submerging him in the group.[7]

Similarly, an important element of organizational growth, as well as individual growth, is the way in which work is accomplished with and through people. In this sense, groups should not be viewed as necessary evils, but rather as offering a viable opportunity for organizational growth when there is enough insight and knowledge to cause them to be productive.

The need for team building is a must for any temporary or on-going work in the organization, but such team development will depend upon a dynamic balance being achieved in the group on four levels. Without implying an order of importance, these levels are:

1. ORGANIZATIONAL EXPECTATION LEVEL. The organization has certain expectations of the work group. These may be in the form of production goals, quality work, company loyalty, creativity, or some other expectation of those who manage the organization or set up the objectives that govern a particular group in the organization.

2. GROUP TASK LEVEL. Most groups confront a task, and exist primarily to carry out that task. They are sometimes so conscious of the need to accomplish this particular task that they ignore or are unaware of the three other levels which are always operating simultaneously.

3. GROUP MAINTENANCE LEVEL. As people work on a task together in a group, they are also doing something *to* and *with* each other. Consequently, a group needs to have a growing awareness of itself as a group, of its constantly changing network of interactions and relationships, and of the need to maintain within itself relationships appropriate to the task. "Maintenance level" refers to what is happening to the members of the group as the task is being accomplished, and this has a direct bearing on the continuity of the group as a group.

4. INDIVIDUAL NEEDS LEVEL.   Each member of a group brings with him a particular set of needs which impinge upon both the group and its task. Individual needs may relate to all of the different levels of man's "hierarchy of needs." A group member may be getting his psychological and safety needs met through external sources of a guaranteed annual wage, good physical working conditions, safe work environment, and an adequate living standard. It is very likely, however, that the work group will be appropriate to meeting his social, ego, and self-fulfillment needs.

As a group balances these four levels, it becomes a more effective and mature group. It acquires group teamness, and thereby contributes to organizational growth. When one or more of these levels is neglected, the efficiency of the group is impaired and its growth thwarted.

While he might resent anyone else saying so, a manager or supervisor may very well admit privately the ineffectiveness of many of the group problem-solving situations for which he is responsible. Usually only a few members of his work group speak up in a frank manner, and one or two persons seem to dominate the decision-making process. Too much time is spent on details and minor differences, and too little on the critical matters that are supposed to receive the group's attention. Under these circumstances, consideration of organizational growth makes it appropriate to define factors affecting group leadership and group functioning. In other words, how can the functioning of a task group and the relationships of its members be improved? It is pertinent here to examine briefly some of the characteristics of a task group—any task group; these characteristics are neither "good" nor "bad," but as part of the reality of group behavior must be examined by the leader and the members in terms of their effect on group action:

GROUP BACKGROUND.   There is a history to each group situation before it even starts. Each member of the group brings to the group a "mental set." One might approach a group meeting saying to himself, "I wonder how long *this* meeting will take?" or "I'm not going to let *anyone* jam anything down my throat!" Someone else will be thinking, "I hope I can get *my* idea pushed through this time," or "The boss isn't going to pull a fast one on me *again!*" And, "This isn't the way we used to do it." These attitudes affect the behavior of all the participants.

GROUP PARTICIPATION PATTERNS.   Communication failures in group situations usually are the result of individual inability to express ideas clearly or significantly. The succinct statement is a rarity; rambling in search of a point is commonplace. The member who uses a technical or high-flown vocabulary to talk over the heads of others sometimes makes it nearly impossible for a group to function meaningfully. Non-verbal means of communications—postures, facial expressions, and glances—can be disruptive and discouraging, or helpful and revealing.

GROUP COHESION.   This is an immediate factor in group productivity and morale—how effectively the group functions as a team, how well it sticks together when the going gets rough or a crisis of decision arises. Groups are cohesive because of a variety of individual motivations that are strengthened in a cooperative situation in which each member has and is aware of responsibility—without abdicating his right to independent thought. Cohesion depends more on goal commitment, wanting to belong to the group, and respect for others, than whether or not a member of the group agrees with or "likes" the others.

SUB-GROUPS.   In any group situation, it is normal that sub-groups of two or more members may be formed. Sometimes these sub-groups are based on friendships, sometimes they gravitate around common agreement about a particular issue or common dislike of a situation. Individuals frequently change from one sub-group to another in the same group—agreeing with certain members on one issue, and then identifying with different members on another issue. When management is interested in organizational growth, it must be concerned with sub-grouping which thwarts problem-solving or healthy interpersonal relationships—particularly those sub-groupings which tend to isolate or shut out other members of a group.

GROUP ATMOSPHERE.   This does not refer to the temperature or humidity in a room, although these comfort factors may be related to the group situation. Group atmosphere refers to the freedom or informality of the group situation, the permissiveness and friendliness that prevails in the work group. It bears on the frankness with which the members express their real feelings about issues, and the existence of an environment in which the members of a group feel free to speak when they have something to say.

GROUP STANDARDS.   Here we refer to the mode of operation that the group adopts or is forced into, the sense of responsibility or non-responsibility it possesses as it carries out its assignment or chooses its goals. It might be a standard of coming to work on time, quality performance, or a standard of being willing to "talk back" to the boss. Group standards are likely to be established fairly quickly, and to persevere. Various kinds of standards will emerge in any work group and affect the patterns of work, and they can be discerned by the leader and the group.

GROUP PROCEDURES.   It is inevitable that a group will follow certain procedures, formal or informal, helpful or hindering. In most task group situations, except those involving large numbers of participants, there is little need for formality and, generally speaking, informality encourages a permissive atmosphere. Even small and informal groups, however, require some ground rules.

GROUP GOALS. Goals can be immediate, short-range or long-range; they can vary in their clarity and in the value which the group places upon them; they can emerge from the group or be imposed on it; they can be realistic in relation to the resources of the group or completely unrealistic. Effective groups must continually check the clarity and validity of their goals.

GROUP LEADER AND MEMBER BEHAVIOR. Leader behavior in a group can range from almost complete control of the decision-making by the leader to almost complete control by the group, with the leader contributing his resources just like any other group member. A leader can assume most of the functions required to provide leadership for the group; or these functions can become the responsibility of the members as well.

These characteristics affect all work groups as they strive to get their many objectives achieved, and try to meet the four levels of needs mentioned earlier. The leader and the members of the group should be constantly sensitive and skillful to see that the task *and* maintenance role functions are being assumed in the work of the group. These functions have been characterized as follows:

TASK FUNCTIONS. Specific group functions facilitate and coordinate group effort in the selection and definition of a common problem and in the solution of that problem:

- *Initiating.* Proposing tasks or goals; defining a group problem; suggesting a procedure or ideas for solving a problem.
- *Information or opinion seeking.* Requesting facts; seeking relevant information about a group concern; asking for suggestions or ideas.
- *Information or opinion giving.* Offering facts; providing relevant information about group concerns; stating a belief; giving suggestions or ideas.
- *Clarifying or elaborating.* Interpreting or reflecting ideas and suggestions; clearing up confusions; indicating alternatives and issues before the group; giving examples.
- *Summarizing.* Pulling together related ideas; restating suggestions after group has discussed them; offering a decision or conclusion for the group to accept or reject.
- *Consensus testing.* Sending up "trial balloons" to see if the group is nearing a conclusion; checking with the group to see how much agreement has been reached.

MAINTENANCE FUNCTIONS. Functions in this category describe group activity necessary to alter or maintain the way in which mem-

bers of the group work together, developing loyalty to one another
and to the group as a whole:

- *Encouraging.*   Being friendly, warm, and responsive to others and
  to their contributions; showing regard for others by giving them an
  opportunity for recognition.
- *Expressing group feelings.*   Sensing feelings, moods, relationships
  within the group; sharing feelings with other members.
- *Harmonizing.*   Attempting to reconcile disagreements; reducing tension by "pouring oil on troubled waters"; getting people to explore
  their differences.
- *Compromising.*   When one's own ideas or status is involved in a
  conflict, offering to compromise one's own position; admitting error;
  disciplining oneself to maintain group cohesion.
- *Gate-keeping.*   Attempting to keep communication channels open;
  facilitating the participation of others; suggesting procedures for
  sharing the discussion of group problems.
- *Setting standards.*   Expressing standards for the group to achieve;
  applying standards in evaluating group functioning and production.

Groups are likely to operate at maximum efficiency when members
perform *both* task and maintenance functions and when these functions
become the responsibility of *all* the members, rather than of the designated leader alone. These two types of functions are not necessarily
mutually exclusive. Very often in performing a task function, the member is also answering a necessary maintenance need (for instance, in
summarizing related items one may also express the feelings of group
members). Generally, it doesn't make any difference in a mature working
group *who* renders a particular function as long as all the appropriate
functions are performed. In certain group settings, of course, the official
position of a member or the particular personality of a member will influence the functions that that member performs.

Generally speaking, the task assigned to or chosen by a group deals in
some manner with a situation or a problem, and the resolution or solution usually involves effective teamwork. Herein lies one of the essential
reasons why many leaders and managers decline to try to take advantage
of group action when confronting organizational situations. The frustrations he anticipates in securing teamwork—perhaps not without reason—
are simply more than he cares to suffer. Insofar as organization renewal
is concerned, however, these frustrations should and can be overcome.

Nevertheless, helping a group of people to work together is a difficult
and complex undertaking, and a primary managerial decision is deciding
when a group should be asked to solve a problem or implement a program. To choose not to use work group action may block program or
policy implementation, because the people involved in the program or

affected by the policy had no hand in its development. Or it might reveal that the manager has no confidence in his own leadership and ability to work with people—or that he has no confidence in the members of his own work group. More importantly, it could suggest that he is not developing those people who work with him into the kind of a team needed for the renewal process to be initiated. Teamwork, in this sense, is manifested in the way a group is able to solve problems.[8] Let's examine some of the characteristics of teamwork and ways to achieve it.

1. TEAMWORK REQUIRES AN UNDERSTANDING AND COMMITMENT TO THE GROUP GOALS.   Whether a regular work group, a project team, or a special task force, the need for the group to determine and understand its goals will be a prerequisite for effective team building. It is not just an understanding of the immediate task, but an understanding of the role of the group in the total organization, its responsibilities, and the morale objectives to which they are related. As indicated earlier, those goals operate at the level of the organization, task group, and individual. They will be both long- and short-range in nature. The members of the group, to achieve teamwork, will need to not only understand these goals but have a degree of commitment to them so as to work effectively toward their achievement.

Obviously, it is not a task-oriented group unless it has a goal or combination of goals—to solve a specific problem, to plan a specific action, to produce a specific report, to make specific recommendations, and so forth. Obviously, too, such goals do not exist in a vacuum, but are a part of the larger goals of the organization within and for which the group exists. The first requirement of team effectiveness is that these goals must be clearly defined. The time spent in arriving at a goal definition here, by a member or by the group itself, helps make the time used by the group meaningful. Writing down goals is not the same as preparing an action plan, but a better plan can be prepared from a well thought out statement of goals. The second requirement is that all members of the group must know and understand with equal conciseness what these group goals are. This is often not the case, and where even a few members have only a general idea of the group's goals, they tend to have quite different ideas about group achievement.

2. TEAMWORK REQUIRES THE MAXIMUM UTILIZATION OF THE DIFFERENT RESOURCES OF INDIVIDUALS IN THE GROUP.   When a manager is confronted with a situation demanding change, he needs to ask himself whether the various aspects of the problem can be most effectively resolved through a memorandum, a report, or in an individual, person-to-person fashion. The group may be used effectively for problem-solving when the type of problem to be solved is one in which there is a quantitative and

qualitative need for various points of view and opinions. This might be especially true where there is a complex problem that has no easy solution within the resources of a single individual. Similarly, inasmuch as people tend to better carry out decisions in which they share, a decision might best be made in a group when the people comprising it will be the ones who will carry out what is decided. Thus, a leader or administrator will find it extremely worthwhile to involve in the process of making the decision those who will ultimately implement it. Different people in an organization will have had different experiences, background, and technical knowledge which frequently will be helpful in arriving at a decision.

> Frequently, in modern organizations, the complexity of a problem requires the specialized knowledge and experience of all the individuals in the group to find a realistic solution. A team knows the different resources of the individuals in their group. A supervisor and leader is the coordinator of these resources in getting group action. A good question [for the manager] to ask is: "Have I heard the ideas of everyone who can make a significant contribution to the solution of this problem." [9]

It has frequently been said that many groups fail because the "wrong people meet the right problem." All too often the people who can best contribute to the solution of a problem are not asked to work on it. This does not mean that there are not many instances where, due to the pressure of time, type of decision, or deferred area of responsibility, an individual may most appropriately make a decision. In other words, there is a place for individual as well as group decision-making in most organizational situations. Teamwork, however, will maximize the utilization of individual resources to achieve group goals.

3. TEAMWORK IS ACHIEVED WHEN FLEXIBILITY, SENSITIVITY TO NEEDS OF OTHERS, AND CREATIVITY ARE ENCOURAGED. A group of persons does not spring into mature group action just because its members happen to be assigned to the same section of the building or to a similar function. A group of persons may need to deal with some of the emotional problems of its members' interpersonal relationships before it can reach decisions effectively. Team action is a complex thing. Group decision-making, at its best, depends on the kind of working relationships in which disagreement, creativity, and shared responsibility can flourish. When such an atmosphere is established, the group normally is ready to reach decisions effectively.

The old cliché that "two heads are better than one" is not always true. In some cases a manager can implement, develop, or think through various plans without getting the advice and suggestions of others. Conversely, when working on a new or complex problem, or a situation that affects a large segment of the organization, more effective resolution might be achieved if a number of people participate in a group problem-solving situation. A creative group should release the potential mental ability and resources of all group members:

> Creativity needs to be developed and nurtured, with the proper motivation to be creative, with the stimulation of other people. With the courage to let ourselves go and try new things, much progress can be made.[10]

The interstimulation of a number of persons can frequently emerge with an idea which is the outgrowth of the group process and not that of any single individual. Many people have their best thoughts stimulated by the thoughts of others. This kind of creative thinking is the goal of good group teamwork, and it is one of the crying needs of management today. Too many conferences, groups, and task groups are sterile because they stick to a rigid agenda and tight procedures, and because they have poor interpersonal relationships.

4. TEAMWORK IS MOST EFFECTIVE WHERE SHARED LEADERSHIP IS PRACTICED.   A group of persons brought together in a problem-solving situation will not function at maximum efficiency if its members are "rubber-stamp" or "yes" men for a manager or leader. In such a situation a group leader is merely communicating his own ideas. If a supervisor is interested both in assuming his own responsibility for leadership, and in developing the membership of a group so that the functions of leadership are shared, his attitude will go a long way toward achieving effective decision-making.

This criterion might be embarrassing to many who are reluctant to exert a team type of leadership. If a manager's motivation in calling together a group is *to get his own way,* he should not pretend to be seeking a group decision. If he has already made up his mind, he should not imply consultation; he should announce his decision and communicate it to those who need to know. It is another matter if he is asking a group of people to think and act together as a means of helping him to reach a decision. Leadership, however, will make or break the work of such a group. The supervisor, or anyone having the duty of guiding the group, must observe certain leadership fundamentals (discussed in Chapter 5) that are prerequisite to developing groups of persons into effective work teams.

5. TEAMWORK REQUIRES A GROUP TO DEVELOP PROCEDURES TO MEET THE PARTICULAR PROBLEM OR SITUATION.   We are all familiar with the use of a voting procedure in group decision-making situations. There have been a number of research studies showing that in many cases it is not the most appropriate tool for group action. In fact, in many settings it is

only a way by which the leader can keep control of the group—or, at its worst, an ideal procedure for "railroading" ideas. In most situations in which group action is taken, there is little need for a voting procedure.

This is not to say that parliamentary procedures are not appropriate in certain situations, for instance, for a working legislative body or a policy body such as a board of directors where there is a need for a historical or legal record. There are also some situations in which a group will not be using strictly parliamentary procedure but will decide on an issue by a vote; or it might develop some procedure such as a majority or two-thirds rule. The creation of a minority group in such a situation, however, frequently poses problems later on, unless the group members show an unusual degree of maturity, or the decision to be made is so inconsequential that no one really cares who wins. To get away from the vote-taking situation, there has been a great deal of talk about trying to get "unanimous" group decision. As laudable as this might be in group decision-making, it is extremely difficult and may be impractical. People being as complex as they are, it is unlikely that one can get unanimous decisions very often; in many cases, it would take a great deal of time and an extraordinary amount of patience for a group to reach perfect unanimity. There is a difference between unanimous decision-making and a "consensus" decision. In a consensus-type decision, the members of the group agree on the *next steps,* with those who are not in agreement reserving the right to have the *tentative* decision tested and evaluated for later assessment. In other words, certain members of the group will agree that on a "provisional try" or a "first-time" basis the organization might try out a particular alternative; *but* they want to ensure certain evaluative means for testing whether or not the feelings of the majority indicate the most appropriate action. In a very real sense, this is different from compromise, where the decision is taken from two opposing points of view and becomes something quite different from either of them. In the consensus decision, individuals in the group might be saying that they are "not sure" of the best decision, but, realizing the need for action, they will accept agreement to one of the alternatives for action after thorough discussion and minority points of view are heard, and with the understanding that the temporary decision will be reviewed and evaluated at a later date.

6. TEAMWORK IS CHARACTERIZED BY THE GROUP'S ABILITY TO EXAMINE ITS PROCESS SO AS TO CONSTANTLY IMPROVE ITSELF AS A TEAM. When two or more people work together for a purpose, there tends to be interaction, interpersonal relationships, group goals, and communication, all with varying degrees of success. Someone has made the observation that a collection of normal individuals can make a neurotic group. In this sense, the word "neurotic" is used to describe a group which is unable

to focus on the problem, is erratic in group discussion and unable to reach a decision, and which constantly bickers and fights. Such ineffective behavior is only one example of the pattern of forces and group dynamics which every task group inevitably exhibits. The leader and each group member might well ask himself some pertinent questions so as to learn from interaction:

What are the motivations of the various members of the group?
What are the real reasons for these people wanting to be members of the group?
What are the various relationships among them?
Are there underlying animosities which will reduce the group's productivity?
What effect will conditions of status have on the group?
Will any members of the group have difficulty in communicating with other members?
Can the group maintain a clear purpose?
How cohesive is the group?

By setting up a process of analyzing its own actions a group can learn from its experiences how to improve its teamwork. A manager should always devote some time to developing group effectiveness—by helping the group confront its own process and initiating appropriate team building opportunities.

7. FOR A GROUP TO FUNCTION EFFECTIVELY AS A TEAM, THE CLIMATE OF THE ORGANIZATION SHOULD ENCOURAGE THE MANAGER TO UTILIZE THE PRACTICES OF PARTICIPATIVE LEADERSHIP. Most managers behave in accordance with the example set by their superiors, and with the implicit and explicit reward systems existing throughout the organization. If the top management of an organization tends to feel that the only good decisions are individual decisions, a subordinate manager probably will feel uncomfortable in using groups very frequently to aid in the problem-solving process. On the other hand, if top management puts value on those leaders who utilize and develop others through team experiences, he will feel encouraged to use group action whenever it seems to him to be appropriate. Even for top management, however, this is not always a clear-cut issue:

An organization built on the assumptions and values of *self-actualizing man* is more likely to create a climate conducive to the emergence of psychologically meaningful groups because of the organization's concern with the meaningfulness of work . . . . The effective integration of organizational and personal needs probably requires a climate based on the assumptions of *complex man* because groups are not the right answer to all problems at all times. Those organizations which are able to use groups effectively tend to be very careful in deciding when to make use of a work team or a committee and when to set up conditions which promote or discourage group formation. There are no easy generalizations in this area, hence a diagnostic approach may be the most likely to pay off.[11]

8. TEAMWORK UTILIZES THE APPROPRIATE STEPS AND GUIDELINES FOR DECISION-MAKING IN THE SOLUTION OF PROBLEMS. As work groups, task forces, management teams, project groups, or other types of groups initiate and decide an action in the renewal process, they should use the appropriate steps and guides in decision-making that can be identified as follows: [12]

A clear definition of the problem. If the problem is ambiguous and the group is unable to understand it, the decision-making process will be greatly impeded. In many cases, a problem is so general that the group is unable to come to grips with it. A problem should be defined clearly, the limits of group responsibility should be set, and any clarification relative to the problem should be encouraged.

A clear understanding as to who has the responsibility for the decision. When a group is asked to assume responsibility for a decision, it should have an understanding as to its freedom to act and the degree of its responsibility.

Effective communication for idea production. It is important to get the ideas of the group out in the open. Too often the group will seize on the first solution or suggestion to solve a problem, but too early evaluation of an idea can block effective decision-making. Such methods as brainstorming and encouraging the group not to associate ideas with people, are often valuable.

Appropriate size of group for decision-making. If a group is too large for decision-making, it should use sub-groups in trying to reach a decision. A group often gets "bogged down" because of its size.

A means for effective testing of different alternatives relative to the problem. If a group is to effectively make a decision, it should have some means of getting data about the effects of the different alternatives it is considering. It is unfair to ask a group to make a decision without adequate data. It might be that a group needs to postpone making a decision until it can get additional data.

A need for building commitment into the decision. A group needs to realize that reaching a decision is only one step in a process which also involves implementation. There is a need to build in to its planning some responsibility, and the delegation of it, for carrying out the indicated action. Frequently, failure to pin down responsibility renders a decision pointless and necessitates further meetings, with resultant frustration and apathy on the part of group members.

Honest commitment of the manager or leader to the group decision-making process.   A leader should be essentially interested in the process and not in a predetermined idea or opinion of his own. This does not mean, however, that the leader, or any other status person, does not have the right to make a contribution, although for him to do so too early is a mistake. If the group members feel he has a particular solution, they will tend to react to it and not creatively introduce new ideas.

A need for agreement on procedures and methods for decision-making prior to deliberation of the issues.   Issues which are particularly controversial, or likely to cause a "split" in the group, make decision-making a real problem. It is helpful to have the group spend some time at the beginning of the meeting to reach agreement on the methods and procedures it will use in reaching its decision. If it can agree on the criteria and standards it will use, it will have established the basis of agreement for later decision-making It is advantageous for a group to take time to prepare itself so that it does not make a hasty decision before there is true readiness for group action.

9. Teamwork requires trust and openness in communication and relationships.   As discussed in Chapter 5, an important dimension of effective leadership is the ability to develop a trusting relationship among one's associates. Such a trust relationship will encourage open and frank communications. It will manifest a high tolerance for difference of opinions and personalities. Teamwork is manifested best when such behavior is common to all members of the group, including the leader.

10. Teamwork is achieved when the group members have a strong sense of belonging to the group.   A degree of cohesiveness is needed for teamwork to be manifested. Such cohesiveness will be built upon commitment to the goals, commitment to the group, and respect for the members of the group. This sense of belonging is not just a matter of blind loyalty, but a sense of wanting to work with other members of the group in accomplishing goals which are meaningful to the individual member. It is not predicated on everyone's liking each other, a highly unlikely occurrence, but is a more mature level of respect and openness which emerges out of common commitment to the task and to working together to accomplish the goal.

It should be apparent from all that has been discussed so far that teamwork depends as much upon the behavior and contribution of each member as it does on the skill of the leader, but this is not to say that the leader is unimportant. The group supervisor or leader is an essential factor in effective group functioning and growth. Different types of situations unquestionably demand different responses by the leader, but organizational growth requires the leader to exercise at least six basic functions:

1. Help the group to decide clearly its purposes and objectives.
2. Help the group to become conscious of its own procedures in order to improve its problem-solving capability.
3. Help the group to become aware of talents, skills, and other resources existing within its own membership.
4. Develop group methods of evaluation, so that the group will have ways of improving its process and become aware of how others think and feel.
5. Help the group to accept new ideas and new members without conflict, to learn to accept discipline in working toward long-range objectives, and to learn to profit from failure.
6. Help the group to create new task forces or sub-groups as needed, and to learn to terminate them when it is wise to do so.

Such leadership skills will be needed to effectively develop the teamwork necessary for a group to cope with its responsibility in the process of organization renewal.

Appropriate inter-group relationships are vital to organizational growth:

> Although the small group lies at the foundation of society and persists despite the rise and fall of institutions in the larger social structure, it is also true that the effectiveness of large scale organizations depends, in large measure, on the development of effective small groups. Not only must groups build their own cohesion and continually resolve their own internal problem, they must also maintain a positive identification with other groups and with a larger organization. The fact that small groups satisfy important human needs assures their survival as a form of organization. But this does not assure the development of effective groups and consequently effective organizations in the larger institutions of society.[13]

There are several kinds of groups within the usual organization, each with its own pattern of behavior, communication, cohesion, goals, procedures, leadership, and membership which contribute to developing a complex of organizational processes and substance. These groups can be categorized under three principal styles of member activity: [14]

> INTERACTING GROUPS: Requiring the close coordination of the members in the performance of the primary group task, i.e., the ability of one member to perform his job may depend upon the fact that another member has first completed his share of the task. The leader's role is one of directing,

channeling, guiding, refreshing, timing, and coordinating the activities of the members.

CO-ACTING GROUPS: While the members of this kind of a group have a common task, they each act independently of the others, i.e., each member is on his own and his performance depends on his own ability, skill, and motivation.

COUNTERACTING GROUPS: Individuals who are working together to negotiate and reconcile conflicting opinions and purposes, i.e., some members representing one point of view and others an opposing or divergent point of view, and each individual working to achieve his own or his party's ends at the expense of others.

Thus, there is a varying mixture of cooperation and competition among the members of groups. This can be extended further to mixtures of cooperation and competition between groups. Such intergroup relationships can either promote or block organization renewal. The latter is particularly likely if the members of competing groups see one another as "the enemy." Distorted views of group values and loyalty can develop, together with stereotyped behavior in which the members of one group refuse to listen to the other.[15] Interaction, rotation of members from one group to another, avoidance of win-lose situations, and focusing on total group goals are useful ways to lessen intergroup conflict and to develop the collaborative relationships essential to organization renewal.

A critical question, therefore, deals with how groups can be beneficially influenced. One answer, of course, is coercive, autocratic control predicted on McGregor's Theory "X";[16] but this, as has been mentioned, immediately tends to obviate the reasons for group action. Another answer is control through benevolence and persuasion, predicated on a distorted view of McGregor's Theory "Y." This can take the form of obvious paternalism or pseudo human relations practices, and this manner of approach has received considerable support, not only by Robert McMurray[17] but also by countless theorists thereafter. A third approach has been referred to variously as "helping," "problem-solving," or "confronting." These express themselves where one finds a consultative system at work. The effects of coercive, benevolent, or consultative ways of influencing individuals or groups are measured by the degree to which each method helps change their ability to achieve goals and meet evident needs. In any consideration of organization renewal, the amount of problem-solving help offered to meet individual, group, or organizational needs by any renewal stimulator is a key factor in the process of confrontation and change.

One of the most hopeful solutions to this way of coping with situations has been to increase the effectiveness of all sizes of face-to-face groups at all levels of the organizational complex. Management's development of "teamwork" is particularly important in the interaction of individuals who regularly must solve problems, face issues, and creatively meet their own needs as well as those of their group and their organization. Here the behavioral scientists are inclined to emphasize the importance of permitting personal individuality, and to increase the role of the individual as an influence within his organization. Recent behavioral experiments confirm that organization renewal requires that opportunities be provided for the individual to contribute to overall goals. This has been accentuated by the productivity and morale studies conducted by the Institute of Social Research at the University of Michigan.

> Studies in the fields of psychology, sociology, and social psychology clearly indicate that if an organization is to make maximum use of its human resources and meet the highest level of man's needs, it must provide conditions where the individual can relate effectively to all of his organizational groups—whether he is a member, peer, or a leader. Emphasis on proper development of groups within an organization can be an aid to individual growth . . . .[18]

But before task groups can develop the kind of climate that brings about the achievement of both individual, group, and organizational goals, they must have leaders and members who work together in the mature manner that is frequently referred to as team effectiveness.

Teamwork requires some kind of coordination among its members; in some cases more, in some cases less. This coordination is not so much concerned with an individual's wielding of strong leadership as it is the most advantageous utilization of the performance of each member of the group.

When people are presenting ideas in a problem-solving group and, as is usually the case, working against time, some way must be established to sort out that which is useful and that which is not. Also, some way should be found to determine periodically what progress the group has made toward the accomplishment of the task before it. Group effectiveness is enhanced when this is done easily and smoothly. A concise statement of goals provides a criteria by which the appropriateness of each member's input can be evaluated, and a simple planning chart, always kept current, will serve to show the team how much remains to be done.

Frequently overlooked, perhaps because it seems like contemplating the obvious, is the need to have some way of knowing when a decision has been made either by the group or for the group. How often have you known a few members of a group to pursue a task at full bay, in the wrong direction, somehow unaware that a different decision has already been reached by the others. And similarly, how often have you known the members of a task group, in whole or in part, to cease to function because they erroneously think the group's goal has been achieved. In both cases, of course, there is an absence of effective leadership, communication, and trust in the group. They have not become a team.

In a very real sense the clarity of the group's goals, communicative openness, and decision-making process grows out of all four levels of needs considered earlier in this chapter (see page 102). As these needs are being met, the group members will be continually working on four problems inherent in their "psychological contracts:"

1. PROBLEM OF IDENTITY. Questions each person in a group seeks to answer are "Who am I in this group?" "What kinds of resources do I have that will be useful?" "What roles will I play or be called upon to play?" "How will this group affect the way I see myself?"

Probably the most prevalent impediments to productive group action are the circumstances under which a new member may enter the group or a current member be severed, the kind of disciplinary action that can be taken against a member of the group, when the group is to convene, and who has the authority to use the group's resources. These problems tend to direct attention toward influence within the group.

2. PROBLEM OF POWER AND INFLUENCE. Members are concerned about who will have power and influence; how much others will exert influence; how much others can be influenced.

This leads us to the matter of group power and influence which, like goals, need to be understood by every member of the group. The important power and influence considerations are these: who has the final word, what actual authority does the group possess, how is a decision to be arrived at (e.g., secret vote, open vote, consensus, or judgment of the leader), and by what means and under what conditions may a decision reached or action taken by the group be reversed or overruled. This problem will remain a major block whether or not one finds an "openness" in communications. Members of a group have different abilities and varying degrees of fear in expressing themselves. While it is certainly not true that all members should participate equally, it is true that all members ought to have an *opportunity* to contribute if they wish to do so. Many a group has silently, but not so mysteriously, disintegrated because one or two members *apparently* were not permitted to have their say and influence the decision. A special effort may be required to help a reticent member to communicate his thoughts and, conversely, to help an overly outgoing member to curb his tendency to dominate. The most difficult channels of intra-group communication to keep open are those through which personal feelings are expressed. These may actually be important to group effectiveness, but normally they only thrive in a warm and permissive atmosphere. This brings us to the third contributing problem that challenges all work group relationships.

3. PROBLEM OF GOALS AND NEEDS. "What are the needs of others in the group?" and "Will any of my needs be met?" are questions con-

stantly asked by both the leader and members. In many groups little information is available to answer these questions because members are unaware of their needs or are unwilling to share their concerns and feelings. Whether needs are being met will be related to group *cohesiveness*, that is, keeping the members of the group together so that they function as a group. In some organizations, this might be accomplished authoritatively or as a condition of continued employment, but these forces are not always available. In voluntary groups, for example, the leader must necessarily consider a great many human characteristics to keep the group from falling apart at the seams. Even where authoritative rule *can* be applied, organizational growth requires that certain human requirements and characteristics be considered. One requirement would be the tolerance of different needs and goals. No matter how homogeneous or unified the members of a group may be, different points of view or preferences will arise among them. Whether or not a group remains intact and, to a large extent, its effectiveness depend upon the tolerance within the group of these differences, and the means used to compromise them.

4. PROBLEM OF ACCEPTANCE AND INTIMACY. A group often confronts persons with the issue of their needs, difficulties, hopes, and feelings of adequacy and inadequacy in forming close, trusting, and intimate relationships with other persons. For some persons, to be alone is threatening; while to others, to be close is difficult. The problem of achieving appropriate levels of intimacy is often worked out covertly as the group works on its task. Openly expressed, honestly stated feelings toward each other are a necessary ingredient of group effectiveness. Neither an individual member nor the groups as a whole wisely can be taken for granted. Acceptance can be expressed—in many forms and at any time—by one member to another member or to the whole group; by the group to one of its members; by the group to itself; or by some outside source to the group and its members. It can deal with large or small contributions. It is, in effect, a reward of membership, and it is needed by both the group and its individual members. Shallow flattery or pseudo-humorous, left-handed references, however, can do more harm than good.

As complicated as groups may be, they are a major key to individual and organizational change. Only by becoming convinced that we can work with people effectively through increasing our skill of diagnosing particular operational situations can managers find fruitful results through use of work group teams. Increased insight into one's own ability, sensitivity to others, diagnostic ability about the problems the group faces, and the practice of effective leadership skills make possible the effective utilization of people in teams to achieve organization renewal.

NOTES

1. Harry Levinson and others, *Men, Management, and Mental Health* (Cambridge: Harvard University Press, 1962).
2. Rensis Likert, *New Patterns of Management* (New York: McGraw-Hill Book Co., Inc., 1961), p. 99.
3. Gordon L. Lippitt and Edith W. Seashore, *The Leader Looks at Group Effectiveness*, Looking Into Leadership Monographs (Washington, D.C.: Leadership Resources, Inc., 1961), p. 1. Reprinted with permission of Leadership Resources, Inc.
4. *Ibid.*
5. Portions of this section of the chapter are adapted from the author's previous article, "Individuality and Teamwork," *The Federal Accountant*, 1964.
6. Likert, *Developing Patterns of Management* (New York: American Management Assn., Inc., No. 182, 1956), p. 7.
7. Leland P. Bradford and Lippitt, "The Individual Counts in Effective Group Relations," *NEA Journal*, November, 1954, p. 487.
8. Adapted for this section of the chapter are portions of the author's previous article, "Guidelines for Managing Groups," *Credit Union Executive*, Winter, 1965. Used by permission.
9. Warren H. Schmidt, *The Leader Looks at the Leadership Dilemma*, Looking Into Leadership Monographs (Washington, D.C.: Leadership Resources, Inc., 1961), p. 9.
10. Irving R. Weschler, *The Leader Looks at Creativity*, Looking Into Leadership Monographs (Washington, D.C.: Leadership Resources, Inc., 1961), p. 10.
11. Edgar H. Schein, *Organizational Psychology* (Englewood Cliffs, N.J.: Prentice-Hall, Inc., 1965), pp. 72 and 73.
12. Lippitt, "Improving Decision-making With Groups," *Y Work With Youth* (a publication of the Program Services Dept., National Council of YMCAs), April, 1958.
13. Abraham Zaleznik and David Moment, *The Dynamics of Interpersonal Behavior* (New York: John Wiley & Sons, Inc., 1964).
14. Fred E. Fiedler, *A Theory of Leadership Effectiveness* (New York: McGraw-Hill Book Co., Inc., 1967), pp. 18–22.
15. Robert E. Blake and Jane B. Mouton, "Reactions to Intergroup Competition Under Win-Lose Conditions," *Management Science*, Vol. VII, 1961.
16. Douglas McGregor, *The Human Side of Enterprise* (New York: McGraw-Hill Book Co., Inc., 1960), p. 19.
17. Robert N. McMurray, "Case for the Benevolent Autocrat," *Harvard Business Review*, January–February, 1958.
18. Bradford and Lippitt, *op. cit.*, p. 487.

PART THREE

Process of Interfacing

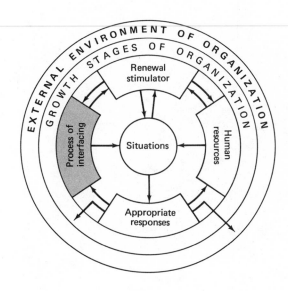

Organization renewal will be initiated and maintained if human resources solve problems in a climate in which genuine interfacing takes place.

In Chapter 7 the essential elements of interfacing are explained as consisting of dialogue, confrontation, search, and coping. The way this process is related to the problem-solving process and change is considered in Chapter 8. The ethical implication of interfacing and change is discussed in Chapter 9.

7 DIALOGUE, CONFRONTATION, SEARCH, AND COPING

> It is my impression that no one really likes the new. We are afraid of it. . . .
> In the case of drastic change the uneasiness is of course deeper and more last-
> ing. We can never be really prepared for that which is wholly new. We have to
> adjust ourselves, and every radical adjustment is a crisis in self-esteem: we
> undergo a test, we have to prove ourselves. It needs inordinate self-confidence
> to face drastic change without inner trembling.
>
> ERIC HOFFER, 1902–

Fighting, hostility, and controversy, all of which can be called conflict, are nearly everyday fare for individuals and groups, although they do not always openly evidence themselves. Too often, there is emotional effort and involvement by many people that go largely unrewarded because they move in restrictive rather than constructive channels. By the same token, conflict releases energy at every level of human affairs— energy that can produce positive, constructive results. Two things should be recognized here. First, that such conflict is an absolutely predictable social phenomenon. Second, that conflict should not be repressed, but channeled to useful purposes. Both of these realities lie at the heart of organization renewal.

The goal of organizational leadership is not to eliminate conflict, but to use it—to turn the released energy to good advantage. The role of the behavioral scientist is to study, analyze, and report why people behave as they do, and to suggest ways in which research can be applied practically.

Conflict is almost always caused by unlike points of view. Because we have not learned exactly alike, and because we therefore see and value things differently, we vary in our beliefs as to what things are or should be. Because conflict, large or small, is inevitable, the extreme result at either end is a situation that is undesirably abrasive or dialogue that is creatively productive.

> The biggest block to personal communication is man's inability to listen in-
> telligently, understandingly, and skillfully to another person. This deficiency
> in the modern world is widespread and appalling.[1]

The process of conflict occurs to man at several plateaus: Intrapsychic (the aversion to being involved personally), interpersonal (the internal manager-vs.-controller controversy), community (where to build the new parking lot), interracial (how Negroes are to be promoted), and others. At any of these levels, the energies released by conflict can be used for good or evil. The problem is to make the conflict creative for organizational good. Most of the workable approaches discovered by behavioral scientists have centered on changing the psychological climate of conflict.

In establishing a helpful psychological climate, a manager should minimize—never try to eliminate—the threat that always underlies conflict. Actually, threat is a stimulus to creative conflict as much as to destructive conflict. It is impossible to eliminate threat in the face of real differences. But one satisfactory way to minimize threat is to surround the protagonists with an atmosphere conducive to interfacing. Here attitudes of respect, understanding, and communication must prevail. The main purpose in doing this is to break a vicious cycle that is characterized by reciprocal threat, resistance, and aggressiveness.

It is important to depersonalize conflict by insuring that the disputants do not sit in judgment of each other, and to focus the conflict on the basic issues by concentrating disagreement on factual ground. Progress in this direction, however slight, is usually self-continuing, and tends to reduce wholesale indictment to retail packaging. This limits conflict to manageable areas that are more likely to be subject to negotiation, accommodation, or compromise. When people are introduced to what they recognize as fact, they tend to become more objective—sensible, if you prefer. Unsupported opinion and implication generally cause an opposite effect. The leader himself, as a rule, should look at the issues coldly and at the people involved warmly.

Conflict will expand—first emotionally, and then physically—according to how the values at issue change. What starts out to be a relatively insignificant dispute can quickly grow to encompass a larger controversy by feeding upon released energy. The latter is violently demonstrated in the ghetto riots experienced by our cities, but less dramatic examples regularly occur in our organizations. The alert leader will clearly, quickly, and forcefully describe the parameters of imminent conflict, if he can, and in doing this he endeavors to limit the responses to areas with which a group can successfully cope. At the same time, reactions must not be heated by the introduction of assumed intentions, inferred beliefs, and plain untruths. Remember that people in conflict or out are inclined to act on what they want to believe.

Leadership, in resolving organizational conflict creatively, also requires empathy and equality, but not neutrality. The neutral position is damaging because by its nature it recognizes nothing. Empathy, on the other hand, means that leadership recognizes both the plight and the ideas of both sides in conflict, without necessarily agreeing totally with either. Equality means that neither of the conflicting parties be made to feel inferior, for the alternative is greater jealousy and heightened competition.

Lastly, adopting an attitude of one side winning and the other side losing is like pouring gasoline on the fire of conflict. On the other hand, the provisional try—honest fact-finding (all the facts), exhaustive exploration (both parties working together), and meaningful problem-solving (with a lot of "What if we try this . . . ?" thrown in)—pries open the door to constructive creativity.

These are, of course, fundamental rules. The experienced leader knows that they do not always work as they should. He knows that he must contend with counterforces between those who passively refuse to engage in conflict and with those who deliberately develop conflict as a battleground for hatreds and greeds, as well as those to whom conflict is a healthy challenge for betterment. Nevertheless, management of human conflict is an objective of organization renewal.

In this second half of the twentieth century, man has the opportunity to develop his instruments of communication, and his assimilation of information necessary to communication, beyond any stage yet achieved. This process unavoidably requires more than merely the efficient expansion of *external* technological capabilities. Our critical concern is the need for a process involving internalizing of communication so that something other than information is transmitted. This latter process can be called interfacing, which is a combination of dialogue, confrontation, search, and coping.

In its simple sense, dialogue is "a talking together." [2] That in itself may be a mild exchange of pleasantries or violent recriminations. In its larger, more resultful sense, it is not only the necessity of mankind but also much more than ordinary conversation. In his book, *The Miracle of Dialogue*, Reuel Howe [3] defines it as "the serious address and response between two or more persons in which the being and truth of each is confronted with the being and truth of the other." The need for *confrontation* must also be combined with *search* and *coping*, and these things tend to eliminate the extremes of pleasantry and recrimination.

Confrontation implies a facing up to the tangled web of relationships, issues, problems, challenges, values, and potentialities that invariably hang like a curtain between the entities into which man is divided or into which he divides himself. Unless each entity involved—for the sake of clarity and brevity, conceived here as being, singularly or collectively, an individual, a group, an organization, or a political or natural subdivision of man-made society—sincerely tries to penetrate this curtain, communication rebounds in sterility. Man is an animal; exclusively among all animals, he is capable of receiving, processing, understanding, and acting upon ideas. Because of this unique capability, he is superior to all other animals. Paradoxically and perhaps also inexplicably, however, his attempts at communication in matters of emotion and feelings are often devious and confused where those of all other animals are positive and direct. Man does not always use his exceptional capability of communication to its full extent. If an idea is only received and neither processed nor acted upon, communication ends in a cul-de-sac. If an idea is received and processed in a rational mind but not acted upon, neither man nor his society benefits. But if the elements of receiving, processing, understanding, and acting are present in an exchange of ideas, the first elementary step has been taken in the quest for interfacing. These four processes constitute an overt attempt to reduce to manageable scope the often enormous problem of unlikeness between entities.

This is the aspect of the search for the self and the other in the process of interfacing. Martin Buber's concept of the I-Thou relationship exemplifies the essentials of the search for comprehension and understanding between persons. As he stated, "Existence cannot be possessed but only shared in." The energizing effort to reach out to the other releases oneself in the process. Such a search is the essential linkage between confrontation and coping.

Once this search is under way, the act of coping becomes a mutual attempt to solve, to know, to empathize, to understand, by means of equitable change, whatever relationship is confronted. This is the fourth essential step in interfacing, and together with dialogue, confrontation, and search, it produces a dynamic interaction in which reality is faced, resolution produced, and action effected.

On the other hand, these things have always been so. They are not new, but their implementation has been made vastly more difficult by the increasing complexity of the world in which we live. Educated mankind shares a common worry about the growing impersonality of man's relation to man, the hugeness of institutions, and still what John Locke called "an age at enmity with all restraint." These things generate a feeling of powerlessness to act, to influence either the parade of monotonous events or the constant trickle of small annoyances that mark our all too brief time on earth. Yet it is because men as individuals and mankind as a society have tried to influence events and circumstances that all human progress has materialized.

Those who are compelled by motivations larger than themselves to react, to respond to situations even of apparent hopelessness, to overcome the restlessness and rootlessness which man inflicts upon himself, have turned to interfacing. The mold from which they were cast has not been broken, men are shaped in it still, and theirs is a constant search for ways in which to improve interfacing. Those who would place their feet in these footsteps are numerous, and far more resilient than their acts portray. Desire is strong, but it is essential to the purpose that men first comprehend the elements of interfacing, for it is a skill that few inherit or acquire.

The quest for interfacing is evidenced on all sides of us, by all kinds of entities (Figure 7–1). It is present in a husband's attempt to express love for his wife. It exists when an individual expresses creative disagreement rather than conformity, or when he seeks to influence the direction of an organization by persuasion alone. It is evidenced in the voicing of responsible community action by an individual in a group, and by those who individually contribute to their country through constructive criticism. It is obvious in speeches at the United Nations that urge peace, and in countless hundreds of diplomatic conversations throughout the world between men representing opposing ideologies.

The diagram suggests the many levels at which interfacing takes place. It is a process that involves man at all levels of his existence. Note that

1. **A** and **B** are both sender and receiver in the process of interfacing.
2. Interfacing participants are constantly **processing** through their senses, feelings, ideas, and actions.
3. Interfacing is essentially a dynamic **transaction** with active participation by **A** and **B.**
4. **A** and **B** may be any combination of Individual, Group, Organization, Community, or Nation.
5. **Ecology** describes the complex totality of forces acting on biological man.

FIGURE 7–1

Various Levels of Interfacing

Each of these is in itself but a microcosmic example of interfacing related to change in the various sub-systems of world society. In each such contact between individuals as entities, man is influenced by his grasp of the universe, his understanding of God, the economics of his survival and the ecological factors that affect him as a thinking organism.

The groups which men come to be a part of also engage in interfacing and this is their principal importance. Within the group, by means of interfacing, the individual

> . . . seeks to satisfy our desire for a sense of personal worth and importance primarily by the response we get from the people we are close to, in whom we are interested, and whose approval and support we are eager to have. The face-to-face groups with whom we spend the bulk of our time, are, consequently, the most important to us.[4]

Friendship and social groups, trade and professional groups, civic and task groups, and others, are manifestations of man's inclination to influence not only other men as individuals but also the group and its community of interest. Outside the group, as a societal sub-system, those who comprise its membership collectively try to be an agent for interaction with other groups or sub-systems. Here the group uses dialogue to achieve meaning for its existence.

If one views an organization as an entity made up of several groups, it becomes obvious that organizations, too, look to interfacing as a means of gaining essential objectives. The large and small conflicts between labor and management, between government bureaus and industries, between divergent denominations of the same religious faith, for example, all involve interfacing. Organizations also find cause to gain acceptance, to assess themselves in matters of national policy, to protect their reason for existence from legislative encroachment. As each organization barters or compromises for compatibility with its communities, as each organization explores its purpose, philosophy, and policy, it attempts to develop interfacing as a path to successful performance.

In spite of the tremendous explosion of population that everywhere creates larger, more impersonal, and increasingly harassed communities, an implicit "sense of community" continues to arise whenever events are of sufficient impact to bring it into play. When disaster strikes, when public services are halted, when endemic disease threatens, when law and order are abandoned, when racial alienation cripples, that entity which we call a community reacts and in some manner engages in dialogue, confrontation, search, and coping—it discovers the heart to find a solution in interfacing. A similar situation is created by the geometric growth of megalopolises. In our day, shortages of water, drowning in smog, pockets of poverty, and competing industrial wage scales are illustrations of interregional maladjustments that require interfacing. Sometime soon man must find ways for people in communities to engage in interfacing horizontally across areas of common need, vertically from the poor to the economically affluent community influences, and across the lines of race, creed, or color that divide us.

Because interfacing is a dynamic process not always uncomplicated by confusions and doubts, its implementation involves a complex transaction (Figure 7–2). Dr. Leo Rosten [5] has pointed out that:

> This problem of getting an idea from one head to another is . . . apparently more complicated than any the physical sciences have had to deal with . . . . We go on the assumption that there is something called "the truth" and forget that there are truths. We think we can talk about **facts** and forget there is something called context.

It is the context in which interfacing must take place that makes reality in its execution elusive. Both the entity sending and the entity receiving an idea in the process of interfacing bring to the transaction personal attributes which limit and color their effectiveness.

SELF-IMAGE.   Each entity wears a mantle of self-perception. What a man or a group or a nation thinks of itself—and this is a combination

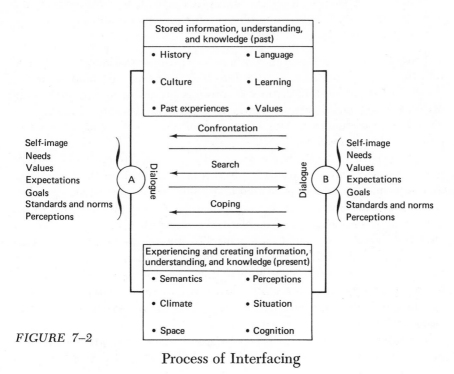

FIGURE 7–2

Process of Interfacing

of such things as its ego, pride, traditions, ambitions—is inescapably reflected in its behavior with and toward other entities.

NEEDS.   Each entity will believe itself to possess unique needs—the need to love, to belong, to give, to be recognized, to be creative, to be secure, to acquire, to work, to be successful, to solve problems—all yearning to be satisfied.

VALUES.   Each entity will subjectively hold dear those things which heritage or education or environment has made valuable to it.

EXPECTATIONS.   No matter how disproportionate they may be, great expectations are consultants sitting at the elbow of each participant in a dialogue. They tend to implant a "mental set" that affects flexibility, they counsel against faith and good will, and they rationalize failure.

GOALS.   Unilaterally worthy though they are, the fixed objectives of an entity can become barriers to vision if no effort is made to take a look from a higher elevation.

STANDARDS.   Each entity will cling to fixed norms that reflect its cultural background and experience, and probably nothing is so difficult to lay down even for the purpose of temporarily trying on another viewpoint.

PERCEPTIONS.   These are eyeglasses worn by each entity that tend to distort rather than to increase conceptual clarity. It is quite traumatic for either entity to take them off even for a moment; still more painful an experience to have the lens reground.

These factors, and sometimes others less pronounced, must be thrown into the scale of balance. In addition, it is necessary to compensate for the effects of outdated or erroneous information and incongruous gaps in understanding which are by-products of faulty education, limiting environment, differences in languages and cultural levels, and in noncomparable value systems.

Man recognizes truth in the axiom *What is past is prologue,* but he does not always find it easy to apply this kind of truth or the knowledge and information which is available to him to a particular situation. Among animals, man alone is not by instinct selectively adaptive to his environment or circumstances. Nature ordains that he must learn by analyzed experience, sometimes painfully, but nature does not provide a means whereby the experiences of one generation are automatically passed on to the next. Thus, with abbreviated memory and no instinct for self-preservation as a society, man has had to learn repeatedly that interfacing is the only effective form of address to problems involving human relationships.

Recently, in the onrush of technological advance, man has devised new ways to store and retrieve information that do not rely solely upon his brain. As this physical process is developed, and as it is controlled and used wisely, there is an increasingly greater chance that each entity participating in interface will come more and more to see the world as it really is, and to evaluate the other's words as more than unintelligible noise.

When this begins to happen, however, interfacing itself will create new information and experience, for its very essence is new understanding. The fundamental action resulting from search and coping is the removal of the curtain that hangs between the protagonists, the transfer of reality from the shadow of suspicion to the sunlight of reason. In a new light, there will be coined semantics and a strange climate, unfamiliar physical and psychological distances, frightening perspectives seen for the first time, and uncertain recognition. These are the challenges, but they are also indicative of the rewards.

Much of the civilized world is already twenty years into an information revolution, and this phenomenon is touching the souls of men and women everywhere in countless and multiplying ways. It is realigning perspectives for both large and small organizations, and for those which are in the birth stage as well as those which have gained maturity. It can serve to protect and enhance the dignity of man and vastly enlarge the mobilization of human energy. Unfortunately, as has been mentioned, information in and of itself, even when communicated, is not enough to establish effective interfacing. Those who attempt to engage in interfacing must fully appreciate beforehand all the conditions that must be obtained, the many hazards that must be encountered, and the roadblocks that must be faced:

COMPLEXITY. Few major problems in human relationships reach the stage where interfacing is imperative without having multiple aspects that are in combination less than simple. For example, when one is dealing with the divergent interests of labor/management, or the entanglements of competitive departments within an organization, or the differing philosophies of succeeding generations, the process of interfacing becomes far from easy.

ANTICIPATION. Prejudgment by peers or the opinions of friends can block out reality to such an extent that behavior is irrational.

LANGUAGE. Modern systems of translation have only partially and imperfectly helped to bring a common denominator to the Tower of Babel. Differences in language still complicate the ability of one entity to relate with another entity at both emotional and rational levels.

SEMANTICS. The ability of each entity to find meaning in a dialogue of words that are mutually invented or understood is crucial to establishing an effective communication process, for it is not the words that are understood that cause trouble but rather the words that are unknowingly misunderstood. The innate desire to communicate is not enough; there must be a sufficient degree of skill.

TRUST. Like a seed thrown on barren ground, interfacing cannot exist under conditions of suspicion, intrigue, and mistrust; and the initial objective must be to establish a climate where these things do not prevail.

ADVANTAGE. Nor will interfacing thrive when it becomes apparent, or is suspected, that a participating entity is striving to gain control, to place the other at a disadvantage; it is natural in these circumstances for resistance to become dominant. Similarly, failure by one entity to make full disclosure to the other, or for either to enter dialogue with incomplete knowledge, makes the search one-sided and inconclusive.

INTENT. Interfacing is not present when either or both entities lack serious intention and merely desire to expose their external selves in an attempt selfishly to gain a goal unilaterally.

EMOTION. Since man is never completely rational, utterances may be heard with ears of anger and jealousy, envy becomes a proud weakness and right more precious than needed solutions; but other emotions are beneficial because they develop the essential energy required to make interfacing dynamic.

EMPATHY. Successful interfacing does not depend so much upon capability of an entity to be compassionate as it does upon its ability in communication to convey cognizance of the other's ideas, feelings, concepts, wants, and needs.

LEADERSHIP. A situation in which interfacing can serve a purpose is almost always one in which nonaggressive initiative is imperative; conversely, a nonsupplicant response is necessary.

DEFINITION. A candid elimination of ambiguity and deception in stating both sides of any issue is an essential aspect of problem-solving through interfacing; without such clarity and completeness, there can be no definite goal and no direction.

Such a list might be extended further, but these items suffice to show the difficulty of interfacing and explain what it is. Whenever most of these factors are absent, one finds failure in communication. The barriers are many and need to be recognized if we are to surmount them. One or the other entity flees from the problem and declares an intention to proceed independently, regardless of cost. Increased alienation, if not actually sharpened hostility, becomes evident. Prejudices and fears lead to defensive behavior, which in turn leads to further solidification of the same policies, practices, and decisions that may have created the problem in the first place. And, too, it usually happens either that a scapegoat is manufactured or resort is made to some unhappy expediency.

There is, in a word, little dialogue or confrontation, inadequate search, and no coping.

Interfacing is an exercise in confidence in understanding, and a key element, therefore, is a readiness to listen while the other entity expresses itself without artificiality, in its own way, out of its own culture, in its own manner and language. At its best, it creates new words and meaning from the shared experience. Since communication is inevitably evaluative, an element most troublesome to achieve is an absence of judgmental attitude. Because each participating entity has a right—in self-defense—initially to expect the other to seek an advantage, it is incumbent upon both to contribute a modicum of trust, not as a gamble but in demonstration of caring, and to suspend judgment until the understanding is as complete as possible. Interfacing itself is experimental, by its very nature a treading on quicksand, for with failure it can and usually does result in disaster qualified only by the practical limits of consequent irrationality.

Many philosophers have been attracted to consideration of this kind of concomitant attempt at communication. Henry David Thoreau touched upon it when he observed that "Any man more right than his neighbor, constitutes a majority of one." Similarly, he wrote: ". . . the man who goes alone can start today; but he who travels with another must wait until that other is ready." Voltaire was incisively critical in stating that ". . . men tend to use thought only as an authority for their injustice, and employ speech only to conceal their thoughts."

Interfacing is worthwhile in human affairs if only to ensure that all terms of reconciliation, understanding, and solution may reflect all circumstances of disagreement. Stress, tension, and suffering are all part of the painful and joyful nature of obtaining such a reflection. This is why Voltaire urged men to allow anyone to talk at length, with open spontaneity, even though what they say may only add to the accumulation of mankind's nonsense. Confrontation by entities without a balance of flexibility is bound to be fruitless, and it should be recognized that acceptance of alternatives is basic to any context of resolution in which the Lewinian concept of "unfreezing, change and refreezing" is to be involved, as it almost always is.

Strangely enough, it is not the absolute truths with which he abides that cause man's travail, so much as it is interpretations of these truths. Someone has pointed out:

> There are subjects—mathematics, physics and the descriptive sciences supply some of them—which can be discussed in terms of verifiable facts and precise hypothesis. There are other subjects—the concrete affairs of commerce, law, organization and police-work—which can be handled by rule of thumb and generally accepted convention. But in between is the vast corpus of problems, assumptions, adumbrations, fictions, prejudices,

tenets; the sphere of random belief and hopeful guesses; the whole world, in brief, of abstract opinion and disputation about matters of feeling. To this world belongs everything about which civilized men care most.[6]

We have so far impersonally explored and analyzed interfacing and its essential features and requirements. Our own lives, however, permit but a small degree of impersonality. As Rufus Jones expressed it, "Already it is clear enough that the 'self' and the 'other' are born together, that personal selfhood is organic with the society in which it is formed. . . ."

The quest for interfacing is not a choice; it is a necessity.

Whether one is examining the communication between one person and another or between one nation in the West and another in the East, there are some common elements essential to interfacing as shown in Figure 7–3:

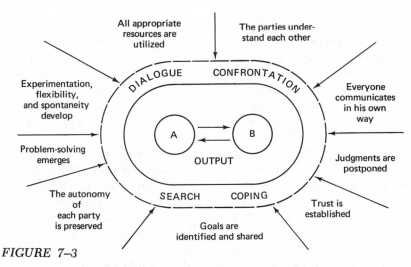

FIGURE 7–3

Elements in the Process of Interfacing

UNDERSTANDING. Interfacing depends on confidence in the parties of both parts that one is being understood. A real expression of interest and a readiness to listen are key elements in this understanding.

COMMUNICATING IN ONE'S OWN WAY. Interfacing permits each person to express himself in his own manner, language, and culture. We may seem to others to be different and incoherent, but the necessity of being allowed to tell one's story in one's own way is paramount.

LACK OF JUDGMENTAL BEHAVIOR. It is difficult in communications not to be evaluative. If, however, we are to establish interfacing, we must not judge the other person, group, or organization. This is one of the most difficult elements for any person to put into practice.

ESTABLISHING TRUST. To be able to establish a modicum of trust is essential. As each party feels that he is influencing the other, the trust begins to emerge. It is only when mutual influence is seen, given, received, and acted upon that trust becomes evident.

MINIMUM ATTEMPT TO CONTROL. Interfacing is a process of jointly coping with a solution to understood problems and not a process of control of one participant over another.

AUTONOMY IS PRESERVED. The need for a person to feel his own independence is an essential thing to protect in the process of interfacing. One remembers the statement of Henry David Thoreau who commented, "If a man does not keep pace with his companions, perhaps it is because he hears a different drummer." We all have the right to hear on the basis of our own idiosyncratic nature and to have what we say we hear respected by others.

PROBLEM-SOLVING APPROACH. The interfacing process utilizes the best commitment to problem-solving as a guide for coping. Such a problem orientation communicates a desire to collaborate in the solution of a mutual problem between the parties involved.

EXPERIMENTATION, FLEXIBILITY, AND SPONTANEITY. An essential element of interfacing is that there is no definite answer or absolute in the process. Both parties need to be willing to experiment in a number of ways to cope with the problem they are confronting. In such experimentation, the value of spontaneous approach to the problem-solving process lessens any fear of deception on the part of the other person.

The ability to be open to new alternatives and to be open to change is an essential aspect of the process of interfacing. In coping with change, we find the need for maintaining flexibility of one's position, attitudes, and behavior in order to be able to respond in a creative growth way to the new potentials in the confrontations of life.

Thus far I have endeavored to explore the multiple factors involved in the quest for effective interfacing. Let us also examine what each of us might do to prepare ourselves to achieve the interfacings of life with a greater consistency and frequency than in the past.

WE MUST START WITH OURSELVES. To understand oneself is the essential element in mental health, communication, and interfacing. It requires, however, more than just knowing oneself. It also involves the giving of oneself. The character, Cristina, in Ignazio Silone's *Bread and Wine,* says that "in all times, in all societies, the supreme act is to give oneself to find oneself, to lose oneself to find oneself. One has only what one gives." This is a starting place for any of us.

WE MUST DEVELOP OUR ABILITY TO DIAGNOSE SITUATIONS. The increased knowledge from the social sciences makes it possible for each of us to be more knowledgeable in our ability to diagnose our problems in communication. Such knowledge is a prerequisite for effective implementation of our intent.

WE MUST EXAMINE OUR PHILOSOPHY AND OUR BELIEFS. We need to ask ourselves what it is we really believe. It is an easy thing in today's world for people to scorn idealism. We should not be afraid of looking at our ideals, goals, and objectives. It is when we understand these objectives that we know where we stand in the quest for interfacing.

WE NEED TO BE GENUINE. Interfacing requires us to be genuine in our relationships with others. A person needs to be exactly what he is, not a facade, a role, or a pretense. It is only by providing a genuine reality in dialogue that interfacing becomes possible. If the other person senses falseness, he will become cautious and wary, and interfacing will not develop.

WE MUST DEVELOP OUR CREATIVE LEADERSHIP. As never before, the world needs creative leadership that is looking for new paths, new methods, new approaches, and the search for innovations that are yet to come. We must accept modern technology and use it rather than be afraid of it. To see such technologies as tools to improve mankind, not to control man, is the attitude.

The quest for interfacing is almost always worthwhile, but not always successful. Doubts or rejections are usually founded on knowledgeably assumed intractability on the part of one side or the other of a problem-solving confrontation. The ultimate end of such intractability is extremism and dissension under circumstances that are likely to be unpleasant. This can occur within an organization—between individuals, among the members of a group, or between groups—and it can occur between the organization and some element in its environment. Like it or not, a leader in or of an organization must learn to endure such conditions and to operate efficiently under them. If he can gird himself with the necessary courage, arm himself with the skills of leadership, and be prepared to act appropriately in each situation, the menace of extremism—either of method or of issue—will assume its proper proportion.

Conscientious leaders strive to take action and make decisions without losing touch with sound basic principles. Constructive disagreement is a part of dialogue—freedom of speech must be preserved, and the viewpoint of the smallest minority should be duly heard and considered. But the inherent problems are these:

When does dissent become dissension?
How does one identify destructive disagreement?
When does freedom of speech become harassment?

The behavioral sciences can contribute some answers by helping to distinguish between legitimate, responsible, representative individuals and groups and those which might be characterized as "only trouble-makers," and by pointing out some ways the irresponsible influence of the latter can be reduced.

The organizational leader should initially look for and evaluate the ultimate objectives of a questionable splinter group. If he finds none, or if what he finds is immaterial or plainly subversive to a recognized good, it is reasonable to conclude that the members of the group are primarily interested in enhancing their own egos, "hurting" someone else, or exercising their ability to gain "power" through harassment. Typically, those who are only troublemakers cause discord and disruption for its own sake. They disdain the obligation to earn the right to wield influence. Rather than being interested in coping with a problem, they purposefully block any form of mutual accommodation that might lead to problem-solving.

This is not to say that all dissenters are suspect, nor that all outspoken small groups in an organization belong to the lunatic fringe. History shows us that some individuals and minority groups have stood against the majority, and the established way, in prophetic and sublime correctness. To confound the problem, we live in a world in which the most obvious truths have been gained only by the most extreme measures. Most of the trouble caused by extremists is generated by their unwillingness to proceed in accepted ways, and unwillingness to exercise the patience needed to bring about change. By these reluctances they can be known.

There are modes of counterbalance against those who would destroy but not build. Although each situation of this type must be judged by its own demerits, these guides to intelligent action in response to incontinent criticism can be outlined briefly:

EVALUATE THE CRITICISM. Is the source respectable and answerable? Can it fairly be demonstrated not to be so? Is the attack plausible? Or is it self-defeating by its own implausibility? Is it of substantial prominence in general acceptance? Or will denial create attention where none exists materially? Is there a risk of misunderstanding within the organization, even though the allegations are invalid? Does the criticism touch upon a legal or moral obligation? What effect does the criticism have upon the organization's appearance where appearance counts?

USE FACTS AS A SUPPRESSANT. The best course is to promise a full response without delay. Then get facts quickly and accurately. Delay enflames the issue and strengthens the position of the critical. They rely upon an inability to respond in time with indisputable, unslanted factual information. Avoid an immature, hotheaded response like the plague, but remember that wholesome indignation is generally looked upon as a healthy sign of mature concern.

ADMIT FAULTS AND ACCEPT VALID CRITICISM. Almost every attack by destructive persons depends upon a golden thread of truth, cleverly interwoven in a fabric of objective falsity. Find this thread and use it. No organization expects any man to be perfect, and its respect is enlarged by an unpanicked admission of oversight when it is accompanied by timely, appropriate action. Promptly acting upon the element of truth that it must have, often so weakens the position of extremism that its adherents fade away, on that particular front at least. Essentially, however, the strongest rampart of defense is propriety in all past actions; the quickest road to disaster is fearful capitulation.

AVOID CREATING A MARTYR IMAGE. It is a part of the calculated plan of most disruptive individuals and groups to seek a semblance of martyrdom; an underdog posture gains sympathy for them that later may be hard to overcome. On the other hand, their very nature tends to make them talk themselves into a corner, to overplay their position so badly as to arouse disgust and rejection. No one is belittled by taking sincere and persistent steps to engage extremists in effective interfacing; on the other hand, stature is gained when they evade reasonable confrontation.

KEEP THE ISSUES OUT IN THE OPEN. A small minority attacking from an extreme angle must necessarily narrow the field of action in order to achieve concentration. From this concentration, which usually fails to consider broader issues the leader must keep in mind, it hopes to receive disproportional attention and, as a consequence, generate pressure upon its target. It will succeed in this tactic if an attempt is made to hush up the disagreement. Candor is disarming. Increase interest in the specific issue quickly, taking care to place it clearly in context. Do not widen the rift by borrowing from other issues, and do not generalize from individual or group to the whole organization. If the opposition is in the right, entirely or partially, the leader should act or explain satisfactorily why he cannot act on the issue on which they are right. If they are in the wrong, entirely or partially, he should try that part in which they are wrong before the bar of open interfacing.

In *The Strange Tactics of Extremism,* Drs. Harry and Bonaro Overstreet indicate that the principal countermove to extremist and lunatic groups and disruptive individuals is linked to the phrase: Don't be afraid!

Don't be afraid of controversy.
Don't be afraid to set standards of procedure and stick to them.
Don't be afraid to say some kinds of action are beyond the pale.

Assuming I have established an understanding of the need for interfacing in organization renewal, it seems appropriate to examine separately these things which are called confrontation, search, and coping.

Confrontation has been called a process of interpersonal relating in which the behavior, the presence, or the mere existence of one person makes a difference in the behavior of another because they openly "face up" to the situation in which they are involved. To be productive, this process relies upon all the individuals involved communicating honestly and with integrity; but even so it generally tends to be inversely related to the intensity of *domination* which the involved individuals bring to bear. The highest levels of confrontation are found in human interacting in which conflict, threat, and domination—and hence the psychological necessity for defense—are negligible. Conflict, of course, is antipathetic to interfacing but, nevertheless, little interfacing takes place that is totally void of conflict, domination, or attempts to influence. "Direct confrontation of relevant situations in an organization is essential. If we do not confront one another, we keep the trouble within ourselves and we stay in trouble." [7]

Harold H. Anderson,[8] of Michigan State University, has listed four levels of domination-in-conflict which are common to confrontation, and which affect the performance of individuals in an organization:

1. DOMINATION-RESISTANCE. At this level the domination from persons in the environment is sufficiently strong to be perceived as frustration; that is, the domination obstructs the person's pursuit of a goal. If the person cannot avoid or ignore the obstruction, his tendency then is to resist. The resistance is not different psychologically from the original domination by the persons in the environment. Differences in the expressions of domination and resistance depend upon the power and situational opportunities of the adversaries. This is the relationship found in a fight. The more frequent examples of domination-resistance, however, take on symbolic and indirect forms where the attack, the degrading, the delimiting, or the frustrating of the other person can be attempted with less risk.

2. BALANCE OF POWER IN CONFLICT; VACILLATION; INACTION; ANXIETY. If the domination is increased, with correspondingly greater threat, the dominated person becomes confused in his percepts and his evaluations, both of power and strategy. He hesitates or vacillates between resistance and submission. This level of relating is seen in the behavior of children and of adults. It represents an uncertain balance of power in conflict expressed in daydreaming, inaction, indecision, worry, "nervousness," and anxiety.

3. SUBMISSION; SEVERE PSYCHONEUROSIS. If domination is further increased in severity, the spontaneity and resourcefulness of the domi-

nated person shrink even more. A child in this situation loses his sense of personal worth, is said to have low ego strength, becomes submissive, dependent, bored, and apathetic.

4. DISINTEGRATION; DETERIORATION; FUNCTIONAL PSYCHOSIS. Some individuals, now found mostly in hospitals and institutions, have lived in a dominating environment, frightening and terrifying in the inconsistencies of its demands. As a consequence, the dominated individual builds a psychic protective wall around himself. He encysts and insulates himself in such a way as to be out of communication with persons in his environment in order to be at greater peace in a fantasy world of his own devising.

It can be seen, therefore, that undue domination of *any* individual in problem-solving dialogue tends to be negating. At one end of the spectrum domination leads to unconcealed hostility, and at the other end it leads to total withdrawal; neither extreme can be tolerated in organization renewal. On the other hand, intraorganizational confrontation requires openness in expression and emotion, encouragement of spontaneity, the legitimatization of back talk, candid competitiveness, and some form of reward for mental nonconformity. The best of organization renewal calls for face-to-face interaction in which discussion is kept related to identified goals, no matter how different these goals may be seen by the confronting parties.

Although I have already dealt with *searching* at length, it may be well to review some of the prominent factors. Basically, what must be looked for by all concerned is an understanding of the position taken by the other person or group. Each person must do this in his own way, communicating clearly and avoiding judgmental behavior so as to help establish a relationship of trust. If each person's autonomy and independence is to be preserved, there must be a minimal attempt by anyone to control anyone else. A problem-solving, goal-oriented, continuously experimental approach must be adopted, and there must be considerable flexibility with respect to the acceptance or rejection of the ideas of others.

Contrasted to the questions of attitude and procedure, *coping* brings us down to the action in interfacing. To cope with a situation requires an appropriate response to the situation, issue, problem, or relationship that has been confronted. Appropriateness may be in the "eye of the beholder," but in the context of organization renewal, appropriate response is related to solving the problem in such a way that the person involved learns from the process; the human sub-systems are strengthened by the coping; the organization is aided in its growth; and in some minor or major way, the resolution or solution contributes to the environmental forms affecting the organization.

Successful coping does not mean that everyone ends up satisfied or in complete agreement. It does mean, however, that the persons involved in or related to the situation feel that the essence of the situation was brought out for confrontation, and extensive steps were taken to make the search part of the interfacing process as complete and realistic as possible. The problem solution that led to coping may be tentative, experimental, and given for review, but it is an action that is felt best by the parties involved *at this time.* Here again the existential nature of coping with situations is reinforced.

The process of interfacing is a requirement for organizational functioning. It may be difficult to achieve, but the capability of an organization to better review itself through the interfacing process makes the endeavor well worth the challenge.

NOTES

1. Carl Rogers and Fritz Roethlisberger, "Barriers and Gateways to Communication," *Harvard Business Review,* July–August, 1952.
2. This portion of the chapter (pp. 125–136) is adapted from Gordon L. Lippitt, *Quest for Dialogue* (Philadelphia: Religious Education Committee, Friends General Conference, 1966).
3. Reuel Howe, *The Miracle of Dialogue* (New York: The Seabury Press, 1963).
4. Rensis Likert, *Developing Patterns of Management* (New York: American Management Assn., 1956), p. 7.
5. Leo Rosten, quoted from *Newsletter,* Ohio State University, Vol. XXXII, No. 4, January, 1967.
6. I. A. Richards, *Practical Criticism* (New York: Harcourt, Brace & World, Inc., 1929).
7. Sheldon A. Davis, "An Organic Problem-solving Method of Organizational Change," *Journal of Applied Behavioral Science,* Vol. 3, No. 1, 1967, p. 13.
8. Harold H. Anderson, Paper presented at 9th Congress of the Inter-American Society of Psychology, December, 1964.

8 PROBLEM-SOLVING AND CHANGE

> No great improvements in the lot of mankind are possible, until a great change
> takes place in the fundamental constitution of their modes of thought.
>
> JOHN STUART MILL, 1806–1873

More man-hours and more dollars are spent on managing organizational
affairs than on any other peacetime activity in the United States. For the
most part, this managerial leadership is undertaken in small and large
organizations alike without special training in the skills required to cope
with problem-solving and change. The very behavior of those trying to
achieve change often erects an impenetrable barrier between the led and
the leaders.

Such a condition exists even though we have numerous management
development programs and increasing numbers of persons in managerial
positions who have college degrees in such areas as business administration, public administration, or engineering.[1] A major reason for the
dearth of more effective managerial leadership is a lack of ability to cope
with the processes of change that are rapidly taking place in today's
business or industrial organizations.

Today, we live in a world of rapid change. In less than two decades,
modern technology has leaped from conventional to nuclear power, from
the piston age to the jet age, from "earth men" to "space men."

Change brings with it challenges for those of us who manage people.
Coping with change mainly involves the proper understanding and
utilization of the human resources of the organization. Clarence B. Randall,[2] former board chairman of the Inland Steel Company, has laid
much of the failure to cope with change squarely on management's own
doorstep:

> The timorous and hard-pressed executive, who deep down inside resents
> and resists change . . . seeks refuge in meaningless statistics. Not sure of
> his own thinking and hesitant to plunge boldly ahead on a plan that would
> put his personal status in hazard he takes protective covering in conformity
> with whatever general level of conduct seems to be emerging.

An organization can be described as the way in which people arrange themselves and their relationships in order to get something important accomplished and to solve problems either for themselves or for society. An industrial organization is such an arrangement, usually with the goal of manufacturing and distributing a consumable product. A voluntary organization brings together persons interested in some social need and in providing a service or promoting a common interest. A neighborhood civic group may be a small organization in that people work closely together in their common action, but it is still an arrangement of persons for a useful and productive activity.

Success in accomplishing improved productivity, greater efficiency, or better service—all examples of indirect results of organization renewal—depends on management's mastery of human resources in order to cope with changing demands. The human resource upon which so much depends is the potential response of a person as an individual or in consort with other individuals. Thus, the basic human resource is the individual: a single, complex organism working in a variety of ways to supply his own needs. He can do this alone, or in informal or formal face-to-face groups made up of other individuals working in a variety of ways to supply their common needs.

Frustration is experienced by those who think success in mobilizing human resources, or in initiating organization renewal, is simply a matter of education and, perhaps, of using persuasive stimuli reinforced by annual picnics, newsletters, and adequate coffee-breaks. A newly identified but actually old-fashioned key to obtaining commitment for a new idea, method, or procedure, is to involve the human resources in face-to-face situations for the purpose of self-determination. This general principle, however, requires specific explanation of the process of change. We know a great deal about change. Some think that like the weather, it is a subject everybody talks about but nobody does anything about. This is not true. Many useful beginnings have been made and various approaches to problems of social change have been suggested.

Change may be studied in a variety of approaches and dimensions. This chapter considers the problem-solving approach to organizational change, especially as it relates to complex organizations. Economically, politically, religiously, recreationally, and throughout other aspects of American life, the individual finds himself increasingly involved with a multiplicity of such complex organizations.

Wilbert Moore [3] has summarized some of the major characteristics of contemporary change. Their meaning for organizations may be stated as follows:

> Organizational changes are isolated neither in time nor space. They interact, and their consequent impact both on the organization and on systems is increasingly distant.

The proportion of contemporary organizational and other change that is either planned or results from the consequence of deliberate innovation continues to increase.

The range of technology and social strategies is expanding rapidly, and the net impact on organizations and their functioning is cumulative despite the rapid obsolescence of some procedures.

As we examine the needs of organizations to cope with change, it is evident that there are two basic categories of social change. One type is *unplanned change* which will happen to and in all organizations. A tornado that blows down a warehouse, a new interest rate on bank loans, a power failure—these are situations to which the organization *must react*. In its reaction it will try to maintain homeostasis which, by definition, is the tendency shown by an organism or a social system to seek a new balance when its elements have been disturbed. Homeostatic change, then, is reactive response to outside stimuli when they occur and it may be competitive or cooperative, but it is not anticipatory. The goals of homeostatic change are the *goals of adjustment,* holding on to a balance of material and psychological expenditures and rewards. Examples might be: management introduces a new computer system solely because a competitor has taken this step; an educational system re-looks at itself because the Soviet Union puts a Sputnik into space; a training director forces himself to buy and use video tapes in his training programs because a well-known figure in his field has made advantageous use of them.

A second category of change is *planned change,* the type of change involved in the process of organization renewal. It can be defined as a conscious, deliberate, and collaborative effort to improve the operations of a system—whether it be self-system, social system, or cultural system—through the utilization of knowledge. It usually involves both a renewal stimulator and some kind of organization, which are brought together to solve a problem or to plan and attain an improved state of functioning in the organizational system by utilizing and applying valid knowledge. A person, a group, or an organization can be a renewal stimulator in the renewal process.

The manager, consultant, or social scientist engaged in planned or inventive change has some social "goals" (objectives) and he has a well-structured "design" (scheme) for achieving this end. Planned change, therefore, involves inventing a future, and creating conditions and resources for realizing that future.

Changes, planned and unplanned, are ubiquitous aspects of modern organizations. Unplanned changes occur because of maturation, depressions, accidents, death, or loss of resources. Planned changes occur because of the need for improved technology, new organizational structure, or new procedures. Suppose you are a responsible member in an organization where organization renewal involving change occurs or is contemplated. What might you expect? What might you do? How could you start?

The changes that can be observed in an organization are of endless variety. Examples are changes in tools, in procedures, in the structure of the organization, or in its policies.

In general terms such changes imply, for each of us, uncertainty about our future role and our behavior in that role. These changes also imply, in our relations with others, uncertainty about who will be doing what, what we can expect of others, and what relations other persons will have with one another. Such ambiguity is unsettling; it generates a need to give meaning to the situation, to try to understand it; it also generates a tendency to react in terms of the meaning we discover, whether or not it is correct.

Two decades of research and experience by social scientists have provided some guidelines as to why people reject ambiguity and resist change. It is my contention that people do not resist change itself; rather they balk at the methods organizational leaders use to put changes into effect. Much of this concern was started early in life when most of us resented the dominance and manipulation of parents, teachers, and other authority figures.

We can no longer shrug our shoulders and say, "You can't change people." Research shows we can change people. In fact, people *like* change. What they resist are the *methods* which are used to put changes into effect. The word and concept of "change" is feared because it upsets a way of doing things and threatens security. This feeling is balanced by a desire for new experiences and for the benefits that may come as a result of change.

The practical reality of life is that people resist change in light of prosperity, growth, new situations, and the inadequate skills of leaders. As Albert Schweitzer [4] said:

> Anyone who proposes to do good must not expect people to roll stones out of his way, but must accept his lot calmly even if they roll a few more on it. A strength which becomes clearer and stronger through experiences of such obstacles is the only strength that can conquer them. Resistance is only a waste of strength.

While he implies that resistance is foolish, I suspect that any initiation of organization renewal and change must identify existing resistances, diagnose them, and confront them with planned change. Some of the more typical reasons for resistance to change have been identified in research: [5]

WHEN THE PURPOSE OF THE CHANGE IS NOT MADE CLEAR. Mystery and ambiguity cause suspense and anxiety. Fear of change can be as disrupting as change itself, because it produces identical worries and unrest. The boss who says, "There's going to be a reorganization around here," will create more anxiety than the one who announces, "Department 47 will be moved to the new building on August 25th."

WHEN PERSONS AFFECTED BY THE CHANGE ARE NOT INVOLVED IN THE PLANNING. It's human nature to support what we create. We're all too ready to follow our own suggestions. A number of studies indicate that when people are "told," they will resent the pressure. When they have a "say" in the planning, or can send a representative to the planning process, acceptance is more likely.

WHEN AN APPEAL FOR CHANGE IS BASED ON PERSONAL REASONS. The supervisor who says, "Won't you come through for good old Charley?" is met with suspicion. The attitude immediately is, "What's Charley getting out of this?" Loyalty is a desirable trait in subordinates, but few people will change solely because of it. They will only respond to a personal plea if, at the same time, they see that it solves a problem . . . gets something done . . . reaches a goal. For example, the office manager who put the following on the bulletin board was not pleased with the results: "I have always felt that a clean desk top is an important indication of an employee's work habits and performance. I will feel better if you all keep a clean desk." This personal "plea" was resented and rejected because it was clearly based on a personal whim. It is desirable for an initiator of change to identify the nonpersonal needs which justify it.

WHEN THE HABIT PATTERNS OF THE WORK GROUP ARE IGNORED. The textile mill burlers and menders who can talk to each other as they work side by side, the group of office girls who eat lunch together, the utility crew that has appropriated a favorite truck—all are stubbornly against anything that will alter their working relationships. As Zander [6] points out:

Every work situation develops certain customs in doing the work or in the relations among the workers. The administrator who ignores institutionalized patterns of work and abruptly attempts to create a new state of affairs which demands that these customs be abolished without further consideration will surely run into resistance.

A person trying to plan and initiate change will find it desirable to be knowledgeable and insightful about the norms and standards of those who will be affected.

WHEN THERE IS POOR COMMUNICATION REGARDING THE CHANGE. Even though it will affect only one or two in a work group of ten persons, all of them need to know about the change in order to feel secure and maintain group cooperation. When people are not informed or kept up-to-date they will fill the void with rumor:

> The grapevine is particularly active when unpleasant news is being "parceled out." The organization has a large piece of bad information to release. The manager reasons: "If we release the bad information all at once, morale will suffer. So, we'll release it piecemeal." This is done. Usually the morale problem is worse. Employees become accustomed to receiving bad news each week. Even when all the bad news is released, they won't believe it. While waiting for all the news, what employees invent to make the partial information make sense is usually much worse than the actual bad news.[7]

People expect, need, and want to be informed about changes so that they can react and adapt to them.

WHEN THERE IS FEAR OF FAILURE.   Today people are predominately concerned with whether they have the ability to master new skills. Fear of failure is especially strong when people are threatened with "punishment" such as a demotion, loss of status, lower pay, or the displeasure of the boss. They should be reassured that they will be given sufficient time and training to adjust to new procedures or assignments.

WHEN EXCESSIVE WORK PRESSURE IS INVOLVED.   Often such pressure results when we don't plan changes far enough in advance, or are uneasy about these changes ourselves. When people are busy, under stress, and feeling pressured, the advocated change may well be the straw that breaks the camel's back.

WHEN THE "COST" IS TOO HIGH, OR THE REWARD INADEQUATE.   For example, people without children may be reluctant to vote for a school bond issue because it will raise their taxes even though they approve of better schools. Persons on a job may see that a change in a procedure will not bring them *higher status, higher pay, or psychic rewards.*

WHEN ANXIETY OVER JOB SECURITY IS NOT RELIEVED.   When a large bank recently introduced automated bookkeeping equipment, the expensive computers averaged 50 percent down-time in the first few weeks of operation. Servicemen found that the machinery was being sabotaged by the insertion of paper clips, even apple cores. The employees who had formerly done the bank's bookkeeping believed their share of the "cost" of the new equipment would be their own expendability. No one had made it clear to them that they would not be laid off, but would be trained for new positions when the automated equipment was fully operative.

WHEN "VESTED INTEREST" OF THE INDIVIDUAL OR A SUB-UNIT OF THE ORGANIZATION IS INVOLVED.   Individuals or sub-units of an organization have an interest in protecting their own "empire." At budget time, one department may want to resist economy steps because they perceive a threat to their own department. A production group may want to protect themselves from "those design engineers with the crazy ideas."

WHEN THERE IS A LACK OF RESPECT AND TRUST IN THE INITIATOR. When those being exposed to an attempted change view the initiator as someone they dislike or mistrust, a lack of acceptance and enthusiasm for the change will quickly become evident.

WHEN THERE IS SATISFACTION WITH THE STATUS QUO.   When an individual, group, or organization is satisfied with the present state of affairs, it is more likely to resist change. It's only human to take the attitude, "Don't stick your neck out," "We never had it so good," or "Why upset the apple cart?" It has been my experience that individuals and organizations satisfied with their present performance are the least likely to initiate or endorse steps leading to the renewal process.

The most obvious way for people to understand and favorably anticipate a change is to obtain information, to ask questions. Even full information, however, is seldom wholly satisfactory since parts of it are likely to contradict prior preferences or decisions. This contradiction between existing beliefs and new ideas creates a state of dissonance which can hardly be tolerated easily. Such dissonance is most easily reduced by attributing favorable qualities to the change that are not obvious and attributing less favorable qualities to previously held ideas. Adverse meanings in change may be found in the hidden purposes of those who advocate it, or in the implications concerning others' evaluations of the work that has been done, which is often feared to be negative.

Depending upon the meaning we give to a change, a variety of reactions follow. We may fully accept the change, but even when we do, remaining uncertainties may generate flight, withdrawal, rigidity, apathy, or a counterplan. Clearly the frequency and vigor of these reactions is a function of the security an individual feels in the part he is to take in the proposed change. Many of these reactions are efforts to protect ourselves from the consequences of the contemplated change. Energy put into such reactions is drained from the efforts to implement the change.

It is apparent from the foregoing that changes in persons must occur at several levels if the change in the organization is to occur effectively. Changees must understand both the problem which generated the need for change and the nature of the change and, somehow, reduce their negative attitudes. Changees must have an opportunity to learn their new functions; that is, they need to practice the needed new skills where new skills will be required.

There are three psychological levels affecting the reception of change, all of which must be involved if performance is to be maintained *after* change is effected:

KNOWLEDGE.   This level involves the cognitive, semantic, and conceptual ability of an individual or group to understand and appreciate the effected or planned change.

SKILL.   This level involves the motivation or behavioral response that goes with knowledge of change. It is more difficult to achieve than mere knowledge or understanding.

ATTITUDE.   This level involves perceptions, feelings, and values. Favorable results are considerably more difficult to achieve at this level of change.

Of course, even though these three levels are more or less achieved by the individual, the organizational system may not be ready to utilize them to effect change in performance.

Persons who are responsible for stimulating change in an organization have a variety of methods available to them. The choice of method depends upon a diagnosis of the possible sources of resistance, the relative importance of resistant acts to successful introduction of change and, when necessary, ways in which resistance can be reduced. Consider the conditions under which several different methods may work:

ISSUE INSTRUCTION.   This will work where the change is relatively minor, the attitudes of individual groups are likely to be favorable, and the right to give such instructions is seen as within the renewal stimulator's legitimate domain of authority.

FORCE COMPLIANCE.   This will work if the change is a public one, if negative attitudes are unimportant and if new skills are not needed by those who must make the change.

PROVIDE OPPORTUNITY FOR OTHERS TO SHARE IN THE DECISION.   This will work if the problem is not too complicated, if those affected believe that their own ideas are being used, and when those affected are comfortable in the position of decision-making.

Studies of change [8] regarding the transfer of acceptance from one system to another—with significant meaning for organization renewal—suggest that this transfer is enhanced by: (1) its simplicity; (2) its consistency with existing values; (3) the prestige of the bearers of novelty; (4) an already changing situation in the receiving system; (5) lack of close integration of the receiving system, such as actual or incipient conflict among existing groups or ideologies; and (6) long and continued contact.

Studies on overcoming resistance to change reported by Goodwin Watson [9] seem to indicate the following steps as being helpful: (1) encourage participation; (2) start with top officials; (3) show that change will reduce rather than increase burdens; (4) connect proposal with tradi-

tional values; (5) bring out novel and exciting aspects; (6) give assurance
that autonomy will not be threatened; (7) include participants in diagnostic efforts; (8) try for consensual decisions; (9) empathize with
resistors and reduce their apprehensions; (10) build in feedback mechanisms so officials are aware of difficulties before they become serious;
(11) build mutual trust among participants; and (12) keep a pathway
open for reappraisal and revision.

A number of these items bear re-enforcing as we think of ways in
which an organizational leader can lessen resistance to change:

INVOLVE EMPLOYEES IN PLANNING FOR CHANGE.   Resistance to change
will be less intense when those to be affected, or those who believe
they might be affected, know why a change is being made and what
the advantages are. This can be done most effectively by letting them
participate in the actual planning. Besides helping them to understand
the when, what, where, and why of a change, participation eases any
fears that management is hiding something from them. In addition,
participation can stimulate many good ideas from those who probably
are best acquainted with the problem that necessitates the change. It
also alerts a leader to potential problems that might arise when the
change is implemented. Such an approach, because people tend to
better understand what they create, also advantageously involves people in the diagnostic and creative processes. Thus, if they help make
the diagnosis, they more readily accept the prognosis—which is to say
that employees can seldom be successfully treated like a doctor treats
a patient, by mysterious prescription.

PROVIDE ACCURATE AND COMPLETE INFORMATION.   When workers are
kept in the dark or get incomplete information, alarms and rumors
start to circulate. This creates an atmosphere of mistrust. Even when
the news is bad, employees would rather get it straight and fast than
receive no news at all. Lack of information makes them feel helpless,
while the whole story—even if it's unpleasant—lets them know where
they stand.

GIVE EMPLOYEES A CHANCE TO AIR THEIR OBJECTIONS.   Change is
more easily assimilated when a supervisor provides an opportunity for
employees to blow off steam. A gripe session also gives leaders a useful feedback which may reveal unsuspected reasons for opposition.
For example, a man may balk at using another machine only because
he will be moved away from a window.

ALWAYS TAKE GROUP NORMS AND HABITS INTO ACCOUNT.   For example, a leader should ask himself if a contemplated change will:

Break up congenial work groups.
Disrupt commuting schedules or car pools.
Split up long-standing luncheon partners.

Unfavorably affect anticipated vacations, priorities, preferences.
Require temperamentally incompatible employees to work together.
Violate a value norm of the group.

MAKE ONLY ESSENTIAL CHANGES.   Most employees can tolerate only
so much change. When they are confronted with many trivial or un-
necessary changes, their reaction will be irritation and resentment.
Even more important, they will be less receptive to major changes.

PROVIDE ADEQUATE MOTIVATION.   Motivation affects a person's willingness as an effective *human resource* to give or not to give of himself to his organization. Resistance may be reduced if these factors are
taken into account seriously:

Meaningful reward.   It varies with individuals. They may be concerned with self-expression, recognition, the need to feel useful and
important, the desire for new knowledge, the need to meet new
people, or a genuine desire to meet unmet needs.

Relationship.   However small it may be, the individual must be
able to relate his contribution to a total effort.

Importance.   Has the contribution had any real meaning to the
organization, or was it a wasted effort? The human resource may not
particularly care whether the answer to this question is happily
"yes" or miserably "no," but he does want to feel that he himself is
important enough to be told which it turned out to be, and he
doesn't want to repeat a wasted effort. He works best in a warm
but work-oriented atmosphere where his efforts are obviously
needed and appreciated.

Initial success.   A little succeeding goes a long way toward maintaining interest in new ways of doing things. The jobs people are
given to do must be within their skills and experience, because
frustration at the outset is sure death to efforts to stabilize or initiate change.

Opportunity to grow.   Interest stops when stagnation is produced
by doing the same thing over and over again; and continued involvement demands new challenge to learn and grow on.

Appropriate involvement in decision-making.   People should be
allowed to take part in this process. One of the hardest jobs a leader
has in organizational management is to refrain from making most of
the decisions all by himself.

Keep people informed.   When an individual contributes even a
small response, he automatically develops an interest in what happens to it; he will feel more intimately involved if he shares in
knowledge of the organization's problems and crises as well as its
achievements.

LET PEOPLE KNOW THE GOALS, THE REASON FOR CHANGE. A story is told of a man who successfully initiated a change in his work crew. He carefully planned how to tell them all the whys and wherefores, and provided answers to all the ifs and buts. Later, as he advanced in his job, he failed miserably when he had to sell a group of his foremen on a change. Why? He felt that because of their superior intelligence, they would not need an explanation. But, the fact that a person or a group is intelligent does not necessarily mean they will better understand and accept change. Because people use their extra intelligence to rationalize more reasons why a change should not be made, the opposite is often true. The more clever and precise the goals of change, the more an individual, group, or organization can cope with it.

DEVELOP A TRUSTING WORK CLIMATE. Mistrust arises when people have inadequate or incomplete information, when they are kept in the dark, when rumors disseminate false alarms. One major reason for this is that they feel helpless—they can't influence the situation. To build a trusting climate, tell the truth. It's been proven time and again that people would rather have bad news than no news. Given the facts, they feel they may be able to *do* something about a problem. In one case, a company was threatened with going out of business because its high costs made it impossible to compete with a similar product made in Japan. Top management decided to give its employees the facts. The employees immediately increased their productivity—and reduced costs—to the point where the organization got back on its feet and is flourishing today.

LEARN TO USE THE PROBLEM-SOLVING APPROACH. Research in behavioral science furnishes some useful guidelines in solving problems that arise from implemented change. First, identify the real problems. A leader may think, "If I could only get Mary to retire, the morale of the group would improve." But deep-seated attitudes rarely are caused by a single individual in a group. Second, be aware of timing. It's much easier to influence people favorably toward new data processing equipment before it is installed than afterwards. Third, help people solve problems to their own satisfaction. They will react negatively to such advice as "You shouldn't take that attitude" or to such persuasion as "I'm sure when you have all the facts, you'll see it my way." Adjusting to change is sometimes difficult under the best of conditions, but it can best be confronted when the initiator of change commits himself to the problem-solving approach and process.

In a very real sense, effective organization renewal must be related to the *process of solving the real problems* facing the organization. Usually, problem-solving proceeds in this direction, by fits and starts, rationally and irrationally, but the phases of the process can be seen to proceed through several steps. They do not always appear in order nor are all of them always present, but the appearance of and the course taken by several phases of the problem-solving process generally produce a better understanding of real problems and workable solutions.

Basic to the problem-solving process is the fact that it starts from motivation—the feeling held by an individual or a group of individuals that some state of affairs is unsatisfactory. Some groups get stuck here. They feel strongly motivated but what they do may have no real effect in removing the dissatisfactions. The felt need often remains strong, or it appears in a different form in a different place. This will require meaningful interfacing where dialogue exists. Starting with a felt need, however, problem-solving may go through the following typical phases:

DEFINING THE PROBLEM. Exploring, clarifying, refining, and rationalizing the problem so that it becomes a group property and, ideally, so that each member is committed to doing something about it.

COLLECTING IDEAS. Gathering a wide range of ideas and possibilities, including very tentative alternatives and solutions. Postpone evaluation or testing of these ideas. Immediate evaluation of one idea tends to inhibit production of new ideas—for while an idea may seem silly or ridiculous, it may actually be only different and new.

TESTING IDEAS AND DEVELOPING ALTERNATIVES. Assembling information, opinions, and data which may be necessary for evaluating ideas; looking at alternatives, estimating consequences of various actions (predicting what will happen rather than outright criticism), and reality testing.

DECIDING. In view of previous considerations, choosing the most desirable action, determining who makes the decision and what procedure is to be followed.

PLANNING ACTION. Decisions must be implemented to be meaningful, and all sorts of evidence show that implementation is quickest and most effective when the implementers have a voice in the decision. How much voice? How is such a thing possible in a large organization? Evidence indicates that steps should proceed in a series of short steps, with feedback after each step, to be sure that the plan resulting from the decision is working.

TAKING ACTION. Spell out action steps and designate who is to do what. Stick to the action plan; there is no way to know its worth if it is not really tried.

ASSESSING CONSEQUENCES. In the light of the results of the decision, objectively evaluated, what modifications or changes are desirable? Objective evaluation means being clear and honest about aspects of failure, negative evaluation often involves hostility; but care must be exercised because evaluation that is too tactless, too realistic may result in destroying the group that reached the decision.

REPLANNING AND CONFRONTING NEW PROBLEMS. Problem-solving is a way of life in an organization. The solution of one problem usually leads to another challenge.

The question is frequently asked about the decision-making phase of problem-solving. Who really makes the decision? Who should be involved? One way is for the decision to be made on the basis of authority; the chairman, the superior, the person with most status or power makes it. This method is frequently used even when it is not the one intended; unless a group has reached a certain stage of maturity, work group members are likely to look to the boss without being fully aware that this is what they are doing.

A second way is by some form of vote. The usefulness of this method, as well as its limitations, is quite well known.

A third way is by consensus. This way of reaching a decision requires some explanation since it is easily misunderstood and misapplied—as well as frequently difficult to obtain. This word is derived from *sensus,* meaning a mental process, not from *census,* meaning counting. Thus, it refers to a "meeting of minds."

Consensus has been reached when the group, as a group, agrees to take a given action. Some may have doubts about the wisdom of the action, but are willing to commit themselves to implement the action because: (a) the consequences of failure seem to be not too great, (b) the group can learn from failure and improve its next attempt, and (c) a next attempt will be possible.

Thus, to be "for" the action means that one is willing to implement for any reason—especially when (a) the consequences are severe, (b) it will not be possible to learn from failure, or (c) there can be no second chance—even when there is no opportunity to use any learning. To be "undecided" means that one is not yet sure about whether he is willing to implement the plan.

Another way decisions are made is by avoidance, not confronting the problem. The situation may end inconclusively with no one knowing what was decided, members may propose getting more information, or they may schedule another meeting. Unfortunately, this frequently happens without the members realizing that their action constitutes avoidance. Sometimes both individuals and groups avoid coming to grips with a situation or problem. Recent research suggests a wide variety of blocks to efficient problem-solving.[10] The perplexing reality to problem-solvers in groups lies not only in the great number of difficulties that confront them, but also in the need to diagnose the specific blocks and to take facilitating action. Several problems may operate concurrently,[11] and at both the *task* and the *maintenance* level discussed in Chapter 6.

Among many obstructive factors, six are singled out here for consideration:

LACK OF CLARITY IN STATING THE PROBLEM. As has been found, much of the effort of decision-making groups is initially directed toward efforts to orient members to the problem. This phase is extremely important, occasionally deserving lavish expenditure of time and effort in order to identify the problem and refine it, and through this process to secure member internalization and comment. Groups frequently are foredoomed to failure, even tragedy, when they inadequately clarify the nature of a problem.

PREMATURE TESTING OF ALTERNATIVES IN MAKING A DECISION. Upon hearing a proposal, it is a natural impulse to evaluate it promptly (and often, most naturally, negatively). For most of us, ideas are fragile creations, easily blighted by a chill, or even indifferent, reception. As groups proceed in their problem-solving activities, unless they are unusually sophisticated, more often than not they will evaluate idea by idea, neglecting to build a supportive climate for idea production and the pooling of a wide assortment of ideas before the important testing phase is introduced.

LACK OF DECISION-MAKING SKILLS. Decision-making is a highly demanding and extremely complicated *cognitive* and *emotional* process. It needs continuously to be seen in these two dimensions. It appears to proceed most effectively under leaders who have been trained. Group members, as well as leaders, should become skillful diagnosticians and interveners, but sophistication in group decision-making appears to suggest a behavior cycle: (a) sensitivity to a difficulty (e.g., a block); (b) an effort to diagnose the source(s) and reason(s) for the difficulty; (c) assessment of consequences of the intervention; (d) subsequent action that seems appropriate in view of the foregoing.

SELF-ORIENTED BEHAVIOR. One way of classifying behavior of group members during the decision-making process is in terms of whether it is *group-oriented* or *self-oriented*. Group-oriented behavior is related to task or maintenance roles, whereas self-oriented behavior orients to the individual *qua* individual. For example, in terms of the group's needs and goals self-oriented behavior appears, in effect, to be behavior which is blocking, dominating, recognition-seeking, and aggressive. The degree of the individual member's unawareness relative to the orientation of his own behavior (self vs. group) is often remarkable, but feedback is a commonly used device for clarifying the effect of one's behavior upon the decision-making effort. There can be no serious quarrel with the generalization that self-oriented behavior correlates negatively with the effectiveness of problem-solving groups.[12]

THE WORKING CLIMATE.   Undoubtedly, many variables contribute to the overall social-psychological atmosphere in which decision-makers conduct their business. Whether the relationships are cooperative or competitive in specific situations seems to make some difference.[13] Style of leadership—that is, whether it essentially is democratic, laissez-faire, benevolently autocratic, or autocratic—has significance for the creative production achieved by a group.[14] How repressive, threatening, or hostile the group is affects the group product. So, too, do status needs and sociometric sub-groups. Cartwright [15] has suggested a formula which identifies the determinants of *security*, which generally contribute to the productivity of a decision-making group:

$$\text{Security} = f \frac{\text{Perception of own power} + \text{friendly forces}}{\text{Unfriendly forces}}$$

CONFORMITY AND HOMOGENEITY.   Many influences calculated to produce compliance and likeness bear upon the individual in decision-making groups. Some are direct, most are subtle. The need for security is often paid for in the currency of conformity. Other self needs and interests are satisfied by a similar kind of barter. Judged by a desire for creative and effective solutions, groups may unknowingly drive questionable bargains as they strive for conformity, in spite of the fact that heterogeneity of views is needed in order most effectively to test the reality of alternatives and expand the range of choices. Groups interested in better decisions might advantageously endeavor to expand their norms so as to increase their tolerance for idiosyncratic and less conventional contributions. Out of an enlarged repertoire of alternatives, better choices should emerge.

In improving group problem-solving a number of challenges confront the manager-leader: the *orientation* challenge, arriving at a common perception of the problem situation; the *evaluation* challenge, achieving an accepted value system by which the various alternative solutions can be judged; the *control* challenge, efforts by the group to influence each other; the *decision* challenge, achieving the final decision out of the choice of alternative solutions to the problem at hand; the challenge of *managing tensions*, handling the tensions which arise in the group as a result of its task activities; the *integration* challenge, preserving the social cohesion of the group as it relates to the total organization.

A useful concept, theory, and method for thinking about change has been developed by social scientist Kurt Lewin. He looks upon a level or phase of behavior within an institutional setting not as a static habit or custom, but as a dynamic balance of forces working in opposite directions within the social-psychological space of the institution. He indi-

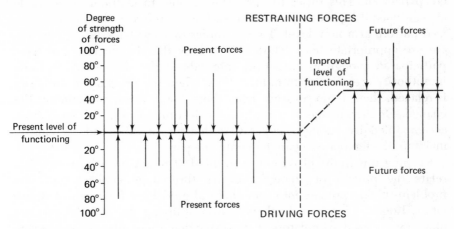

FIGURE 8–1

Force Field Analysis

cated that we should think diagnostically about any change situation, in terms of the factors encouraging and facilitating change (driving forces) and the factors against change (restraining forces). These forces may orig- inate inside the organization, or in the environment, or in the behavior of the renewal stimulator.

We can think of the present state of affairs in an organization as an equilibrium which is being maintained by a variety of factors that "keep things the way they are" or "keep me behaving in my customary ways." The renewal stimulator must assess the change potential and resistance, and try to change the balance of forces so there will be movement toward an improved state of affairs.

Looking at patterned behavior as illustrated in Figure 8–1, it can be seen that change occurs when an imbalance occurs between the sum of restraining forces and the sum of driving forces. Such imbalance *un- freezes* the pattern and the level changes until the opposing forces are again brought into equilibrium. An imbalance may occur through a change in the magnitude of any force, a change in the direction of a force, or the addition of a new force.

Lewin pointed out that the effect of change will be maintained if the initial set of forces is unfrozen, initiates the change, and then refreezes at the new level. In many situations, however, the evidence of change is only temporary. Everyone knows that change in an organization is often followed by a regression toward the old pattern after the pressures effecting change are relaxed. A company or school system may imple- ment the recommendations of a study under pressure from the board or manager, but as soon as vigilance is relaxed the old patterns usually creep back in. This raises the problem of how to maintain a desirable change once it has been accomplished, how to refreeze the institutionalized pattern at a new level. Two examples of ways backsliding may occur are appropriate here. Those affected by the change may not have participated enough to have fully internalized the change which those in authority are seeking to induce; thus, when the pressure of authority is relaxed, there is no pressure from those lower down to maintain the change. Or the change of a part of the institution may not have been accompanied by enough cooperative changes in other sub-systems to maintain the temporary change in only one part.

Keeping this frame of reference in mind, it might be helpful to interrelate the process of change, Lewin's three-stage concept, and the problem-solving process into some helpful guidelines for renewal stimulators. Ronald Lippitt and others,[16] after studying the actual behaviors of many renewal stimulators, have expanded these phases into seven. Here, in some respects, the term "aspect" may be preferable to "phase," for the latter has too much the sense of an unalterable sequence. There is a good deal of evidence that a renewal stimulator and an organization work on problems in a rough order of priority, but it is important to keep in mind that they may subsequently, again and again, come back to the same concerns and processes that were in evidence at the onset of the relationship. For example, I believe that confrontation, search, and coping must take place at each of these "aspects":

DIAGNOSIS OF THE ORGANIZATION'S PROBLEM. It is not easy to overstate the importance of diagnosis in the renewal process, although in the same breath we must note that diagnosis generally does not stand as an end in itself and that in most cases it must be translated into a course of action for change. The history of planned change shows that most renewal stimulators approach each problem with predetermined diagnostic orientation. Some of them always feel the basic problem is either a maldistribution of power, caused by faulty interchange of ideas, or the result of poor utilization of energy by the organization. It seems almost axiomatic among industrial consultants that poor intraorganizational communication lies at the root of low productivity. A renewal stimulator with a particular diagnostic orientation undoubtedly will find data to fit his preconception; this does not limit the usefulness of his diagnosis provided he changes it in the face of contrary data.

Ronald Lippitt has pointed out that renewal stimulators vary greatly in the extent to which they feel it is necessary to share their diagnostic insights with the organizational system. Some contend that disclosure of data might stimulate so much resistance within the organization as to endanger the solidifying of change. On the other hand, the more psychologically oriented renewal stimulators hold that all data gathered represent a part of the reality with which the organization must deal in order to introduce necessary innovations. The methods used by renewal stimulators to collect data represent a wide range of skills and approaches. Direct questioning is probably the best way, but it often turns out that the best diagnostic data result from the relationship itself.

ASSESSMENT OF THE MOTIVATION AND CAPACITY OF THE ORGANIZATIONAL SYSTEM TO CHANGE. If change is to occur, it must come about largely through hard work within the organization itself. It is not enough that the organization experiences discomfort. Problem awareness must be translated into a desire to change, and this in turn requires a readiness and capacity to change. In a community, for example, people will have conflicting desires; on one hand they want the advantages that change may bring but on the other hand they do not wish to give up the known security and satisfaction which they currently enjoy. The ability to recognize readiness for change, and to handle resistance to it, requires considerable sophistication on the part of the renewal stimulator.

ASSESSMENT OF THE RENEWAL STIMULATOR, MOTIVATION, AND RESOURCES. From a practical point of view, it is important that the initiator of change clearly assess his ability to help the organization in a particular situation. If he decides that his special skills and knowledge may be helpful, he then incurs a further responsibility for defining what may be reasonably expected from the change project. Perhaps most persons and organizations who seek help tend to feel that once they have contacted the right expert or authority and put the matter in his hands, half the battle is won. Most renewal stimulators know that if no attempt is made to clarify mutual expectations, then the organization's leaders may find that their own expectations are going unmet, become disenchanted with the whole process, and withdraw.

Beyond the question of professional responsibility and personal motivation is the problem of professional ethics. People may ask what right has one person to remake another? This issue is treated in depth in Chapter 13 of this book. At this point, however, it is enough to say that the renewal stimulator may provide the tools and support, but alone he does not and cannot create change. To emphasize this, some stress the means by which change objectives can be reached and organizational leaders can make decisions about goals. It is a commonly held view of almost all consultants that policy decisions can be made only by these leaders.

SELECTING APPROPRIATE CHANGE OBJECTIVES. The first three aspects of the planned change process have to do with diagnosis: what is wrong and what resources do we have to change what is wrong. A difficult part of the task of the renewal stimulator is the conversion of his diagnosis into action. In the medical field, diagnosis has become a separate specialization. Similarly, some renewal stimulators, emphasizing a methodological approach, feel that little more than diagnosis is enough to stimulate an impetus for change. Most of them, however, are not in a position to stop at this point in the change process and must go on to handle the question: "Knowing this, what should we do first?"

Many renewal stimulators state that after diagnosis, the movement toward the final goal is a sequential process which requires a number of sub-goals and, therefore, that the place to begin must be chosen in terms of an overall strategy. This starting point is frequently referred to as the *leverage point*. This may be a person, persons, or a group especially salient or accessible to change, and therefore receptive to communication. On the other hand, we may think of the leverage point in terms of patterns of behavior, or in terms of organizational facts of life. Renewal stimulators and organizations work from one problem area to another or from one leverage point to another.

CHOOSING THE APPROPRIATE TYPE OF ROLE FOR RENEWAL STIMULATOR. Tied up with the selection of leverage points is the selection of the appropriate help role. In what way will the renewal stimulator relate to the problem? There are a number of possibilities. One way is for him to make possible new connections and to reorganize old ones. Another role that he often assumes is that of an expert on procedure or method. He may, for example, provide the organization with techniques which will enable it to find out more about itself through the use of community self-surveys or self-education devices for small groups. Or consultants in human relations may advise skill training or a program of supervisor training. There is the danger, however, that in a culture such as ours, where self-improvement is so valued, follow-through procedures may become ritualized and sterile unless they are accompanied by the means of obtaining fuller understanding of motivation.

We should note the advantage of creating a special environment for change. Sometimes environment is a direct impetus toward change, in other cases it may be merely a necessary background which must be present to promote the effectiveness of other change forces.

ESTABLISHMENT AND MAINTENANCE OF THE RELATIONSHIP WITH THE ORGANIZATION. A further important problem the renewal stimulator faces is the maintenance of change once it has been started. Some use the relationship with the organizational system to this end, and continue to offer them support and reinforcement. Even though the renewal stimulator should not stand at the elbow of an organizational leader while he is trying something new, he can provide periodic opportunities to review the change attempts.

Another way of reinforcing change is to build into the organization means by which change may be maintained. This may involve the inception of an ongoing training program in an industry or the freeing of communication so that feedback may be made available to policy-makers. It is also more conducive to establishing lasting changes in one part of a system if other related parts are prepared for change. At the community level it is always more effective to attempt change among a large group rather than a few isolated individuals. Persons who have a similar change experience can reinforce each other's efforts. The renewal stimulator can also help to maintain change by · helping the organization to accept the legitimacy of seeking help when needed. Everyone needs support while working for change, and this usually can be provided if the person desiring change is assured that experimentation in new directions is useful and desirable.

TERMINATION OF A SUPPORTIVE RELATIONSHIP. The problems sur-rounding the termination of the helping relationship are more pro-found in those cases where it is used directly to effect change, as is the case in psychotherapy. Even with larger organizational systems, the resolution of dependency needs on the part of both may be a matter of concern. Generally, there is likely to be considerable depend-ency in the early stages of the relationship and if thereafter the or-ganizational leaders come to rely heavily on the renewal stimulator for support and guidance, the termination is likely to be a painful affair.

I have already mentioned that a special effort is sometimes made to build into the permanent structure of the organizational system a substitute for the renewal stimulator. This may take the form of pro-cedures, or training programs, or the possibility of continued consulta-tion on new problems and new personnel.

In this chapter I have attempted to relate the problem-solving process into a workable frame of reference for those initiating and implementing planned organization renewal and change. These guidelines, mainly from behavioral science research, may also help the professional renewal stimulator.

In the spirit of the words of Dr. Oppenheimer,[17] today's organizational leaders should realize the following:

> In an important sense this world of ours is a new world, in which the unity of knowledge, the nature of human communities, the order of society, the order of ideas, the very notions of society and culture have changed and will not return to what they have been in the past. What is new is not new because it has never been there before, but because it has changed in quality.

The changes facing our society, our organizations, our leadership will demand the maximum knowledge, skills, and courageous attitudes by those of us who bear the responsibility of managing complex problems with the human resources available to us today.

NOTES

1. This chapter utilizes portions of the author's previous articles on change: "Managing Change: 6 Ways to Turn Resistance Into Acceptance," reprinted by permission of the publisher from *Supervisory Management*, August, 1966 issue, © 1966 by the American Management Assn., Inc.; and "Overcoming People's Suspicion of Change," reprinted from *Nation's Cities* (the magazine of the National League of Cities), Vol. 3, No. 12, December, 1965.
2. Clarence B. Randall, "The Myth of the Magic Numbers," *Dun's Review of Modern Industry*, March, 1961, p. 34.
3. Wilbert Moore, *Social Change* (Englewood Cliffs, N.J.: Prentice-Hall, Inc., 1963).
4. Albert Schweitzer, quoted from *This Week*, September 26, 1966.
5. Alvin Zander, "Resistance to Change—Its Analysis and Prevention," *Advanced Management*, Vol. 15–16, January, 1950, pp. 9–11.
6. *Ibid.*
7. Leslie E. This, *Communicating Within the Organization*, Management Series Monographs (Washington, D.C.: Leadership Resources, Inc., 1966), p. 22.
8. Moore, *The Conduct of the Corporation* (New York: Random House, Inc., 1962), pp. 199–201.
9. Goodwin Watson, "Resistance to Change," *SEC Newsletter,* Ohio State University, Vol. 1, No. 7, May, 1966, p. 5.
10. Gardner Lindzey, ed., *Handbook of Social Psychology*, Vol. 2 (Reading, Mass.: Addison-Wesley Publishing Co., Inc., 1954), pp. 735–785.
11. Norman R. F. Maier, "The Quality of Group Decision as Influenced by the Discussion Leader," *Human Relations*, Vol. 3, 1950, pp. 155–174.
12. See, for example, N. T. Fourienzos, M. L. Hutt, and H. Guetzkow, "Measurement of Self-oriented Needs in Discussion Groups," *Journal of Abnormal Social Psychology*, Vol. 45, 1954, pp. 682–690.
13. See, for example, M. Deutsch, "A Theory of Cooperation and Competition," *Human Relations*, Vol. 2, 1949, pp. 199–232.
14. Ronald Lippitt and R. L. White, "An Experimental Study of Leadership and Group Life," in G. E. Swanson and E. L. Hartley, eds., *Readings in Social Psychology*, 2nd ed. (New York: Holt, Rinehart and Winston, Inc., 1952), pp. 340–355.
15. Darwin P. Cartwright, "Emotional Dimensions of Group Life," in M. L. Reymert, ed., *Feelings and Emotions* (New York: McGraw-Hill Book Co., Inc., 1950), pp. 439–447.
16. Ronald Lippitt, J. Watson, and B. Westley, *Dynamics of Planned Change* (New York: Harcourt, Brace & World, Inc., 1958), Chapter 6.
17. Robert Oppenheimer, "Prospects in the Arts and Sciences," *Perspectives USA*, Vol. 11, Spring, 1955, pp. 10–11.

9 ETHICAL IMPLICATIONS

You know that medicines, when well used, restore health to the sick: they will
be well used when the doctor, together with his understanding of their nature,
shall understand also what man is, what life is, and what constitution and
health are. Know these well and you will know their opposites: and when this is
the case you will know well how to devise a remedy.

LEONARDO DA VINCI, 1452–1519

In contemplating, designing, and implementing organization renewal,
we are confronted with the process of some individual or group being
a renewal stimulator to initiate reflections, data collection, analysis,
revolution, and, out of all that, change.

First of all, who is a renewal stimulator in an organization? It is any-
body who deliberately sets out to help himself and others to achieve
change for the betterment of the organization. Certainly every personnel
or training director is a renewal stimulator because he operates with
other people to try to train or influence them to behave differently in
the organization. Certainly every manager falls into that category. The
various specialists in the organization, the accountant, the lawyer, the
company doctor, and almost everyone in a leadership position falls into
this category at one time or another.

Next, what is the central ethical problem of the renewal stimulator?
What right does he have to try to make an organization different from
what it would otherwise be? On what grounds does he base his value
judgment to influence others to change in this direction rather than
that? This question is closely connected to the earlier, more technical
question of *how* he effectively helps others to change. But they are different questions. Value judgments on which one bases an attempt to influence the thinking, behavior, and attitudes of others require one to
re-examine the controlling values, as well as the grounds for their valida-
tion and justification.

Recognizing that many words have achieved evaluative weight, it
might be well to divorce, for the moment, our necessary value judgments
from the processes these words describe. Manipulate, for instance, means

the arrangement of conditions so that change in a certain direction will take place. The school teacher who arranges his classroom setting, provides certain selected pieces of handwork, asks certain questions, demands certain homework, and creates certain motivational drives, is "manipulating," whether he is teaching physical fitness or higher mathematics.

In *The Ugly American,* the authors have Father Finian write in his diary, "What we discovered is that men are persuaded of things by the same process, whether the persuading is done by the Catholic Church, Lutherans, Communists, or democrats." This would indicate that there are observable processes and forces at work in every organizational situation. By observation and analysis, these forces can be understood and, to some extent, their effect can be predicted from the nature of their influence. Further, skills can be developed to use, direct, or otherwise control present forces to meet desired, although not necessarily desirable, ends. Men can and do influence and sometimes control such forces. This is a nonjudgmental statement; it is observable data.

This line of reasoning suggests, then, that the question is not merely one of the values of the forces themselves, but rather the value system which motivates a leader to use or not use them, and the ends he attempts to achieve. From this point of view, each man, acting or refusing to act as an influence for organization renewal places his basic beliefs and, stemming from those beliefs, his ethical system under judgment.

If we accept this line of reasoning, if we recognize that our commitment to a specific job in the organization often makes us a potential renewal stimulator, then I submit that the question usually asked, "What right have I to try to make persons and groups different from what they are?" must be reversed. The basic question which we cannot avoid is "What right have I to withhold myself, my skills, and my convictions in a changing situation from helping that change to take place in a direction consistent with my convictions?"

Society has always been concerned about the ethics of those who wield power and influence. As man's control of his environment has increased, his intense interest in the motives and values of leaders has also mounted. Today's massive organizations, mass advertising, and automated systems are controlled increasingly by professional managers who live in a world of continual tension and change. How do such men self-guide their actions? What rules can be laid down to help the executive choose whether to put his country above his company, his family above his job, moral honesty above profit? Price-fixing scandals may arouse the public for a time, but the day-by-day struggles to find the right way to lead are fought on the lonely battleground of the manager's conscience.

Research in the area of ethics is very limited, with most of the data obtained by questionnaires and depth interviews. Studies [1] of business managers and organization leaders reveal that a majority of them:

Admit to numerous accepted practices in their organization which they consider unethical.

Often disagree about the ethical thing to do in regard to specific business practices.

Tend to consider the average manager less ethical in general than they consider themselves.

Feel that top management must lead the way in reducing unethical practices.

Would welcome a written code for their industry, but state that it must have teeth in it for enforcement.

Believe that the most important factor in influencing an executive to make *ethical* decisions is his personal code of behavior.

Believe that the most important influence toward making unethical decisions is the behavior of his superior.

Think that close or tight supervision tends to produce higher standards of conduct.

Research into ethics usually follows one of two approaches:

DIRECT QUESTION APPROACH

"Would your superior expect you to go against your own standards of conduct to get a job done?"

	Yes	No	Sometimes
Top management	9%	66%	25%
Middle management	6%	70%	24%
Lower management	18%	40%	42%

"Would you expect a subordinate to go against his own standards of conduct to get a job done?"

	Yes	No	Sometimes
Top management	5%	68%	27%
Middle management	4%	70%	26%
Lower management	7%	55%	38%

CASE EXAMPLE APPROACH

Imagine that you are the president of a company in a highly competitive industry. You learn that a competitor has made an important scientific discovery which will give him an advantage that will substantially reduce, but not eliminate, the profits of your company for about a year. If there were some hope of hiring one of the competitor's employees who knew the details of the discovery, would you try to hire him?

	What I would do	What others would do
Probably hire him	48%	70%
Probably not hire him	52%	30%

Lawrence Stone, a member of the Board of Directors of Scott Electronics Corporation, has just learned that the company is about to announce a 2–for–1 stock split and an increase of dividends. Stone personally is on the brink of bankruptcy. A quick gain of a few thousand dollars can save him from economic and social ruin. He decides to take advantage of this information concerning the stock split by purchasing stock now to sell in a few days at a profit.

Approve	30
Somewhat approve	18
Somewhat disapprove	15
Disapprove	37

Once the awareness of the complexity of many ethical problems is granted, the very difficult task of defining what is ethical, and what is not ethical, arises. One definition of "ethics" given by Webster is that it is "the study of ideal human character, actions, and ends." The problem lies in the fact that differing ideas exist as to what is ideal human behavior.

Ethics is frequently interpreted as being "in the eye of the beholder." When a person wins something in competition with another individual or group, it is the superiority of his ability; when the other person wins, it is easy to perceive "shenanigans" and to wish to expose him as unethical. Some people use the definitions of "legal" or "illegal" as an adequate definition of ethical behavior. Dr. James Owens [2] of American University defines ethics as "a set of standards, or code, or value-system by which free, human actions are determined as ultimately right or wrong, good or evil. . . . If an action agrees with these standards, it is an ethical action; if it does not agree, it is an unethical action." He goes on to say:

The word "ultimately," used in this definition of ethics, carries a special meaning. It suggests that the "good" (used above) refers to something more than merely good looks or a good taste or a good (pleasurable) feeling or being "good at" a skill; it refers rather to the "good" in the most ultimate sense in which any of us can conceive of it. This may seem vague, since the concept of the good or goal any of us seeks constitutes the meaning of human life and remains unclear for most humans in a way that is both exasperating and overwhelming. The idea of the ultimate good is sufficiently clear, however, for us to use it in most concrete life situations. For example, the doctor who demonstrates an almost impossible skill in experimental surgery upon healthy, unwilling prisoners in a prison camp is clearly a good surgeon, but his action is wrong in any ultimate sense of the word. Similarly, a good salesman could be using tactics that are ethically wrong; and a good lawyer could be unethical. We are all aware that in many areas of leadership good intentions are not enough.

Actions take on moral value in relation to the circumstances of a particular situation. Both theologians and practitioners have been focusing the modern concern for ethics on "situational ethics" rather than on absolutes that put all ethical confrontations in "black and white" terms.

Can our complex ethical heritage be interrelated with the dynamic realities of modern organization life? Is there a place for "ideals" which are consistent with the "practical necessities" of organization management? All too often organizational forces compromise the manager, and because of our heritage, he is left with a bad conscience. How did the present state of ethical dilemma develop? From what did most ethical norms emerge? Ethical behavior is based on moral tradition and beliefs. Our culture has given us a heritage of ethics that sometimes puts us in a position where any course of action we pursue will violate some ethical principle.

Writing in 1960, Samuel H. Miller,[3] Dean of Harvard Divinity School, delivered an introductory indictment of the oversimplified approach to ethical awareness adopted by many of the teachers, researchers, and leaders in the management field:

> We have reached a stage in our civilization where many different strands of ethical tradition have been woven together. Imbedded in the culture which conditions us and our relationships, and imbedded also in us as civilized, educated persons, are several distinctive ethical patterns. These sets of moral attitudes are contradictory enough to be competitive—both in their institutional forms and in their personal aspects. . . .

Let's look at some of these "different strands of ethical tradition" which make their impact on the modern leader and those he leads:

Hebraic culture, based on the Ten Commandments—the "covenant" with the group was very important.

Christian system, based on the Beatitudes of Jesus Christ, with emphasis on redemption of the individual born into the Kingdom.

Medieval way of life, based on penance, with emphasis on the future life.

Renaissance culture of the Reformation, based on the individual and his freedom.

Industrial Revolution, based on the technical application of science to production and distribution.

Scientific approach, based on the empirical method and the reign of law.

There is an enormous gulf between the superficial ambition and prestige attitude of the Industrial Revolution and the fundamental ideas of the beatitudes of the Christian culture. The Industrial Revolution remains with us, but it has been altered somewhat by the latest form of culture—the scientific approach. This approach, based as it is on empirical methods and laws, sometimes finds past cultures questionable as suitable foundations for building and renewing a society today.

Consistent with all of these cultural influences has been the emergence of a social ethic and individualistic ethic. The individualistic ethic glorifies the freedom of the individual, competition between one person and another, and self-determination as the value goals of life. The social ethic elevates the importance of the individual to the group, community, and larger society. It assumes that the group is the primary way of meeting man's needs.

In some cases people feel a clash between these two values. The social ethic advocates adaptation, equilibrium, and solidarity. Competition is no longer exalted. While the individual is not neglected, his satisfactions are seen as derived from participation and membership in organized relationships—e.g., groups, clubs, or organizations. Organization management has built upon both of these ethics for its values and practices. The individualistic ethic has focused attention on hard work, responsibility, individual goal achievement, self-development, and many other practices commonly or less commonly found in organizational life. One intensive survey made by the Church and Economic Life Commission of the National Council of Churches [4] enunciated those individual values that are relevant to our economic system:

SURVIVAL AND PHYSICAL WELL-BEING (PRODUCTIVITY). Each individual should have access to the conditions necessary for health, safety, comfort, and reasonable longevity.

FELLOWSHIP. Each individual should have a variety of satisfying human relationships.

DIGNITY AND HUMILITY. Each individual should have the opportunity to earn a position of dignity and self-respect in society.

ENLIGHTENMENT. The individual should have opportunity to learn about the world in which he lives. He should be able to satisfy his intellectual curiosity and to acquire the skills and knowledge for intelligent citizenship, efficient work, and informed living.

AESTHETIC ENJOYMENT. The individual should have the opportunity to appreciate aesthetic values in art, nature, and ritual, and personal relations. Many aesthetic values are attainable through both production and consumption.

CREATIVITY. The individual should be able to express his personality through creative activities. He should be able to identify himself with the results of his own activity, and to take pride in his intellectual, aesthetic, political, and other achievements.

NEW EXPERIENCE.   An important goal of life is suggested by such words as variability, spontaneity, whimsy, novelty, excitement, fun, sport, holiday, striving against odds, solving problems, innovations, and invention. Each individual should have opportunity for new experience.

SECURITY.   Each individual should have assurance that the objective conditions necessary for attainment of the above goals will be and continue to be reasonably accessible to him.

FREEDOM.   Freedom is the opportunity to pursue one's goals without restraint.

JUSTICE.   The religious concept of love does not imply neglect of the self. The individual is to be as concerned about others as he is about himself—neither more nor less.

The preceding goals are stated in terms of the kinds of life experiences people wish to have; they can also be translated into the kinds of persons we wish people to be. Goals can then be regarded as qualities of human personality and, accordingly, a desirable personality would be defined as one that is favorably conditioned toward the various goals.

Fulfillment of such a list of individual values is a challenge to any manager, group, or organization, and it indicates some of the forces at work in initiating organization renewal. The individual values that have emerged in our culture sometimes conflict with a second trend which focuses on social ethics.

The social ethic has emphasized the value of cohesive work units, use of specialists combined in team situations, associations in product and professional areas, responsibility to customers, and numerous other practical applications. In this context, management has differing responsibilities to various segments of society as it establishes goals, policies, and practices. These obligations try to secure and maintain a compatibility between management's relationship to society by legal and nonlegal means. The basic problem results, as management pursues its operations, from the tension between organizational self-interest and social obligation. Some of the social responsibilities of organizational management are:

ETHICAL RELATIONS WITH CUSTOMERS.   Whether an organization is providing services or widgets, it has an obligation to provide what is advertised, requested, or promised.

ETHICAL RELATIONS WITH EMPLOYEES.   Management bears the obligation to provide a fair wage, proper working conditions, opportunity for promotion, appropriate fringe benefits, equal employment opportunity, and good personnel relations.

ETHICAL RELATIONS WITH SUPPLIERS.   Managers have a responsibility to treat suppliers with the same consideration given to customers.

ETHICAL RELATIONS WITH POLICYMAKERS, SHAREHOLDERS, OR SPONSORS. Almost every organization has a group of persons who have invested capital, trust, or energy into the life of the organization. The responsibility to inform, consult, reward, and be influenced by those groups is a prerequisite of ethical management.

ETHICAL RELATIONS WITH COMPETITORS. To work with one's competitors in such a way that fair practice results is another part of management's responsibility. This means avoiding price-fixing, not stealing industrial secrets, cooperating in presenting one's field, and contributing to the development of the profession of management.

ETHICAL RELATIONS WITH THE COMMUNITY. In the past ten years, management has become more aware of its responsibility in community planning, community relations, and community problem-solving. It is necessary for today's leader to consider the importance of individual and social ethics. To apply these ethical standards to the organization, the group, and one's self is an essential undertaking. It is an even greater challenge to relate these ethical values to organization renewal and change. It is also important, I think, to clearly understand that there are some underlying assumptions supporting the need for organization renewal:

1. In today's organizations there are unavoidable human problems which involve varying degrees of interpersonal and intergroup tension and conflict that keep the organization from functioning most effectively.

2. It is better that such human problems be solved than that they remain unsolved.

3. Deliberate planning of solutions to these problems, which necessarily involve changes in the people, the groups, and institutions concerned, is necessary to a degree that it has not been in the past. Trial and error processes of historical accommodation are no longer adequate to the organizational needs of today.

4. The most promising source from which to derive principles of ethical control in the planning of the changes that we must make is in our system of democratic and scientific values. These values can be translated into norms or principles of method which can be used in the guidance and direction of organization renewal, of deciding what changes are needed, and in evaluating the changes produced. The alternatives are to identify "democracy" or "scientific" with one substantive solution or another. Some people who favor public housing will argue for it as "democratic"—others will identify private housing with the "democratic" way. Let us translate these values into norms of method acceptable to both sides. Through conflict they may work out a solution which may not be what either held in the first place, but which hopefully will be mutually satisfactory to both.

Several colleagues have discussed the implications of democratic leadership [5] and the scientific method.[6] I have attempted to relate this thinking to some guidelines for those who must plan changes which lead to organization renewal. The first guideline concerns motivation. A planner can be motivated, in part, by such individual needs as status, security, and prestige. One's own awareness of these motivations may clearly demonstrate his role. The approach to problem-solving should be task-oriented rather than prestige-oriented. The essential concern should be that the new condition achieved be better than the first, not that the person initiating change should receive credit or have an enhanced standing in the eyes of others in the organization.

The processes by which organization renewal is planned should be collaborative, they should involve ideally all the people affected by the change. For example, as we set out to produce a change in the pattern of staff meetings in corporate headquarters, insofar as possible, the changes planned and instituted should be arrived at collaboratively. All the people affected should have an opportunity to express themselves concerning the problem, and to contribute to shaping the solution in terms of their particular relation to the decision. Many times resistance to collaboration operates within the people with whom we deal, as well as within ourselves. Attempts at complete self-effacement in the renewal stimulator may be a kind of dodge that covers up his own self-interest in producing change. Widespread resistance to his attempts to influence should lead him to re-examine his position and re-enter the change arena with approaches that permit and sustain collaborative planning of change.

In order for the renewal stimulator to conform to democratic and scientific values, the methods of problem-solving should be experimental. Though this norm may be most difficult to derive from basic democratic values, it is still very important. The opposite tends to be a kind of absolutist conviction that one's present views are right beyond question. Such an attitude often prevents genuine collaboration. If a human problem is a genuine problem, there is no single, pat solution. There may be many principles that apply but no one knows in advance exactly which combinations best fit reality. An experimental attitude means giving any reasonable but novel plan a try; it also means building into the plan methods of evaluation which will reveal whether the altered practices approach the desired change goals. Almost always, solving a problem in human relations involves some interadjustment in all the people concerned, including the renewal stimulator.

The method used for organization renewal, if it is to be democratic and scientific, must be educational and/or therapeutic for the people involved, leaving them better able to face and control future situations. We are not trying to solve present problems to get away from future problems, but rather to know better how to deal with the latter as they arise. The idea is not to get away from problems, which is to get away from reality, but rather to know better how to confront, diagnose, and solve problems.

Finally, it is my feeling that a person initiating planned change must always be aware that he is accountable. In the first place, he is accountable to himself. The responsibility rests with him to examine his motivation, the results he desires and the methods he employs, to see how consistently they correspond with the value response required of him. Secondly, he is accountable to those who are affected by his efforts. In this it is a help, and further guide, to accept the fact that the renewal stimulator is always involved in and affected by the change he produces. He does not stand over and above—a little God who calls the shots and determines the destiny of others. He, too, is involved and affected, whether he be an outside consultant or a part of the system. He can never disassociate himself from the profoundly inextricable relationship he has with his fellow men.

Let us take these guidelines for working in a democratic and scientific manner, as well as an operational definition of ethics, and apply them to the work of a renewal stimulator as he works with the all-important groups in an organization.

Leading or consulting with groups is required of all those who accept responsibility in changing the organizational systems of modern society. Today, fortunately, recent research results and new research techniques permit us to diagnose the behavioral phenomena associated with the achievement of constructive group action. With present knowledge, it is indeed now possible to develop the diagnostic skills required for group leadership and consultation.

As leaders develop their capacities to improve group performance, it is well to examine the fundamental ideas and beliefs that undergird them, lending their efforts a value and central meaning. Group leadership skills have been largely developed, to my way of thinking, as they have been because they were successfully related to a set of cultural and religious values. Only when he has some value pattern to guide him, is it possible for a leader to judge and evaluate his work with groups in meaningful terms. I have identified below some of the value orientations I believe to be desirable in a renewal stimulator who is working with groups: [7]

WORTH OF EACH INDIVIDUAL IN THE GROUP. In Western society, a belief in the individual is an imperative in the development of group relation skills. We see the individual as an end in himself, not as a means to an end—not as a pawn to be moved about as it may please an authoritarian to do.

It is essential, in leading groups, to be sensitive to the motivations and needs of the individual members, as well as those of one's self. To understand individual needs is to be aware of the complexity of personality, its structure and capacity for growth toward self-hood. As Rollo May [8] has said:

It [self-hood] means achieving a dynamic unity which is manifested chiefly in the potentialities in productive work and the expanding meaningfulness of one's relations with one's fellowmen.

The implications of the Western concept of individual worth are quite clear. If he is to be successful, the group leader must consider each member indispensable to the group, and he must help each member to fulfill himself within the context of the group. The psychological concept of Maslow's "hierarchy of needs" has all men desiring self-fulfillment at their highest level of need. It is a modern form of the classical Judeo-Christian doctrine of the infinite value of the person, calling forth the affirmation of one's self as created in the image of God—and the recognition and affirmation, through redemptive fellowship, of the "self" in others. An effective group leader will want each member of the group to be involved, to take part, and to contribute to the achievement of the common goals.

GROUP RELATIONSHIPS SHOULD BE AUTHENTIC AND SATISFY THE YEARNING FOR ACCEPTANCE. Of the many reasons why people participate in groups—for example, to secure representation, support, knowledge, experience, or to focus responsibility—perhaps the most basic reason is to obtain personal satisfaction. Kenneth Berrien [9] has indicated that people search for social satisfactions through "the development of close relationships which anchor the individual securely in some stabilizing continuing group." When groups are ineffective it is often because they are not satisfying the personal needs of members. Such failure, understandably, leads to apathy, loss of time, indecisiveness, and poor attendance at meetings. People yearn for acceptance in a fellowship. Such motivation has caused the formation of religious organizations, voluntary agencies, fraternities, and similar subdivisions of society. The history of the two ethics in Western culture—the individualistic and social—instructs us that both are of great significance in the life of man.[10] Fellowship requires acceptance, authentic and natural, where people associate without sham or malice. In Pasternak's novel, *Dr. Zhivago*, we hear the hero saying of the modern age: "These days I have such a longing to live honestly, to be productive. I so much want to be a part of all this awakening."

The great challenge to working with groups is that of developing honest, nondefensive, and authentic fellowship in the life of the group.

Ross Snyder [11] has paraphrased Martin Buber in describing the authentic relationship:

Authentic existence is meeting each fresh situation with a spontaneous wholeness; responding out of the depths rather than in terms of previously decided rules or images, or from compulsive emotion; and the response is such as to call out potentialities of the Kingdom of God that are hidden within this situation and moment.

The group leader or consultant, it appears clear, should strive for unembarrassed communication among individual members of the group, with free exchange of ideas and feelings. In such an atmosphere, the sociological term, "sense of community," takes on flesh and meaning. Frank expression and argument are viewed within this context by a mature leader as positive values which he not only tolerates but encourages.

MEMBERS MUST BE ABLE TO INFLUENCE GROUP DECISIONS.   Individuals should be allowed the right to influence the group, and group leaders should create a climate favorable to the exercise of that right, *if* the decision is a group responsibility. In cases where the responsibility is in fact the leader's, or a decision already has been reached, people ought not to be manipulated and led to believe otherwise at group meetings.[12] Whenever the group is asked to reach a decision, its freedom to act and degree of responsibility should be made clear. The renewal stimulator should guide, not direct; he should seek opportunities for group, not personal achievement. As Lao Tse indicated in the *Book of Tao* in 600 B.C.:

> A leader is best
> When people barely know he exists . . .
> When his work is done, his aim is fulfilled.
> They will all say, "We did this ourselves."

THE SEARCH FOR TRUTH AND USE OF MAN'S MIND.   The search for truth is another ethical principle that should guide group leadership and group actions. Group decisions must be based *not* upon friendship, not upon likes and dislikes, hunches or intuition, but rather upon the objective search for the right answer. Frequent references have been made to a supposed contradiction between the scientific method and religious values. It appears to me that this is essentially a semantic disturbance, a confusion of dogma and creed—which may indeed offend science—with the essence of Judeo-Christian thought. The scientist Wernher von Braun [13] put it this way:

I am certain that science, in its search for new insights into the nature of the creation, has produced new ethical values of its own. . . . Personally,

I believe in the ultimate victory of truth. . . . The better we understand the intricacies of the atomic structure, the nature of life, or the master plan for the galaxies, the more reason we have found to marvel at the wonder of God's creation.

Leaders and consultants who believe in the search for truth will encourage full play of members' minds in solving problems of the group. A good mind, encouraged to work, will penetrate half truths and enlarge the incomplete view to encompass a broad perspective. Effective group action depends upon facing hard facts, sensible interpretation of them, and ideas—all a part of the problem-solving process. Man must indeed use his mind in order to survive. As has been written:

Man's mind is his basic tool of survival. . . . He cannot obtain his food without a knowledge of food and of the way to obtain it. He cannot dig a ditch—or build a cyclotron—without a knowledge of his aim and of the means to achieve it. To remain alive, he must think.[14]

While we seek new knowledge, we should also make the best use we are able of what we already know, always working toward the improvement of ourselves, other individuals or groups, the organization, and mankind itself. An effective renewal stimulator will employ problem-solving techniques to bring out the best in the minds of the members of the group.

A GROUP LEADER SHOULD STIMULATE CREATIVE FREE EXPRESSION. Most religious values underline the importance of man's "free will" and his "free choice." All members of the group should be free to dissent, to be in the minority, or indeed to stand alone, and to differ with the leader without fear of reprisal. In short, the member of the group should be stimulated to release his creative best. Group activity is often criticized, and sometimes only too accurately, on grounds that it encourages conformity with the views of the leader or the hierarchy of the organization. An effective leader, however, usually is one who provides a climate which releases the creative potential of individuals in the group, and encourages spontaneity.

Expression of one's personality through group action is a rewarding experience that adds an immeasurable dimension to life. Such an experience is all too rare, but it lends life excitement and novelty as well as deep satisfaction. As the philosopher Hocking [15] said:

The tightest of organizations depends on individual creativity. When that creativity is limited to a few at the top, we have despotism. But organization as such does not trust the individual. Most of us spend time under a master, and if he tells us to do something that is morally wrong, we must refuse. Creativity exists as long as the servant has any moral initiative of his own. Individualism grows and spreads with responsibility. You can only make men free when they are inwardly bound by their own sense of responsibility.

Man wants to take pride in his achievements be they intellectual, manual, aesthetic, political, or any other. This pride has a special value in group performance when a member's ideas or actions tend to be supported by the others during the problem-solving phase. Leaders and consultants should work to have the pardonable pride of individuals serve and advance the group objectives.

TOLERATE DIVERSE BEHAVIOR AND DO NOT SIT IN JUDGMENT OF OTHERS. A prime tenet of Western culture is the toleration of diversity; the recognition that many beliefs, attitudes, and personalities form the web of mankind. Most value systems caution that we judge not for we may also be judged. The concept of forgiveness, turning the other cheek, is prominent in our religious philosophy. While an effective group leader will develop his perceptions of another person, and feelings toward him, these perceptions and feelings should *not* affect his judgment of a member's contribution, nor of his individual worth. As much as anyone else, the leader should exercise tolerance of people's behavior and recognize that hostility, aggression, and personal ill will are to be expected in group activity. He will forgive as he hopes to be forgiven. Beyond forgiving another, the group leader must try to understand him, in order to communicate and progress. It is not unknown for a leader to use precedent as a substitute for democratic action when the group decision differs from his own. This, of course, is a poor way to "win," and organizations themselves should be flexible enough to prevent it. As Rollo May [16] has said:

Achieving [group maturity] means arriving at the psychological and spiritual integrity which is characterized by the capacity—and practice—of judging [group] actions by one's own, inner criteria rather than by vain and narcissistic standards of public (and organization) acceptance and applause.

This section of the chapter has attempted to identify some of the basic life values and methods that can provide guidelines for the responsible group leader and renewal stimulator. These have support in both psychological and religious knowledge; they put the leadership of groups in a frame of reference that indicates that growth of persons, freedom of will, use of man's mind, meaningful fellowship, and the importance of the individual are the dynamic dimensions of qualitative group functioning in today's organization. It may well become evident in the organization renewal process that there is a need to confront the overall values and operating ethics of the total organization.

In light of the complexity of organizational ethics, there is a temptation to feel that one "can't do anything." There are, however, a number of steps that ethical managers can take:

They can explore with policy groups the philosophy of their organization. Incorporating the guiding principles of an organization into a creed can be a valuable tool. The process of formulating this creed is often more valuable than the statement itself. In such a process, management is able to begin the assessment of its goals.

They can carry out the process of management by objectives, which means the setting of goals in all aspects of the organization. These goals can be examined in terms of the philosophy of the organization.

They can include concepts of management ethics and philosophy as an integral part of training and executive development programs. This important part of leadership training is frequently neglected.

They can initiate a program of two-way communication with employees, clients, suppliers, and the community—relative to needs, problems, and standards.

They can develop a process of internal reporting and evaluation of ethical problems that confront the organization. These can be discussed as part of leadership responsibilities in the organization.

They can develop a code of ethics. Many organizations have developed a code of ethics to guide the individual behavior of their employees. The problem is to put "teeth" in the enforcement of these codes without forcing management to perform police functions. The most effective kind of enforcement is that provided by one's peers, as is the case with many professional groups.

Many people feel that the increasing knowledge of human behavior and increasing bodies of tested techniques for dealing with human situations are inherently dangerous in that the more knowledge we have of why people behave as they do, and of how to effectively influence their motivations, the more danger there is of misuse. Actually, our knowledge about people and techniques for influencing people is still all too limited. We need to extend research and study to augment social knowledge and technology. If this increases the risk of misapplication, a moratorium on research is not the answer. We must make every effort to disseminate this knowledge to more and more people so that a few people who possess it exclusively cannot use it against the others who are ignorant of it. We must try to learn more and more through field experimentation and evaluated practice, but we must try to spread the knowledge gained and not hoard it. It should become a common resource that all can see. We will probably not be able to share it completely, however, and there probably will always be the need for the renewal stimulator. Concurrently, though, we need better ways for organizations to control the experts they need.

We can develop techniques for dealing with people that have ethical controls built into them. If, for example, a committee is helped to get better command of the forces working in their situation, and to build into their agenda time and devices for evaluation of their work, including the leadership, this in itself becomes a technique which operates against the leader's unconscious or conscious misuse of his power as a renewal stimulator.

Both research and practical experience underscore the fact that the single most important factor in the practice of ethical behavior is the individual's personal code and standards. Each person represents in his own life the influence of his environment and his experience, and this contributes to the criteria he uses to appraise the ethical implications of particular situations. Some people have used certain tests to evaluate the proper decision in a particular situation:

> THE TEST OF COMMON SENSE.   Does the action make sense? In view of the situation, how will the proposed action look in practice and result in practical consequences? This common sense test may help to determine whether the proposed action is appropriate.
>
> THE TEST OF HURTING SOMEONE ELSE.   Will the action contribute "internal pain" to someone to the extent that it may endanger the integrity of a personality or cause excessive discomfort?
>
> THE TEST OF ONE'S BEST SELF.   Each of us has a self-concept which may or may not fit our actions. As we consider a decision, we might ask if this action will fit the concept of ourselves at our best.

Persons operating as renewal stimulators can best guard against misuse of their own skills and knowledge, if they are aware of their own major motivations. Many times we conceal our motives from ourselves. We are more likely to violate our ethical norms when we use our knowledge and skill for purposes which we cannot or do not admit to ourselves. If we are concerned with ethical change, self-knowledge is very necessary. There is no royal road toward self-awareness, yet this is of primary importance for the person concerned with his ethical or non-ethical motivation toward changing other people's behavior. We are more likely to fool others, the more skilled we are in fooling ourselves. Self-knowledge does not necessarily make one more ethical but it does put the renewal stimulator in command of the forces operating on and through him so that he can bring his way of dealing with them into line with his ethical commitments.

> THE TEST OF PUBLICITY.   A simple test to apply to any contemplated action is to determine how the act would stand up to the light of

public knowledge. What if people knew what you were doing? This is a searching and healthy test for any leader to ask himself when confused about the ethics of a situation.

THE TEST OF ONE'S MOST ADMIRED PERSONALITY.   Most of us have one or two people who mean a great deal to us—such as parents, teachers, or bosses. What would such a model do in this situation?

THE TEST OF FORESIGHT.   An important test of any decision or action is to explore the possible consequences of the behavior. What is likely to result from this action?

Managers and others who assume renewal responsibility have many other responsibilities to the organization and society of which they are a part. Legal and social obligations of management are to operate the organization in accordance with goals, objectives, and rights under which it operates. Equally important are its obligations to employees, customers, government, the community, and the public at large. These may at times be momentarily in conflict with the decisions and policy-making of management. However, the goal of management should be that its complex obligations and responsibilities should never jeopardize the application of high ethical standards.

The ethics of any decision-making situation are determined by looking at the effect of the decision on the decision-maker and on those influenced by the decision, as both of these factors relate to the existing values of the culture. A leader must assess each situation in the light of relevant organization, group, and individual ethical standards. Over the past thirty years, organizations have continually attempted to demonstrate their eagerness to fulfill their social and individual responsibilities. They have initiated, and accepted from others, policies which have improved overall standards of conduct. Through these improvements, the requirements of effective leadership have steadily risen over the years. This, in turn, has had a profound influence on the performance of the scientific and industrial society in which we live.

In one sense, however, there is an additional factor that can help make sure that a renewal stimulator will manifest proper ethical practice. This is the extent to which we develop managing, leading, and consulting in the organization renewal context as a *professional* role and function. It is possible to develop adequate professional controls over attempts to produce change. Historically, one of the best methods of safeguarding the public from the misuse of expert knowledge and skill has been professional self-regulation. This is rather difficult for change stimulators to achieve in the organization renewal field because the renewal stimulator may operate in and through professional associations supporting many different disciplines. Here part of the problem is to get the several professional associations more concerned, more commonly aware that perhaps a new body of knowledge and techniques in the social change area is emerging—new knowledge and techniques that should be used for the common good, not for selfish ends, thus laying the basis for an inter-professional ethics. Many of the older principles of professional ethics do not take into account the emerging new body of knowledge about renewal and, when rigidly applied, can delay application of available knowledge to organizational problems, and also delay the working out of new, valid ethical controls.

Many persons responsible for organizational change do not belong to any profession at all. This creates an additional problem to which there is no easy solution, since these people do not come under the discipline of any particular profession which might already have or may develop some appropriate group self-regulation.

It is my purpose to highlight this area of concern in examining the whole effort of organization renewal. Planned change does have ethical implications which should be thoroughly considered by the whole body of practitioners. The moral and ethical standards that have become involved in this problem of individual and social responsibility should be the key to the future advancement in both the private and public sectors of our society. The responsibility for establishing and maintaining high ethical standards rests heavily upon managers and consultants in all kinds of organizations. However, every coin has two sides. This responsibility must, in part, be shared by everyone who has an influence upon the environment of our whole social order.

NOTES

1. The studies which are summarized include research completed by the Reverend Raymond Baumhart on 1,700 managers reported in an article entitled, "How Ethical are Businessmen?" *Harvard Business Review,* July–August, 1961; a study of 143 government and military executives by L. Forbes and H. Y. Lee at George Washington University, 1964; and a study of 103 business executives by James V. Clark at UCLA School of Business Administration, 1965.
2. James Owens, quoted in Gordon L. Lippitt, *The Leader Looks at Ethics,* Looking Into Leadership Monographs (Washington, D.C.: Leadership Resources, Inc., 1966), p. 4. Reprinted with permission from Leadership Resources, Inc.
3. Samuel H. Miller, "The Tangle of Ethics," *Harvard Business Review,* January–February, 1969, p. 59.
4. Howard R. Bowen, "Findings of the Study," in John C. Bennet and others, *Christian Values and Economic Life* (New York: Harper & Row, Publishers, 1954), pp. 47–60.
5. Warren G. Bennis and Philip Slater, "Democracy is Inevitable," *Harvard Business Review,* March–April, 1964, pp. 51–59.

6. Kenneth D. Benne, *A Conception of Authority,* Columbia University, 1943 (unpubl.).

7. The following section is taken from Lippitt, "Ethical Dimensions of Group Leadership," reprinted by permission from the March, 1967 issue of *Pastoral Psychology,* copyright 1967 by Meredith Publishing Co.

8. Rollo May, "Religion, Psychotherapy, and the Achievement of Selfhood," *Pastoral Psychology,* January, 1952, p. 42.

9. F. Kenneth Berrien, *Comments and Cases of Human Relations* (New York: Harper & Row, Publishers, 1951), p. 236.

10. Robert T. Golembiewski, *Men, Management, and Morality: Toward a New Organizational Ethic* (New York: McGraw-Hill Book Co., Inc., 1965).

11. Ross Snyder, *The Authentic Life: Its Theory and Practice,* Religous Education Committee, Friends General Conference, 1959, p. 26.

12. Lippitt, "Guidelines for Managerial Use of Groups," *Executive,* Credit Union Executive Service, November, 1965.

13. Wernher von Braun, "Why I Believe," *This Week,* July 18, 1965, p. 3.

14. Ayn Rand, *Atlas Shrugged* (New York: Random House, Inc., 1957), p. 108.

15. William E. Hocking, *Time,* May 10, 1963, p. 35.

16. May, *op. cit.,* p. 45.

PART FOUR

Conditions, Skills, and Actions in Organization Renewal

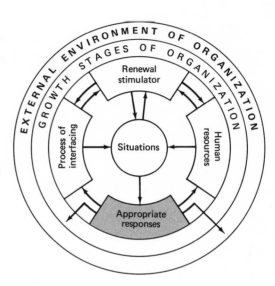

Organization renewal may take place in various ways. To be maintained, however, it will require appropriate conditions for "learning how to learn" from the multiple situations which are confronted.

Chapter 10 presents some criteria and guidelines to use in evaluating organization renewal and its appropriateness. Chapter 11 proposes that organization renewal must focus on the "learning-how-to-learn" concept that will utilize the best from varying research and theories of learning. Chapter 12 presents some of the problems and potentials in using laboratory methods in renewal activities and processes, and identifies the skills required. Chapter 13 presents five different case examples of organization renewal from various types of systems.

10 CRITERIA FOR EVALUATION

This institution will be based on the illimitable freedom of the human mind. For here we are not afraid to follow truth wherever it may lead, nor to tolerate error so long as reason is free to combat it.

THOMAS JEFFERSON, 1743–1826

The assessment of the results of learning or change experiences is a matter of concern to managers, educators, trainers, and professional groups interested in improving organizational productivity, or in providing educational and developmental experiences in organizations. Two aspects must be considered in any meaningful evaluation. The first of these is the effect of learning experience upon the individuals involved. This can be demonstrated to some degree by the use of before and after measurements which can illustrate differences in responses. The second, and more complex aspect, is the assessment of the effectiveness of the change experience when applied to the organizational setting, an evaluation which presents more complicated problems.

Since we know very little about the effect of traditional change processes, it is discouraging to contemplate the difficulties to be faced in evaluating more complex effects of organizational development as stimulated by organization renewal. Tannenbaum, Weschler, and Massarik [1] have said:

> Many organizations spend a great deal of time, effort, and money on various forms of training. This training typically is intended to provide experiences which will in appropriate ways modify the trainees attitudes and behaviors. These expenditures have been made on the assumption that training does effectively change the views and reactions of persons exposed, and that it will make them more skillful in dealing with others. Often a mere judgment of faith is involved. Comparatively little is known of the actual impact that may be ascribed to training.

Developing *criteria* for this purpose typically has been one of the most difficult problems facing researchers. In organization renewal, the task is even more difficult because there is no universal agreement as to how an organization should function, how it should be organized, and how it should be supervised and regulated—even what, really, it should be and do. Different systems, furthermore, are faced with different requirements depending on their structure, resources, size, products, and types of people serviced. On the one hand an organization must be responsive to the values and perceptions of the people it serves; but to be effective, it also needs to exercise leadership and to follow sound human, technical, managerial, and financial practices.

As pointed out by Walther and McCune [2] this need for criteria development is essential for evaluating any organizational change effort:

> While we can recognize that there is considerable controversy among experts on a number of organizational functioning issues and that it may not be possible to develop principles that have universal acceptance, explicit criteria are, nevertheless, intrinsic to any objective evaluation of a change process. Any development program is based on assumptions that certain types of behaviors, attitudes, and decisions will improve performance, but all too often the assumptions underlying a particular change strategy are taken for granted and remain implicit rather than explicit.

Part of the problem is the nature of earlier types of training endeavors that has made us focus on improving organizational functioning, rather than just increasing the skills of individuals. Following World War II organizations in the United States faced the immediate need for additional persons in the managerial ranks, but in the fifties and sixties the nature of this need began to change. The development of greater numbers of more competent managers, and their successful management of the human resources of organizations, has become urgently necessary for business, industry, and government because of technological advancements.

The fewer-than-needed graduates of our institutions of higher learning —who may be potentially qualified to manage in an area where efficient systems, adequate planning, and ever more complex machines are commonplace—are too often too soon obsolescent in the continuing knowledge explosion of today's society. It is for this reason that the initiation, nurture, evaluation, and updating of management development systems received increased attention. Many different types of organizations, public and private, are now developing programs and activities to assure the development of both new and different types of managers, the renewal of experienced managers, and the needed changes in the organizations of which they are a part. For this reason, a start must be made toward devising criteria by which these organizations may guide themselves in this difficult but essential task upon which they have embarked.

That the continuous development of all managers in their ability to initiate and cope with change is a problem with wide implications is now generally recognized. This was once an area of special interest thought to have only intangible practical value. Organizations today are hiring staffs, sponsoring research, and bringing in consultants. But wild approaches, questionable theories, and variable practices have caused many people to look upon organization renewal as a quagmire of confusion—which, in the absence of bench marks, it well may be.

As much as nine years ago, one experienced practitioner [3] observed:

> Thus far, we have proceeded from an initial need the need to increase the supply and improve the performance of managers. From this need, we have gone directly to the mechanics of application, using at first such tools as were available. In the process, two things have happened: we have refined and added to these tools, until now there is a considerable array of fine techniques, methods, and "programs" for doing the job of management development; and in the course of using these tools, we have amassed a considerable body of experience with the developmental process. But we have not extracted from that experience such standards and guides as are needed to help us discipline and organize our application of these tools, as a consequence, we continue to fall easy prey to the fad of the moment, the gimmick peddler, and the charlatan.

I might say, in addition, that organizations often are frustrated in their desire for either management or organization development by the inappropriate use of otherwise sound methods. But from the panoply of approaches, certain basic criteria have emerged that seem applicable to the latest and less empirical aspects of action research and planned change as opposed to pure research in behavioral science. Current synthesis can be isolated by first tracing the trend of the management development emphasis through some of its accumulative phases from the relatively artless to the present diagnostic and manipulative. This trend is a forerunner of the present concern with organization renewal.

Anthropologists and social scientists might argue with the hypothesis that management development was first vicarious, but that progression toward acceptance of commercial and social values, and the economic manifestation of family enterprise, led to what is now known as "on-the-job experience." The latter, in its original form, was concerned with inculcating by understudy and inbred imitation those skills and traits that an incumbent manager considered essential in anyone destined to follow in his footsteps. The process was explicit and did not allow at all for organizational change in keeping with environmental change. In modern form, the understudy learns not only by observing and adapting, but also by questioning, assisting, initiating, and assuming a measure of responsibility in carrying out, in a narrow field of endeavor, preplanned tasks that are progressively more difficult. Almost half a century ago, this method began to be overtaken by technology, and management itself struggled into a recognition that it is a profession in its own right.

Apprenticeship, job rotation, and performance appraisal—historical and still fundamental to management development in military services—became productive innovations in business and industry about thirty years ago. Men who demonstrated management potential were named to junior management boards. Here they had an opportunity to participate with a group in making recommendations to a senior board and, in part by design but largely for self-development, each participant was able to see his own role in a broader context. One of the liabilities incurred in this system, as an outgrowth of having scant means of pre- or post-evaluation, was the tendency to groom "crown princes," whether or not they were basically qualified for higher management responsibilities.

About two decades ago, competition from youthful on-comers and the concurrent pressure from assumed requirements for wider cultural understanding forced incumbent executives back to school for education promising to provide learning outside a narrow technical specialty and outside their organizational affiliations. While none of this effort was altogether wasted, much of it may have been disoriented and topically misdirected as far as individual management capabilities were concerned. Sometime participation in professional organizations, civic and community groups, reading and lecture programs, gradually gave way to perhaps more pertinent economic, environmental, and political studies. At this point, top organization executives in government, community agencies, and industry recognized the probability that their investment of money and the man-hours of subordinate employees might well return dividends in management development. In an overt attempt, rationalized as a means to preserve and strengthen the "free enterprise system," management endorsed the liberal arts adult education movement that stresses the management-directed broadening of the horizons of executives and prospective executives as responsible performers in the twentieth century.

As beneficial as this concept was and is, the science of management soon demanded more specific knowledge and skills, and a greater conceptual understanding of the relationship between the trainee's organization and the controlling aspects of the world in which it exists. Philosophic and cultural achievements alone did not meet the need for such managerial skills as decision-making, planning, and fiscal management, or the imperatives of communication such as faster reading and improved writing abilities, effective public· speaking, and group leadership, let alone the ability to cope with change. With computers coming into general use, data processing systems analysis, information retrieval, operations research, and scheduling methods such as PERT crowded in upon management. Starting late in the fifties, keeping abreast of the state-of-the-art in management became a critical concern. Many organizations, lacking professional guidance and any rationale by which to identify their own requirements, assess the appropriateness of various approaches to training and education for their executives, or measure the results that might be obtained, launched themselves into management development somewhat blindly.

At about the same time, research both within and without the organizational structures, and the pursuit of environmental influences and essential management skills, brought to the forefront in some organizations the need for the executive to better know himself. This led to sensitivity training for laboratory groups with all its variations and debates, and psychological counseling, personality assessments, and medical examinations, and thus to an even greater call for meaningful criteria.

Within the last few years, the trend has been toward both individual executive growth and management team building through the problem-solving process and "management by objectives." [4] This trend reflects a value system that requires heuristic implementation at all executive levels rather than the more common, and paradoxically, hide-bound and piecemeal approach to management development. Today, the progression of methodology, greatly enriched by experience and knowledge derived from the many disciplines contributing to behavioral science, has very nearly circled back upon itself so as to be once more treading in an area not unlike the earlier, even ancient concept of developing situationally oriented abilities in the individual manager. There is, therefore, an urgent necessity to determine on a man-to-man basis whether the application of tailored management development results in learning that is congruent to the *organizational circumstances* in which it is to be used. These succeeding trends in management development reveal a poverty of fundamental guidelines that organizations can now fit to "patterns of work and relationship, structure, technology, and administration [that] promise some of the most significant changes in our society." [5]

As an outgrowth of this trend in management development we have seen emerge what is commonly referred to as *organization development*. Thus, as defined by Buchanan,[6] the new emphasis in organization renewal is characterized as follows:

> Organization development is directed toward developing the capabilities of an organization in such a manner that the organization can attain and sustain an optimum level of performance; it is a problem-solving process; it is undertaken on a collaborative basis by members of an organization and behavioral science practitioners; and it reflects the belief that even in organizations which are operating satisfactorily or adequately there is room for further improvement.

As I mentioned in Chapter 1, "organization renewal" also involves the capabilities of the organization or its sub-systems to achieve whatever may be its next stage of maturity. Some of the key decisions and actions required at various stages of maturity are indicated in Table 10–1. Development efforts should be organically related to the decisions and

TABLE 10–1

Key Management Decisions and Actions

Organization needs	Key decisions and problems	Actions required
To create a new socio-technical system	Marketability of product or service Fiscal procedures and funding Technical procedures Political or legislative needs Organizational leadership	Assess risk alternative Make firm decisions Move with speed and flexibility Employ fluid strategy and tactics, using internal and external opinions Provide for timely entrance of product or service into market
To survive	Focus of operation Accounting and recording procedures Modes of competition Recruiting and training procedures	Meet competition Hire high-quality personnel as cadre Obtain financial backing at appropriate times Introduce delegation Implement basic policies with one eye on future
To stabilize	Long-range planning Proper responses to new competition Technological matters Internal reward systems for personnel Basic public relations policies	Take more aggressive action in market place Use systematic plans and objective setting Try to beat competition Begin R&D as appropriate Train personnel for future needs Begin image building in and outside organization
To earn good reputation	Increasing the quality of goods and/or services Top-notch leadership training Escalation of public relations policies into the community service area	Meet special customer and supplier requests Update policies and philosophy Concentrate on posture and image —internal and external Assure sound financial foundation Contribute to community needs

problems faced by the organization *at the present time.* It becomes of prime importance, therefore, that any organization, plant, or sub-unit first diagnose its present stage before engaging in a development project. Such diagnosis is one of the first steps toward planned change, and whatever efforts are taken to institute and maintain organization renewal, certain criteria might be helpful for management and change agents to keep in mind.

Twelve criteria are suggested to assist in evaluating any contemplated or continuing plan for organization development and renewal: [7]

IS THE ORGANIZATION RENEWAL EFFORT BASED ON AN ARTICULATED VALUE SYSTEM IN WHICH THE PURPOSES OF AN ORGANIZATION ARE CLEARLY

TABLE 10–1 (*Continued*)

Key Management Decisions and Actions

Organization needs	Key decisions and problems	Actions required
To achieve uniqueness	Internal audit of resources and limitations Policies to develop balance in operations	Select and promote one special service or product, or range of services or products Increase delegation Provide for more effective communications including upward flow of ideas Increase advertising and build corporate image Consider optimal size
To earn respect and appreciation	Long-range R&D Determination of self-actualization program for corporate personnel Scope of community and national service	Make heavier commitment in community (e.g., scholarships) Commit executives to national programs and assignments Utilize ideas of total work force Increase contribution to basic R&D, as appropriate Concentrate on long-range direction Flatten internal organization, allowing more freedom for individual responsibility Assess internal direction in relationship to total environment

SOURCE: Gordon L. Lippitt and Warren H. Schmidt, "Crises in a Developing Organization," *Harvard Business Review*, Vol. 45, No. 6, November–December, 1967, p. 111. Copyright © 1967 by the President and Fellows of Harvard College.

RELATED TO THE PUBLIC IT SERVES? One element of an organization's culture is its system of norms and the basic values and assumptions which underlie them. Such values and assumptions deal with the goals of the organization, the means to be employed in achieving the goals, the performance obligations of the members of the organization, and the "correct" way of handling the human resources of the organization.[8] The management of an organization should identify and express the values it espouses and manifests. When this is done satisfactorily, it can then undertake organization renewal with a competent awareness that change or reinforcement of attitudes, skills, and knowledge probably will affect these values, and it will be in a position to control the degree and manner in which new values are inculcated, or old ones modified. However, if study reveals that an organization's value system is the result of dogmatic, authoritarian attitudes rather than rational adjustments, the inability of its present management to keep pace with a changing world may render useless whatever organizational development takes place.

Do THE RENEWAL EFFORTS TAKE INTO ACCOUNT ESSENTIAL NEEDS AT THE PRESENT STATE OF ORGANIZATIONAL GROWTH? An organization develops differing needs for managerial leadership, depending upon the stage of growth at which it finds itself (see Table 5–1, p. 95). A small organization trying to establish itself may need a few dynamic and autonomous executives who behave autocratically in defined spheres of responsibility. A large organization with multi-regional offices may need executives who can coordinate and communicate through others. A well-established corporation with years of success behind it may well want its executives to concentrate on community and other external relations that can contribute to larger service goals. These differences need to be continually assessed in establishing and executing the objectives of organization development efforts.

IS THE RENEWAL PROCESS BASED ON THE REALITIES OF FUTURE CHANGE? Tomorrow's managerial existence in a rapidly-changing industrial-governmental complex requires that today's executives be highly adaptive, and that the managers they develop be creative, tolerant of ambiguity, and capable of timely self-adjustment. A practical awareness of the probable organization of tomorrow, in the near and distant future, should be maintained by those who plan the development of future leaders and groups in organizations.

ARE THE DEVELOPMENT AND RENEWAL PLANS BASED ON WELL-DEFINED ORGANIZATIONAL OBJECTIVES? Management by objectives has been thoroughly propounded in the management literature of the past ten years. Organizational development plans should be translated into individual and group objectives, because success in human endeavor is inevitably related to meaningful achievement of personal and group goals. Those involved in a process of organization renewal need to know and understand their goals, and to have knowledge of the criteria used to evaluate desirable change in their performance.

IS THE RENEWAL PROCESS PREDICATED ON EXAMPLES OF SUCCESSFUL AND UNSUCCESSFUL EXECUTIVE PERFORMANCE IN THE ORGANIZATIONAL SYSTEM? Management thinking is frequently limited by the reluctance of controlling executives, and those on whom they may rely for organizational development, to establish criteria for effective executive performance, both positive and negative. There is no single standard. The kind of managerial performance required in a large steel company may be quite different from that required in a large government agency. Skills or entrepreneurship needed in a small clothing company may differ remarkably from those essential in a small research and development firm. A well-conceived program will be based on the most thorough information possible as to the kinds of managerial characteristics and capabilities needed at each desk in that particular organization.

There is a need, too, to avoid managerial provincialism in the development of managers. Because no organization exists in a vacuum, and because other organizations constantly, subtly bring their influences to bear on whatever value system may be endorsed, it is important that the way things are done outside the organization be not only unsuppressed but explored and evaluated as an avenue toward creating sophistication and balance in the judgments of the individual manager.

ARE THE ACTIVITIES AND PLANS DESIGNED TO CHANGE OR REINFORCE INDIVIDUAL ATTITUDES AS WELL AS TO DEVELOP APPLICABLE SKILLS AND KNOWLEDGE? If a development process contributes only the acquisition of new knowledge or skills, there may be no substantive change in performance—because so limited a contribution provides no foundation of attitude re-formation in the actual practice of new behavioral patterns. The most meaningful aspect of personal change is the examination and alteration of attitudes.

IS THE RENEWAL PROCESS IN ALL RESPECTS SPECIFICALLY DESIGNED FOR THE PARTICULAR ORGANIZATION, GROUP, OR INDIVIDUAL? There probably will never be such a thing as a universally applicable organizational development program. Canned or packaged development and training which emphasizes one skill or another may be of questionable benefit unless it is quite obvious that such skills can be appropriately woven into the fabric of a larger, well-rounded plan that considers multiple needs and precisely fits the growth stages of the organization and the groups and individuals in it.

IS THE DEVELOPMENT PROCESS TO BE PROFESSIONALLY CREATED AND IMPLEMENTED? Any program for developing effective managers, groups, and organizations should make use of all that is known about learning processes and theory, educational methods, group and organizational behavior, and similar fields of knowledge. Whether guidance comes from within or without the organization, professional planning, designing and implementation are vital; more damage than good can be wreaked in this complex field by the inexperienced and unknowledgeable.

IS IT SUPPORTED BY THE LEADERSHIP PRACTICES AND CLIMATE OF THE ORGANIZATION? Productive organization renewal almost invariably means that desirable change will be effected in both individual and organizational practices. Reinforcement and follow-up are essential to refreezing and maintaining management learning and problem-solving at new levels. Two major factors must be present: the behavior of senior executives should manifest support for and belief in the development program so as to establish a climate in which achievement is possible, and desired change in the organization should be rewarded as a concrete indication that progress toward new goals is appreciated in terms of the present stage of organizational need.

DOES THE RENEWAL ACTIVITY PROVIDE FOR EVALUATION IN TERMS OF LONG-RANGE ORGANIZATIONAL GOALS? The future effect of an organization renewal process, as well as its immediate results, should be examined in terms of changing needs. A "happiness ratio" can, and usually is, easily obtained from the comments and testimonials of individuals or groups who are initially involved in a training and development program, but available research methodology for assessment at a deeper level should be used to determine the real effect upon organizational, group, and individual behavior. There is a danger that without the guidance of such deeper analysis, an organizational development program may prove to bring superficial and momentary rather than meaningful change in terms of organizational structure, process, and attitudes. Moreover, the means of evaluating short- and long-range objectives should be devised in advance. Objectives then found not to be compatible with achievement measurement probably will also be found not worth the expense and effort necessary to gain them.

IS THE PROCESS DESIGNED ULTIMATELY TO STRENGTHEN RATHER THAN WEAKEN THE INDIVIDUAL'S DESIRE TO REMAIN PRODUCTIVELY EMPLOYED BY THE ORGANIZATION? For a number of reasons, a badly-handled organizational development program can—and has—resulted in abnormal personnel turnover. This includes both those it makes unhappy, and those who come to think they are good enough to move elsewhere for the money. A more effective process of solving problems and learning from confronting situations should strengthen interest, involvement, productivity, and commitment.

Is it designed to produce greater capabilities in initiative and creativity? It is possible that a poorly-designed organization renewal process, or a misdirected one, could damage an organization's future by inadvertently creating solidified resistance to any further progress or change. This would be a result of "freezing" too hard at some particular level of change. An effective renewal process will create a constant desire for renewal rather than self-satisfaction.

These criteria are almost always applicable to the evaluation of organization renewal, and such an evaluation might quickly be observable when we hear the voice of innovation leading to new products, openness in communication developing more efficient communication, development of work unit teamwork leading to higher morale, or a change in organizational structures releasing the potentiality of newly-promoted managers. Such observations, however, are at the mercy of subjectivity and chance. It would be inappropriate to spend money, time, and effort on organization renewal and not provide for some fact-finding about the results obtained. Too often, however, that is the case.

Indeed it is tempting to conclude, from the literature and from my own experience, that our lack of attention to fact-finding and evaluation derives, in part at least, from our low level of understanding of *how to go about* such evaluative effort. We may even need, in short, research on how best to conduct research leading to evaluation of training and organizational change activities. At the very least, there seems little ground on which to challenge the proposition that some research is sorely needed.[9] And, considering the present national policy emphasis upon training and organizational change, there seems to be an almost urgent need for professionals to make commensurate efforts in an attempt to know how they are doing, and to learn how they can improve in tackling the complex job of helping organizations adapt to changes required to stay viable in the nineteen-seventies.

When a need for evaluation research presents itself, it must be formulated in researchable terms (not as a "should, ought to, value belief" question) and reduced to practical scope in time and cost. The data required must be defined, and the possibility of translating findings into action within the organization should be clearly ascertained.

Specialists are fond of asserting that the only truly effective development program is one that causes obvious and favorable changes in job performance. This assertion is valid. A major dimension of any projected research, therefore, must measure such changes; a before and after performance profile must be obtained in terms of specific criteria to fit a particular organization.

An organization must plan, organize, execute, and test. Testing is fact-finding. Research, usually starting with some stated hypothesis, is that phase of fact-finding which is not the by-product of regular operating procedure and reporting. Using the criteria indicated earlier, those initiating an organization renewal process should be able to develop a research design that can evaluate the organization's efforts and results.

A research design is the method of securing the data that have been defined as needed. Design is aimed at reducing error and bias, and economizing cost of collection. Design will depend on whether the study is:

FORMULATIVE OR EXPLORATORY: i.e., establishing hypothesis or bases for study. Here design must be flexible, will depend much on insight, and can profitably use analysis of "deviate" cases.

DESCRIPTIVE AND DIAGNOSTIC: i.e., describing a situation, and diagnosing reasons for it, and thereby suggesting action to be taken. Here selection or sample for data collection will be of great importance.

EXPERIMENTAL: i.e., testing validity of a hypothesis. Here design can be laboratory or field in nature; involves comparisons of an experimental group against some type of control observations.

In keeping with the schema of organization renewal, the test will be whether the involved efforts solve a problem, improve the functioning of sub-systems in the organization, deepen the process of interfacing, and contribute to the next stage of organizational growth.

The present-day approach to organizational change and development no longer considers the individual apart from his organization or the community in which he lives. As a result of a historic trend away from the purely mechanistic, the directed development of managerial effectiveness in the individual and the group is now flexibly oriented to specific organizational tasks and values in a known climate. Self-understanding and productive relations with others are integrated with an ability to apply a variety of methods and solutions, as well as skills and knowledges, to problems that are themselves multi-faceted.

In the future, those who assume the responsibility for the development of managers will be judged by their overall contribution to developing organizational management teams that create adaptable and viable systems. Such judgments are best made in the light of parallel performance criteria, applicable on the one hand to the achievements of the individual and on the other hand, to the achievements of the organization in solving problems and taking steps toward its own increased maturity. This is why a renewal stimulator needs to concern himself with the criteria involved in the renewal and change process.

NOTES

1. Robert Tannenbaum, Irving R. Weschler, and Fred Massarik, *Leadership and Organization: A Behavioral Science Approach* (New York: McGraw-Hill Book Co., Inc., 1961), p. 22.
2. Regis H. Walther and Shirley D. McCune, *Socialization Principles and Work Styles of the Juvenile Court,* Center for Behavioral Sciences, George Washington University, Washington, D.C., August, 1965, p. 3.
3. Willard Bennet, "An Integrated Approach to Management Development," *Personnel,* Series No. 171, American Management Assn., Inc., 1957, pp. 30–31.
4. Peter F. Drucker, *The Practice of Management* (New York: Harper & Row, Publishers), 1954.
5. Warren G. Bennis, "Theory and Method in Applying Behavioral Science to Planned Organizational Change," *Journal of Applied Behavioral Science,* Vol. I, No. 4, 1965, p. 26.
6. Paul Buchanan, "A Concept of Organization Development or Self-renewal as a Form of Planned Change," *Concepts of Change,* National Education Assn., National Training Laboratories, 1967, p. 1.

7. The following section is taken from Lippitt, "Emerging Criteria for Organization Development," reprinted by permission from the May-June, 1966 issue of *Personnel Administration*, pp. 6–11. Copyright 1966, Society for Personnel Administration, 1221 Connecticut Avenue, N.W., Washington, D.C. 20036.

8. Edgar H. Schein and Lippitt, "Supervisory Attitudes Toward the Legitimacy of Influencing Subordinates," *Journal of Applied Behavioral Sciences,* Vol. II, No. 2, 1966, p. 166.

9. Shirley McCune, Lippitt, and L. Church, "Survey of Evaluation Research Methods Utilized by Training Directors," Center for the Behavioral Sciences, George Washington University, May, 1963.

11 RENEWAL IS LEARNING HOW
TO LEARN [1]

> Intelligent behavior requires an apprenticeship; it is not the expression of ready-made inborn capacity, it is the outcome of learning. And it is not every kind of learning that avails; it must be learning that includes some perception of the relation of things.
>
> SIR J. ARTHUR THOMPSON, 1861–1933

Organization renewal is not merely a matter of good intentions or the identification of new objectives. It involves the improved ability of persons in the organization to *learn* how to solve problems. Some people feel that knowing how to confront problems effectively is an inherited part of man's nature. Considerable research indicates that man must learn skills of problem-solving.

Initiators of organization renewal face the fact that the learning of many persons is "out-of-date." The knowledge explosion has antiquated many of our ideas about human behavior, communication, management, leadership, and organizational functioning. To secure support for new organizational structures, processes, and action it will be necessary for most adults to "re-learn" so as to substitute new ideas, concepts, and realities for the outmoded knowledge, skills and attitudes they possess.

We confront almost any learning opportunity with mixed feelings of wanting to learn and, at the same time, resisting learning. We want to learn for a great variety of reasons. Learning as learning is rewarding. It satisfies curiosity, it provides greater personal power, it gives one a sense of achievement. On the other hand, learning may be uncomfortable. It says that the job of personal development is not finished. Cherished and comfortable assumptions and ways of doing must be questioned. We are obliged to open ourselves to some anxiety and stress as we abandon earlier pointers and fumble in ambiguity toward new attitudes, new insights, and new abilities.

Another complexity in the learning process is that many of us see learning as a passive process in the classic tradition. Because much of our academic and early life experience has led us to believe that we learn out of listening to authorities, there is frequently a need to learn how to learn from real life experience.

As Lee Bradford [2] has observed:

> The learning process should endeavor to help the learner learn how to learn more effectively so that more of his experiences can lead toward learning and change. . . . A basic purpose of education in all learning situations is first to help the individual learner open himself up for learning by being able to bring his problems and needs for learning to the surface and to listen and accept relevant reactions about his problems and behavior. A second purpose is to help the learner gain methods of experimenting, analyzing and utilizing experiences and knowledge resulting from daily problem-solving.

Attempts are often made to distinguish between training and education. Some educators feel that training directors and others similarly involved in organized learning activities are not engaged in education. Most such persons believe they are. Educators tend to make this distinction: training is narrow in scope and involves only learning that is directly related to job performance, while education is concerned with the total human being and his insights into, and understanding of, his entire world. These attempts to distinguish between training and education seem petty inasmuch as both are concerned with the process of human learning.

Berelson and Steiner [3] define learning as "changes in behavior that result from previous behavior in similar situations. Mostly, but by no means always, behavior also becomes demonstrably more effective and more adaptive after the exercise than it was before. In the broadest terms, then, learning refers to the effects of experience on subsequent behavior." From this we can deduce that for the organization renewal planner, learning would seem to imply these kinds of things:

Knowing something intellectually or conceptually one never knew before.

Being able to do something one couldn't do before—a behavior or skill.

Combining two knowns into a new understanding of a skill, piece of knowledge, concept, or behavior.

Being able to use or apply a new combination of skills, knowledge, concept, or behavior.

Being able to understand and apply that which one knows—either skill, knowledge, or behavior.

Since those interested in organization renewal are concerned with learning, it follows that they should be concerned with learning theory. Many training and development people talk rather glibly about the learning theory that underlies their endeavors, but most of them do not have a good understanding of learning theories and their application to our training efforts. Nevertheless, it is from the viewpoint of a training director that I venture into an overview of learning theory. Here I must observe that, as we design training programs, we are confronted by many factors about which we must make decisions:

DESIRED OUTCOMES FOR THE LEARNING EXPERIENCE.   They can range from complex comprehension of organizational dynamics to simple manual skills. Managers who underwrite educational programs normally stipulate entirely different sets of training outcomes. These usually are identified as reduction of costs; increased productivity; improved morale; and a corps of competent promotional replacements. Sometimes these things are confused by training directors as outcomes of training that are affected by learning theory. It seems to me, however, that while they may be results of training, learning theory does not directly relate to them as outcomes.

SITE FOR LEARNING.   Persons involved in planning learning experiences are concerned whether learning best occurs on the job, in a classroom, on or off organizational premises; at a university or other formal site, cultural island, or at home.

LEARNING METHODS.   These are seen as being on a continuum from casual reading to intense personal involvement in personal-relationship laboratories.

GROUPING FOR LEARNING.   Grouping of learners can involve all combinations from individuals and dyads to audiences.

As learning planners deal with and manipulate the variables listed above, they tend to confuse them with *learning theory*. For example, a training director will say "My theory of learning is that employees learn best when placed in small discussion groups at a training site removed from the plant." What is not clear to most training directors is that the variables identified above result in a myriad of devices and techniques that stem from, and are most effectively utilized by, a given learning theory. In and of themselves they are not learning theory.

Just as we confuse learning theory with the variables of site or grouping, the use of the terms "learning theory" and "learning theory corollaries or principles" can be confusing. Usually the learning theory can be stated very broadly—for example, "Learning occurs when a stimulus is associated with a response." From this generalization about how learning occurs, a number of specific laws of learning are derived. For example, "Repetition of a response strengthens its connection with a stimulus." Thus, the statement, "problems are difficult to solve when they require the use of the familiar in an unfamiliar way" is a corollary of the Behaviorist Learning Theory School. It is corollaries such as this that most often serve as application guides.

Some research findings about learning seem to be unrelated to any particular learning theory and will be found in the literature as isolated pieces of research:

Sleep immediately following learning results in more retention than when the subject stays awake after learning, even if he gets the same amount of sleep before the retention test.

Simple facts do not seem to be learned during sleep, even when they are presented throughout the night by tape recording.

I have dealt with corollaries because those concerned with organization renewal sometimes incorporate one or more of them into a learning design. One then says "Here is the learning theory that I am employing in my development activity." Sometimes the corollaries have been borrowed or derived from several learning theories and so would appear to be inconsistent. However, this may be quite valid, because the content and training objectives for a given training program may include both skill and conceptual training. Each of these kinds of training would tend to borrow techniques from different learning theories. The point here, however, is that in planning educational experiences a learning theory corollary is frequently confused with basic learning theory. A learning theory is always greater than the corollary but, in using the corollary, the designer of a learning experience is often unaware of the major learning theory which lies behind it.

As one plows into learning theory literature, one is confronted by the problem of motivation. Can you motivate a person to learn? Is the understanding of learning motivation a prime requisite for educational planning? One runs into difficulty as it becomes obvious that learning theorists do not agree what motivation is or how it is accomplished. Generally speaking, these premises prevail: the learner must be self-motivated; the trainer must motivate the learner through an effective learning climate; not enough is now known about causes of motivation to discuss its role in the learning process.

Most managers and organization renewal advocates believe there is a factor called motivation. They seem to be evenly split as to whether the learner must be self-motivated or whether the training situation or the trainer can develop motivation. Those who believe that learning must be self-motivated usually believe the trainer must provide the conditions under which self-motivation can occur. In practice, there is little to distinguish the training designs of trainers who subscribe to differing philosophies. Designed conditions under which self-motivation can occur look very much like the designs of those who attempt to motivate learners.

As the planner explores learning theory, he is confronted with another discouraging task. If anything is in print discussing, in layman terms, individual or comparative learning theories, it is conspicuous by its rarity. Learning theories are to be found in courses in educational psychology and require a strong background in psychology, research, and statistics to understand them. Some of the differences seem to be very subtle. It is extremely discouraging to attempt to understand either the individual theories or the difference between the schools embracing several theories. The first thing that strikes home is that most of the research on learning theory has been accomplished by using animals for subjects. Several authors comment that at least 95 percent of learning research has been accomplished on data received from experiments with rats, chickens, pigeons, monkeys, dogs, and cats. It is also interesting to note that research on animals inevitably occurs under one or both of two conditions: the animal is either very hungry or sex deprived. It may very well be that the designers of training programs have been overlooking some excellent motivational factors.

Animal research accepted, two other problems present themselves. First, it is often difficult to differentiate the general schools of learning theory. Second, it is even more difficult to distinguish between individual learning theories within the general schools. This difficulty is compounded because of the technical language and equations used to express the theories. Usually, aspects of the theories are stated mathematically and then expressed in prose. Neither is done in such a way that a practitioner can easily comprehend. He is then faced with the problem of trying to determine what the technical language expresses and restate it in words he can understand. It may be helpful, therefore, to examine briefly the six general schools in which learning theories seem to fall.

The first school is known as the *Behaviorist School*. Primarily, these theories hold that learning results from the rewards or punishment that follows a response to a stimulus. These are the so-called S–R Theories.

E. L. Thorndike was one of the early researchers into learning and, generally, he held that learning was a trial-and-error process. When faced with the need to respond appropriately to a stimulus, the learner tries any and all of his response patterns. If by chance one works, then that one tends to be repeated and the others neglected. From his research he developed certain laws to further explain the learning process —for example, the Law of Effect: if a connection between a stimulus and response is satisfying to the organism, its strength is increased; if unsatisfying, its strength is reduced.

E. R. Guthrie basically accepted Thorndike's theory, but did not accept the Law of Effect. He came up with an S–R Contiguity Theory of learning. His position was that the moment a stimulus was connected to a response—the stimulus would thereafter tend to elicit that response. Repeating the connection would not strengthen the association. Thus, if

I am learning a poem and learn it sitting down, I can probably recall that poem best when sitting rather than standing. He did not attach much significance to reward and punishment, holding that responses will tend to be repeated simply because they were the last ones made to a stimulus.

Clark Hull introduced a new concept: stimulus and response were not the only things to be considered in learning—the organism itself could not be overlooked. The response to a stimulus must take into account the organism and what it is thinking, needing, and feeling at the moment. We now had the S–O–R concept.

B. F. Skinner is usually identified with the Behaviorist School. Rather than construct a theory of learning, he seems to believe that by observation and objective reporting we can discover how organisms learn without the need of a construct to explain the process. He depends heavily upon what is called operant conditioning. He makes a distinction between "respondent" and "operant" behavior. Respondent behavior is that behavior caused by a known stimulus; operant behavior is that behavior for which we can not see or identify a stimulus, though one may, and probably does, exist. If we can anticipate operant behavior, and introduce a stimulus when it is evidenced, we can provide the occasion for the behavior by introducing the stimulus—but the stimulus does not necessarily evoke the behavior. Thus, the emphasis in learning is on correlating a response with reinforcement. This is at the heart of programmed instruction—a correct response is reinforced.

Other researchers have developed variations of the theories described above. Some assume that the organism is relatively passive but that the response is in the repertoire of the learner. Other theorists pay particular attention to instrumental conditioning. They assume that the organism acts on its environment and that the response may not be in its repertoire. Still others talk about mediating responses in which a period of time may elapse between the stimulus and the response or the response may be a series of responses that stretch over a period of time. For example, a man may be desirous of marrying a girl but will work for ten years to save enough money to support her adequately before proposing.

The second grouping is the *Gestalt School*. These theorists believe that learning is not a simple matter of stimulus and response. They hold that learning is cognitive and involves the whole personality. To them, learning is infinitely more complex than the S–R Theories would indicate. For example, they note that learning may occur simply by thinking about a problem. Kurt Lewin, Wolfgang Köhler, E. C. Tolman, and Max Wertheimer are typical adherents to this school. They reject the theory that learning occurs by building up, bit by bit, established S–R connections. They look at the phenomenon of insight, long-coming or instantaneous. To them, "the whole is more than the sum of the parts."

> Central in Gestalt theory is the Law of Prägnanz which indicates the direction of events. According to this law, the psychological organization of the individual tends to move always in one direction, always toward the good Gestalt, an organization of the whole which is regular, simple, and stable.[4]

The Law of Prägnanz is another law of equilibrium.[5] Accordingly, the learning process might be presented as follows: The individual is in a state of equilibrium, of "good" Gestalt. He is confronted by a learning situation. Tensions develop and disequilibrium results. The individual thus moves away from equilibrium but at the same time he strives to move back to equilibrium. In order to assist this move back to the regular, simple, stable state, the learning situation should be structured so as to possess good organization (e.g., simple parts should be presented first; these should lead in an orderly fashion to more difficult parts).

A third school is the *Freudian School*. This is a difficult school to encapsulate:

> It is no simple task to extract a theory of learning from Freud's writings, for while he was interested in individual development and the kind of re-education that goes on in psychotherapy, the problems whose answers he tried to formulate were not those with which theorists in the field of learning have been chiefly concerned. Psychoanalytic theory is too complex and, at least at the present time, too little formalized for it to be presented as a set of propositions subject to experimental testing.[6]

A fourth school is that of the *Functionalists*. These seem to take parts of all the theories and view learning as a very complex phenomenon that is not explained by either the Gestalt or the Behavioral Theories. Some of the leaders in this school are John Dewey, J. R. Angell, and R. S. Woodworth. These men borrow from all the other schools and are sometimes referred to as "middle of the roaders."

A fifth so-called school is comprised of those who subscribe to *Mathematical Models*. To these researchers, learning theories must be stated in mathematical form. Some of these proponents come from different schools of learning theory but tend to focus on mathematical models such as the Feedback Model, Information Theory Model, Gaming Model, Differential Calculus Model, Stochastic Model, and the Statistical Association Model. As I try to understand this school, it occurs to me that they seem to have no theory of their own but are expressing research findings of other theorists in mathematical terms.

A sixth school is more general in nature and can best be characterized by calling it the *Current Learning Theory School*. Here the advocates are quite difficult to classify and seem to run the range of modifying the Gestalt and Behavioral Theories, accommodating two pieces of both theories, assuming that training involves the whole man—psychological, physiological, biological, and neurophysiological. Some of these are the postulate system of MacCorquodale and Meehl and the social learning theory of Rotter.

Some of the more exciting kinds of current research seem to be in the neurophysiological interpretations of learning. One example of this was shown on a national television program called "Way Out Men." In this research, flatworms are trained to stay within a white path. If they deviate from the white path, they receive an electrical shock. After the flatworms learn to stay within the prescribed path, they are then chopped up and fed to a control group of worms. This control group learns to stay within the white path in about half the learning time. This has led some theorists to talk about the possibility of eventually feeding students "professorburgers."

Additional research is going on in this area and we have recently seen two or three other related pieces of research. It seems to indicate a key as to where memory and instincts are stored so that they can be transmitted to offspring. One is intrigued by this research when one remembers popular beliefs such as eating fish as a good brain food and the practice of cannibals eating the brain of an educated man to become smart or eating the heart of a brave man to become courageous.

One of the problems that often confronts a manager, educator, or training director is the transfer of learning. In learning how to learn we need to know how to transfer "learning from failure" in one situation to achieve success in another situation. The following are some of the major ways in which learning theories attempt to provide for the transfer of what is learned to the work situation:

ACTUALLY DOING THE "THAT" WHICH IS BEING LEARNED. In this instance, the stress is placed on the belief that the transfer is best when learning occurs in live situations. This is so because little or no transfer is needed—what is learned is directly applied. Instances employing this technique are on-the-job training, coaching, apprenticeship, and job experience. This approach is the key to most organization renewal attempts.

DOING SOMETHING THAT IS SIMILAR TO THAT WHICH IS TO BE LEARNED. This transfer principle is applied when we use simulated experiences —the training experience and techniques are as similar to the job as possible. Sometimes we let the trainee discover the principles and apply them to his job. In other instances, particularly in skill training, he works on mock-ups which closely resemble the actual equipment on which he will work. Other techniques employed would include role playing, sensitivity training, and case studies.

READING OR HEARING ABOUT THAT WHICH IS TO BE LEARNED. The trainer or a book gives the trainee the principles, and then discusses and illustrates them. The trainee must then figure out the ways in which what he has heard or read applies to his job and how he can use it. Illustrative training techniques would be lectures, reading, and most management and supervisory training programs featuring the "telling" method.

DOING OR READING ABOUT ANYTHING ON THE ASSUMPTION IT WILL HELP ANYTHING TO BE LEARNED. In this instance there is an assumption that a liberalized education makes the trainee more effective in whatever job he occupies or task he is to learn. This might be termed the liberal arts approach. It assumes that a well-rounded, educated person is more effective, and more easily trained in specifics, if he understands himself, his society, his world, and other disciplines. Obviously, this would be a somewhat costly way of training for organization renewal inasmuch as it would involve perceptual living and generalized education.

Much research has gone into understanding the transfer of learning. Most of this occurs in the S–R Theories. It seems to be less of a problem in the other major theories. This is quite understandable when one compares the theories of learning. For example, the S–R Theories become quite concerned with questions like "Will the study of mathematics help a person learn a foreign language easier and more quickly?" This has led to consideration of the conditions under which the transfer of learning best occurs. It is also applicable to conceptual learning. For example, will learning how to delegate responsibilities to children be useful in the delegation process in the work organizations?

Recent research into adult learning at the University of Nebraska indicated:

> The average older adult in an adult education program is at least as intellectually able, and performs as well, as the average younger participant.
>
> Adults who continue to participate in educative activity learn more effectively than similar adults who do not. This would simply seem to indicate that learning skills require practice to be maintained.
>
> Adults learn far more effectively when they are permitted to learn at their own pace.[7]

The concerns about motivating individuals to learn, and the recognition that there is such a thing as a learning process, have led to exploration of the condition under which learning best seems to occur. Numerous lists of conditions for learning exist. They vary depending on the learning theory school to which the author subscribes. However, there is a remarkable acceptance of some general conditions that should exist for effectiveness regardless of the learning theory employed: [8]

ACCEPTANCE THAT ALL HUMAN BEINGS CAN LEARN.   The assumption, for example, that you "can't teach an old dog new tricks" is wrong. Probably few normal people at any age are incapable of learning. The tremendous surge in adult education and second careers after retirement attests to people's ability to learn at all ages.

THE INDIVIDUAL MUST BE MOTIVATED TO LEARN.   This motivation should be related to personal drives. The individual must be aware of the inadequacy or unsatisfactoriness of his present behavior, skill, or knowledge. The individual must have a clear picture of the behavior which he is required to adopt.

LEARNING IS AN ACTIVE PROCESS, NOT PASSIVE.   In most cases it takes action and involvement by and of the individual with himself, a resource person, or a learning group.

NORMALLY, THE LEARNER MUST HAVE GUIDANCE.   A trial-and-error method is too time-consuming. This is the process of feedback. The learner must have answers to "How am I doing?" if he is to correct improper performance before it becomes patternized.

APPROPRIATE MATERIALS FOR SEQUENTIAL LEARNING MUST BE PROVIDED.   Cases; problems; discussion; reading. Training tools and materials should be available, and it should be recognized that there are limitations in the capacities of these things. It is in this area that so many training programs get trapped by utilizing the latest training fads or gimmicks for inappropriate learning.

TIME MUST BE PROVIDED TO PRACTICE THE LEARNING.   To internalize; to give confidence. Too often there is pressure to "pack the program" —to utilize every moment available to "tell them something." This is inefficient use of learning time. Part of the learning process requires sizable pieces of time for assimilation, testing, and acceptance.

LEARNING METHODS, IF POSSIBLE, SHOULD BE VARIED TO AVOID BOREDOM. It is assumed that there will be sufficient sophistication to vary the methods according to their usefulness to the material being learned. Where several methods are about equally useful, variety should be introduced to offset factors of fatigue and boredom.

THE LEARNER MUST SECURE SATISFACTION FROM THE LEARNING.   This is the old story of "You can lead a horse to water. . . ." Learners are capable of excellent learning under the most trying of conditions if the learning is satisfying to one or more of their needs. Conversely, the best appointed of learning facilities and trainee comfort can fail if the program is not seen as useful by the learner.

THE LEARNER MUST GET REINFORCEMENT OF THE CORRECT BEHAVIOR. B. F. Skinner and the Behaviorists have much to say on this score.

Usually learners need fairly immediate reinforcement. Few learners can wait for months for correct behavior to be rewarded. However, there may well be long-range rewards and lesser intermediate rewards. It should also be emphasized that rewarded job performance when the learner returns from the training program must be consistent with the learning program rewards.

STANDARDS OF PERFORMANCE SHOULD BE SET FOR THE LEARNER. Set goals for achievement. While learning is quite individual, and it is recognized that learners will advance at differing paces, most learners like to have bench marks by which to judge their progress.

A RECOGNITION THAT THERE ARE DIFFERENT LEVELS OF LEARNING AND THAT THESE TAKE DIFFERENT TIMES AND METHODS. Learning to memorize a simple poem is entirely different from learning long-range planning. There are, at least, four identifiable levels of learning, each requiring different timing methods, involvement, techniques, and learning theory. At the simplest level we have the skills of motor responses, memorization, and simple conditioning. Next, we have the adaption level where we are gaining knowledge or adapting to a simple environment. Learning to operate an electric typewriter after using a manual typewriter is an example. Third, is the complex level, utilized when interpersonal understandings and skills are involved. At the fourth level we deal with the values of individuals and groups. This is a most subtle, time-consuming, and sophisticated endeavor. Few work organizations have training programs in which a change of long-standing, cultural, or ethnic values is a specific goal. Many work organizations, however, do have training programs aimed at changing less entrenched values.

The reader will recognize that this listing of the conditions under which people learn contains concepts and principles from most of the learning theory schools. In most organizations the development and training specialists are generalists, and seldom do their activities and programs focus on a constant single-objective outcome. It is perhaps inevitable, therefore, that guiding concepts and principles are a meld from many theories. It is important, however, that concepts and principles derived from theories of learning be used in a way that will accomplish the organizational objectives.

As the learning stimulator and planner explores learning theory, he finds several points of view. There are individual exponents of a given theory who insist that their theory alone accounts for the way people learn. There are those who insist that we do not know what learning theory is and that learning theorists do not contribute to the real problems of training and organization renewal. There are those who will be frank in saying to a training specialist, "You are on your own. Learning theory in its present state will not materially help you. Experiment. If it works and gets you the results you want—don't worry about what learning theory lies behind your success." It is encouraging to note in the two quotations below that some social scientists are aware of this breach between research and practice:

> Knowledge is not practice and practice is not knowledge. The improvement of one does not lead automatically to the improvement of the other. Each can work fruitfully for the advancement of the other but also, unfortunately, each can develop separately from the other and hence stuntedly in relation to the other.[9]

> It should be clear that the linking of social theory to social practice, as well as the development of a practice-linked theory of the application of social science knowledge to practice, is an intellectual challenge of the first magnitude. But it is one that many social scientists—particularly those who rarely leave the university system—have neglected.[10]

It is known that those in learning situations sometimes have better insights into the factors affecting their learning than do those who do the planning. Participants, for example, almost always give a high rating to their interactions with each other, partly because they become aware that their own problems are not peculiar, that it is helpful to learn about and from others, and partly because interaction seems to produce broadened and more perceptive understanding. These things, once thought to be minor in influence, are now viewed as major benefits in many learning situations. Similarly, participants frequently stress that they need time to internalize, digest, reflect, and be left alone. Too often, this need is answered by scheduling more of the same kind of sessions, whereas it is probably true that two hours of learning should be complemented with six hours of relative solitude and freedom.

In the same vein, the learning situation benefits from free-wheeling bull sessions, and from recreation that permits the release of emotional and physical energy. Dyad conversations are useful, even if somewhat forced, because they provide reaction, clarification, and feedback. Although not many organizations will allow costly training time to be used for reading pertinent articles and books, this kind of supporting activity seems to pay off handsomely in the overall process of learning. Lastly, limited experimentation seems to indicate that it is well to bring all of the participants up to at least a common level of basic knowledge before placing them in a learning situation.

Many of us are inclined to think that listening to the comments of participants, and designing training programs to meet their expressed needs, might have very excellent payoff in training programs, even if the training director could not find support for the technique within existing learning theories. I suspect, however, that no single learning theory should be embraced exclusively for any learning situation. This feeling seems to be supported by current trends: [11]

A trend toward a focus on improved performances rather than on increased individual knowledge.

A trend to deal with situations rather than individuals.

A trend to see training as the way management gets its job done rather than as a function of a department in the organization.

A trend toward building up inhouse capabilities rather than dependence on outside experts.

A trend toward insistence on evaluation of the results of training rather than accepting rosy reports on faith.

A trend toward designing learning that will focus on learning-how-to-learn.

A trend toward training that is based on action-learning rather than on one-way communication.

A trend toward training that provides reinforcement and follow-up experience for trainees rather than "graduating" them from a training program.

A trend toward dependence more on the learning to be self-motivated by the learner rather than imposed on the learner by the trainers.

A trend for training to be goal oriented rather than a vague assurance that it will be "good for you."

A trend toward greater homogeneity in the persons being trained.

A trend toward emphasis on the importance of organizational climate as an essential factor affecting change.

Different learning techniques and conditions are applicable to different kinds of training and learning. The training programs within a work organization are not all aimed at the same kind of learning. Perhaps different learning theories apply according to the nature of the subject to be taught and learned, the nature of the organization, the nature of the trainees, and the available teaching resources. This strengthens the idea that no single learning theory can be applied across the board to all learning activities, but the following format might be one that would be useful to a person who is initiating a learning situation:

STEP 1. Determine the desired learning outcome. This will indicate what is to be taught—orientation, problem-solving, decision-making, knowledge, memorization, changed attitude, changed behavior, manual skill, creativity, self-insight, lessened resistance to change, person-to-person relationships, group-to-group relationships, technical knowledge, communication, self-development, executive development, or understanding principles and theory.

STEP 2. On the basis of what is to be taught, select the learning theory most applicable to that content.

STEP 3. Utilize the basic learning theory by examining the derived corollary theories and principles clearly useful in effectively training toward the desired end. These are many, varied, and descriptively named, but not dealt with here in detail. For example: knowing others better, knowing related programs better, reflection time, informal interaction, exercise, recreation, advanced preparation, immediate reward, delayed reward, learning plateau, practice-rest-practice, reading with recitation, meaningful material, "A-ha" phenomena, immediate use, material known previously, important material, pleasant material, concept formation, concrete concept, part-whole versus whole-part, positive instances versus negative instances, general to specific, maturation task relatedness, fatigue factor, and motivation.

STEP 4. On the basis of these considerations, make specific decisions on the following factors:

- Whether the learning site should be on-the-job: classroom on organizational premises; classroom off organizational premises; university or other formal site; cultural island; or home.
- Whether the grouping arrangement should be: related to size—one, dyad, trio, groups 5–8, groups 9–15, groups 16–30, or audience style (any number); or related to the relationships of participants—all male, all female, mixed sex; little experience, much experience, mixed experience; related to age—old, young, mixed age groups; known to each other or not known to each other; same organization —vertical, horizontal, diagonal; other organization—homogeneous, mixed; same educational level, mixed educational level; and same task or mixed tasks.
- Learning methods to be employed—lecture, panel, symposium, debate, laboratory, programmed instruction, experience, coaching, job progression, job rotation, job enlargement, apprenticeship, situational training, personal reading, correspondence, liberal arts, formal school, formal outside program, workshop, conference, institute, seminar, visitation, or discussion groups.
- Training aids to be used—movies, instantaneous replay movies, telephone, loudspeaker, TV, role play, exercises, "in" basket, gaming, film strips, slides, transparencies, tape recorder, blackboard, newsprint easel, flannel board, magnetic board, self-administered instruments, tests and quizzes; case studies—no printed discussion, printed discussion, or incident process; experiments, models, mockups, or group-generated data.
- Type of resource persons or instructors—written material, experience, instrumentation, self, organizational technical expert, outside technical expert, organization renewal consultant, professors, industrial resource people, training department, supervisor, or peers.

- How much attention needs to be paid to transfer of learning: direct transfer; live, simulated reality; principle to be applied; no direct application; known stimuli—opposite response; familiar to be used in unfamiliar way; or principle to be learned and applied.

Believers in change through learning strive very hard to establish response patterns that hopefully will be carried over and continued in the work situation. This is at the heart of one of the criticisms managers sometimes level at organization renewal programs—the behavior of participants in the work situation too often seems relatively unchanged. As one examines this phenomena, it becomes apparent that most organizational training programs—in the conceptual areas of supervision and management—lean very heavily upon Theory "Y" assumptions. I do not know of any programs that pointedly train toward Theory "X" assumptions. Conversely, these same organizations usually have a goodly amount of Theory "X" assumptions underlying both their operations, supervisory, and management practices.[12] This raises two questions:

1. In the current zeal to get away from the mechanistic approach to organizational dynamics, there has been a tendency to underplay the role of the Theory "X" and Theory "Y" factors in the total organization as they affect training outcomes. Training is accomplished as if such realities did not exist and as if the only operable dynamics were the human factors in the training. This has often created a breach between the training office, operating people, and management.

2. The S–R phenomenon not only operates within the training situation but is very much operable within the work situation. People react in the direction of the rewards they receive. The S–R patterns initiated in a training session have very little chance of survival when they come up against different S–R patterns of rewards in the work situation. For example:

"Research papers get you promoted—not supervisory ability or a skill."

"Promotions depend on who you know—not what you know."

"I don't give a damn how your people feel—we've got a job to do."

"OK, you've been to a training program. Say something new."

"Seniority is what really counts around this place."

If an S–R pattern initiated in a training program is to be maintained in the work situation, then it must be rewarded by the organization. If the pattern is in conflict with organizational reward patterns, the newly learned patterns are soon discarded. I believe this accounts for a great deal of supposedly poor results of training. Organization renewal will have a better chance of success if training is planned according to the organization's reward pattern and the goals desired. This would include lessening the stress on perfection and placing the emphasis on the necessity to learn.

Published research into learning theory has indicated a need that has not been fully recognized. An identification of the existing learning theories that appear to be best researched and validated, a statement and comparison of these theories in language that the practitioner can comprehend and understand, and suggested guidelines for ways in which those concerned with organization renewal can utilize these learning theories are very much needed. Such identification could very well make our training and change programs more effective in meeting the needs of organizations.

The sophistication needed to understand and utilize the implications of learning theory have much to say about the kinds of qualifications and skills required for organization renewal. The naive assumption that title and salary make one an educational expert is tragic. Similarly, the managerial assumption that an employee who has the knack of making cute speeches or who once taught elementary school is training director material is inadequate. I would even go further and suggest that there are some questionable implications in taking an employee who never managed even a small sub-unit and entrusting him with the development of other managers.

Operational and organizational climate must support learning. In addition, managers need to be much more realistic and expect that very few entrenched S–R responses can be changed in a week's training program.

We need to re-look at the anxiety about evaluation of training. We are not even sure how people learn and this creates real problems in trying to evaluate the effectiveness of our learning process efforts. We know people do learn but we are not sure why. We also know that people remember and learn best from analyzing failure experiences. When one looks at the tremendous number of complicated, tenuous, and conceptual ideas that are discussed within the span of one week in the average supervisory or management training program, it seems at least naive to expect that very much in the way of established new patterns of behavior could possible emerge. The expectations of management generally are too high, and training directors and renewal specialists sometimes promise too much.

There is one other trap. When a specialist in organization renewal becomes concerned with learning theory, he must expect to find conflicting theories and practices within the field. It is necessary to keep our focus on the objectives and not become enchanted with the theories:

> Theories . . . attempt to organize existing knowledge, they attempt to provide guiding threads of hypotheses toward new knowledge, and they

may also furnish principles by which what is known can be used. This practical outcome is seldom central in the thinking of the constructor of theory, and it is not surprising, therefore, that the person seeking advice from the learning theorist often comes away disappointed. . . . It turns out, however, that many of the quarrels of the theorists are internal ones, not very important in relation to immediate practical problems; there are, in fact a great many practically important experimental relationships upon which the theorists are in substantial agreement. . . . If the theoretical differences are irreconcilable, and one position eventually wins out over the other, there will ultimately be an effect upon practice. But advice for practical people today need not wait for the resolution of these theoretical controversies.[13]

In summary, effective learning methods assume that knowledge, skill, and attitudes have to be *discovered* by the learner if they are to mean anything to him and make a difference in his behavior. Man does not just learn from experience, he learns from *analyzed experience*. The renewal specialist sets up conditions, including dilemmas and unsolved problems, where the learner can experiment, try things out, see what works, analyze, and generalize for himself. The test of learning is not responses on a test, but whether the discovered learning makes any difference in the learner's life work as he is constantly learning how to learn from every situation where his senses encounter opportunities for growth.

This, then, is the challenge to those of us desiring to meet the critical problem of developing effective learning-how-to-learn experiences to meet changing needs of today's organizations.

NOTES

1. This chapter is largely an adaptation of an article by Leslie E. This and Gordon L. Lippitt, entitled "Learning Theories and Training," *Training and Development Journal,* April and May, 1966, pp. 12–18, 26–43. Reproduced by special permission. Copyright 1966 by the American Society for Training and Development, Inc.

2. Leland P. Bradford, "The Teaching-Learning Transactions," *Adult Education,* Vol. 8, No. III, Spring, 1958, pp. 18–24.

3. Bernard Berelson and Gary A. Steiner, *Human Behavior—An Inventory of Scientific Findings* (New York: Harcourt, Brace & World, Inc., 1964), p. 63.

4. Kurt Koffka, *Principles of Gestalt Psychology* (New York: Harcourt, Brace & World, Inc., 1935), p. 110.

5. Pierre J. Marsh, "Selected Learning Theories: Their Implications for Job Training," Masters Thesis, George Washington University, School of Business and Public Administration, Washington, D.C., August 6, 1965, pp. 56–57.

6. Ernest R. Hilgard, *Theories of Learning* (New York: Appleton-Century-Crofts, 1956), p. 290.
7. Alan B. Knox and Douglas Sjogren, "Research on Adult Learning," *Adult Education*, Spring, 1965, pp. 133–137.
8. Composite drawn from Lippitt, *Conditions of Learning Affecting Training*, unpublished notes; and Harry L. Miller, *Teaching and Learning in Adult Education* (New York: The Macmillan Co., 1964).
9. Fritz J. Roethlisberger, Introduction to James V. Clark, *Education for the Use of Behavioral Science*, Institute of Industrial Relations, University of California, Los Angeles, California, 1962, p. 4.
10. *Ibid.*, p. 89.
11. Lippitt, "Changing Trends in Organizational Development," talk before the Public Administration Society, University of Michigan.
12. Douglas McGregor, *The Human Side of Enterprise* (New York: McGraw-Hill Book Co., Inc.), Chapters 3 and 4, pp. 33–57, for detailed explanation.
13. Hilgard, *op. cit.*, p. 485.

12 LABORATORY METHODS AND THE RENEWAL PROCESS

For the last century, not merely have we been able to think of the world as a whole, in time and space, but we have been able through manifold inventions to act in the same fashion. Yet both our thinking and acting have been crude, not to say primitive, because we have not yet created the sort of self, freed from nationalistic and ideological obsessions, capable of acting within this global theater.

LEWIS MUMFORD, 1895–

Inasmuch as the organization renewal process so frequently focuses on the need to strengthen operating groups, laboratory-type group learning experiences and methods are frequently utilized. The laboratory, in this context, is used to create a human behavior learning experience where the actual behavior of the individual or group becomes the "data" for observation, analysis, and practice. As has been pointed out by Bennis and Schein,[1] the method has a number of unique implications:

. . . laboratory training is an educational strategy which is based primarily on the experiences generated in various social encounters by the *learners themselves*, and which aims to influence attitudes and develop competencies toward learning about human interactions. So, essentially, laboratory training attempts to induce changes with regard to the learning process itself and to communicate a particular method of learning and inquiry. It has to do with "learning how to learn."

In most cases of this type of learning, the goal is learning about human behavior. The most frequent and well-known application of laboratory learning has been the T-group or sensitivity training. In an article written in 1963,[2] Leslie This and I probed some of the implications of sensitivity training for today's organizations, and a portion of that article is repeated in this chapter in somewhat revised form.

Some strong opinions have been expressed pro and con about sensitivity training by leaders in the field of management. Douglas McGregor [3] says this kind of training can ". . . bring about significant improvements in the skills of social interaction," while George S. Odiorne [4] feels that many human relations laboratories have become ". . . perverted into psychological nudist camps which end up mainly as self-flagellation societies."

Observations such as these are related to some of the experimental work going on within the field of sensitivity training. Increasing emphasis has been placed by some leaders in the field on *personal growth* of the individual, and on the use of any activity that helps the individual more effectively understand himself. Such organizations as the Esalen Institute in California and others are using body movement, marathon labs, music, and other means to free the individual to new insights and understandings of the self. Such new directions may sometimes be seen as esoteric and dangerous. In the hands of nonprofessionals, the latter may be true. There is a need, however, for experimental work in the field. In my opinion it is not appropriate to introduce organization renewal into organizations by such an application of the laboratory method. Laboratory methods need to focus on *developing teamwork* among the human resources so that they can *accomplish a task;* the goal is not personal growth solely for the sake of personal growth.

While much has been written about sensitivity training, most of the literature is either technical or descriptive of personal experience. Neither approach is helpful to the training director or manager who wants to answer the pragmatic question, "Is this kind of training desirable in my organization and related to my organization's problems, needs, and objectives?"

When trying to get an answer to this kind of question, the organizational decision-maker usually consults someone who has been through a program. Almost inevitably he is told, "Oh, I couldn't begin to tell you about it—you just have to experience it." This is not helpful for effective decision-making. The manager then turns to a professional person, who usually does not distinguish between the direct work-related benefits and the more complex areas of personality integration, social responsibility, self-fulfillment, and other person-oriented values of such training. Let us, therefore, examine some major areas of consideration and questions that have frequently been asked.

In my opinion, the expression "sensitivity training" is an inadequate phrase popularly used to describe a particular theory and method utilized in human relations training. Laboratory training usually includes the methods of unstructured group learning, individual feedback, skill practice, and information sessions. The theory behind such methods is based on a concept of learning which believes that individuals can best learn interpersonal and group skills through actual experience when that experience is analyzed for the benefit of the learner. One of the underlying assumptions is that man best learns these kinds of insights by self-discovery.[5] It does little good to be "spoken to" about or to read many of these kinds of learnings. The learning experience, then, must provide the kind of setting and methods that will best enable men to discover these insights and knowledges for themselves, and the methods used have been found most helpful in the typical type of training program.

SENSITIVITY TRAINING GROUPS.   Here the participants meet with a professional trainer in groups of eight to fifteen. They have no formal agenda or prior-determined leader. Normally, the groups meet once a day for two hours, but may meet twice a day. They struggle with making decisions about how to spend the time profitably and how to provide structure and leadership. They have time to "thresh out" their struggles and examine their group life. As they do, they begin to gain an insight into the forces that are at work—things like the leadership struggle, group structure, group objectives, accommodating individual objectives to group objectives, group standards to guide their conduct, what improves and lessens the appeal of the group, how decisions will be made, how to handle the participation of members, how one's own behavior is influencing the group, and how the behavior of other members is influencing one's own behavior.

As the group pauses to study the parts of their group life that have interest for them, the trainer helps them to understand the forces at work at that moment. From time to time an individual member may want to test out with others the effect his behavior is having on them —how they see him—and may ask for reactions and information (feedback)—and the members try to help him see himself as they see him in the life of the group.

. . . the whole notion of feedback is crucial. Giving persons feedback on how they are doing gives them a choice to do better. Caring plays an important part. Confronting without caring can be a rather destructive process. (See Albee's *Who's Afraid of Virginia Woolf?*) It does turn out that people in general can be very caring of one another.[6]

INFORMATION SESSIONS.   Usually the problems with which the learning groups and individuals are concerned at any given time in the training can be fairly well predicted. Presentations are made, drawing on research and experiences, to further explain the forces or factors involved in a particular area of interest. The design of the program is such that it is flexible and may be modified to meet the needs and interests of the participants. Real life experiences are compared and generalized from other's experiences.

SKILL PRACTICE SESSIONS.   As a participant achieves knowledge about what, for him, may be a better way to perform as a manager, he wants to practice trying out that new way. Skill exercise periods are provided to let the participants try out new ways of behaving, or to test out ways that have been suggested in the presentations or by the groups. Here he has little at stake since he knows he is in a training setting and encouraged to experiment with new ways of behaving. If it seems to him to be better than his old pattern, the chances are enhanced that he will try it out in daily life.

These are the main methods employed in sensitivity training. Other action learning methods are also utilized—case studies, informal group discussions, films, gaming and coaching teams. All of these are utilized as appropriate to a particular program to provide the maximum opportunity for participants to learn.

Sensitivity training does not seem mysterious to those who know what the training is designed to accomplish. As we indicated earlier, however, the learnings about oneself are so highly personal that it is difficult to share them with another person in a meaningful way. How would a superior react if you told him, "I learned that people mistake my seriousness for aggressiveness, and I'm going to try to do something about it"? It is in this respect that it is difficult to explain one's learning. Perhaps it is a reflection of our culture as well as a need for this training that causes us to find it difficult to share our own feelings, emotions, and behavior, but this is the essence of the sensitivity group experience.

On the other hand, there is no excuse whatsoever for misunderstanding the content of the information or skill practice sessions. These one can listen to, talk about, read, and perform; and these activities form an important part of the training. Because the learnings of a personal nature are so vivid and meaningful, in comparison to the substantive learnings, it is understandable that the total training experience tends to be seen as that component of the learning activity in which trainees gain their most meaningful insights.

It seems to me that sensitivity training can serve three distinct purposes in organization renewal:

1. A manager works in a complex organizational system. Organizations are more than the physical "things" that go on inventory lists. It is not possible to think of an organization without thinking of people—their functions and interrelationships. If people are removed from an organization, one is left with a catalogue of items occupying space —little more than a poorly utilized warehouse.

It is people who have organizational objectives; need a division of labor; do the work or give the service; need meetings, directives, policies; need methods for delegating work and controls; need to know how to get the most from other people.

In all truth, too little is really known about the human dynamics of organizations. One of the objectives of sensitivity training is to help the participant to see the informal, unseen, or unnoticed functions, elements, characteristics, forms, authorities, traditions, and interpersonal processes *at work*. The premise here is that the more he understands the nature of the human encounter in the organization, the better equipped the participant will be to utilize release and to control the organization for the attainment of organizational objectives. This is the essence of every renewal process.

2. Organizations accomplish their work through the motivations of people. Most managers know their technical specialty quite well, and they usually are quite well informed about their job functions, such as planning, reporting, and controlling. What they are less knowledgeable about is how to obtain maximum efficiency and productivity from people. Down through history one of the precepts noted by successful leaders has been "Know thyself." Whether a manager recognizes it or not, his behavior, posture, gestures, tone of voice, and ways of reacting to people and situations greatly influence how other people react to him and the jobs he asks them to do.

It would follow that the more a man understands himself, and how his behavior, consciously or unconsciously, will affect others, the more effective he can be in his relationships with other human beings. The objective is not to become an amateur psychiatrist, but to be more sensitive to the influence his behavior has on others, and vice versa.

Such sensitivity is not designed to make a person "thin-skinned," but rather more aware of his surroundings. The human organism has the radar of its many senses, which frequently are dormant or undeveloped; it is in the sharpening of these senses that sensitivity training can assist.

3. A manager frequently works in groups. The work-day life of today's manager is spent with two or more persons in organizational work units, such as project and planning groups, task forces, and similar groupings. Many of the factors at work in individual-to-individual contexts are also at work within groups. As every manager knows, however, when a number of individuals are brought into a group setting they tend to create additional factors and forces. Many of us have commented, "How can people, who individually are such fine persons, behave so ineffectively when I call them together to work on a task?"

There is a body of knowledge about the factors at work when people work in groups, and the more a manager understands these factors, the more effectively he can perform. Rensis Likert has recently summarized much of the research in this area, and its implications for managers and organizations, in his book *Patterns of Management.*[7] As mentioned earlier, the research on morale and productivity indicates that people potentially meet their needs and accomplish work effectively in the face-to-face work units of the organizations.

The need for *team development* is all important in the process of organization renewal.

These three areas, then, are the major areas of learning to which sensitivity training can contribute. Since much of what is learned is peculiar to the individual participant and the group, it is difficult to list what specific learning or insights each will discover. To know oneself better is a different experience for each of us, and that is why a personal insight for one person is not an insight to another. This explains, in part, why participants find it so difficult to agree on what they learned from the human relations laboratory experience called sensitivity training.

People develop their skill and awareness through various learning experiences. Any experience which can further interpersonal competence will need to provide the following conditions for learning: [8]

The recognition on the part of the trainee of a need for improving his own human relations skills.

An opportunity for the participant to interact in a learning situation so that actual behavior may serve as the curriculum.

A supportive and helpful climate for learning created by the total experience.

An opportunity for the trainees to give "feedback" on the effect of their behavior in both structured and unstructured learning experiences.

A basic knowledge of individual, group, and organizational behavior to give guidance to the learner.

A chance to practice new skills of relating in person-to-person and person-to-group situations.

An opportunity to relate his learning to back-on-the-job situations.

In evaluating the contribution to organization renewal made by this kind of training, it is necessary to assume, first, that the training can affect organizational problems and, second, that individuals and groups are organizational problems. Some organizational problems are not the primary province of any kind of training. If the organizational product or service is not needed, wanted, or of an inferior quality—training isn't the answer. If the market falls out from under a product because of technological or marketing factors, training is out of its field in attempting to solve such a problem. There are some organizational matters that are the main province of other facets of organizational problem-solving. Organizational effectiveness, in all its aspects, can never be equated with training or the lack of training, but too often organizations mistakenly see training as the answer to *all* their problems.

If, however, an organization's leaders suspect that the organization's effectiveness is being disturbed or affected by some of the following kinds of problems, they may well consider sensitivity training: [9]

There is an otherwise effective manager whose attitudes, skills, relationships with his work force, relationships with other persons and sub-units, effectiveness in meetings, and ability to diagnose personal relationship problems in their embryonic stage are seen as inadequate.

The basic face-to-face units of the organization do not seem to be achieving a level of morale and productivity that is in keeping with their abilities.

The organization is concerned with public relations, and its staff has enough contacts with outside groups so that the totality of these contacts can materially affect the organization's image.

It is important for communication to flow as uninhibitedly as possible between peers, between subordinate and superior, and between work units even though they appear as separated elements on the organizational chart.

There is good reason to believe that managers in the organization are, by organizational practice or climate, discouraged from being inventive or creative, from exercising or receiving appropriate responsibility, from delegating authority, and from exercising initiative in meeting operational problems.

The organization gets its work done in large measure through the use of group meetings, conferences, and informal group activities.

Generally speaking, before sensitivity training can be useful to an organization, certain internal conditions are prerequisite. For example, the training should be consistent with the organizational objectives, goals, and processes of decision-making. There must be an understanding, beginning with top management and permeating down through the levels to be trained, of the purpose of the training, and acceptance and support of the training objectives. The training program should be designed to help solve one or more identified management problem, and be tailored to fit the needs of the particular organization. The program and design should be carefully worked out and planned. It is usually helpful for some top management personnel to have had personal experience with this kind of training.

The training should be seen as voluntary, and an employee should be permitted to decline to undertake the training without anticipating punishment or embarrassment. There should exist an organizational understanding and climate that will enable a participant to "try out" and practice his learnings in the organizational setting. A qualified staff should be utilized, and this staff should include social scientists with experience in this kind of training, but they should also be provided ample opportunity to become familiar with the organization and to be accepted by all the people in the organization. There should be a well-designed evaluation plan to measure effectiveness. Lastly, the people involved or affected must see the training as a part of the organizational life and be committed to follow-up and supplementary training opportunities that reinforce the process.

All this has developed a number of approaches and issues in its application:

LENGTH OF TRAINING. Some training programs last three weeks; others for as short a period as two days. In recent years so-called "micro-labs" have been carried out in a few hours. There can be little assurance as to how much more learning takes place in a three-week program versus a one-week program, or a one-week program versus a three-day program. Probably common sense is the best guide, and one might expect that more can be learned in one week than in three days. Rarely has this kind of training been undertaken without having at least twelve hours of group learning time, plus other aspects of the program.

In the shorter programs the organization would need to identify what kind of skills, insights, and knowledges are most important and to design the training program for intensive concentration in these predetermined areas. Generally, most organizations seem to find an experience of at least one week's duration most desirable. This is particularly true if one is focusing on personal insight. It takes time to create the group atmosphere and individual readiness that will permit constructive and direct feedback of a helpful nature.

HETEROGENEOUS OR FAMILY GROUPS. Opinions differ as to whether it is better to train men and women from different organizations, within one industry or business, within one department in an organization, along peer lines, or vertically from several levels. There are advantages and disadvantages to each. Generally speaking, the advantage to "family" training is that all members of a work group, or related work groups, get the same kind of training at one time and get to know each other quite well.[10] They can also use the learning process in their day-by-day work to solve operating problems. This application is most relevant to the organization renewal concept.

One of the major disadvantages to family groupings is that participants seldom completely forget the setting and work relationships and, therefore, the interactions among participants may be less intense and direct. It has been proven valuable in heterogeneous training to send a team of persons from an organization to increase impact back in the organization. Which pattern one chooses would depend upon the length of the program, the experience of the persons to be trained, the intensity of training desired, and the objectives of the program. I have conducted sensitivity training using both approaches, with governmental, community, and industrial organizations, and found real impact for organizational change to be possible in either approach, depending on the job or the situation.

USE OF TRAINER OR INSTRUMENTS IN THE UNSTRUCTURED GROUP PHASE OF THE LEARNING. Recently, experimentation has been carried out with so-called instrumental groups.[11] The instruments consist of both individual and group administered questionnaires in which reactions can be coded, analyzed, and then "fed back" to the participants. A trainer does not sit with the basic training group, but does assist in the design of the training activity and provides materials to help the groups analyze their behavior as they work together. The trainer may also lead data-summarizing sessions or presentations as well as assist the group with practice exercises. Results of these programs indicate that learning does take place under such circumstances. A group, through the use of well-developed collection instruments, can feed back data to itself for effective learning.

Many of the specialists in this field feel that the trainer should be present to help with interpersonal feedback and group analysis as well as to prevent attempts at ill-advised therapy or hasty judgments by trainees of each other. It is also felt by some that such training can best utilize a professional at all times during the training. The experience to date would indicate the value in using *both* the trainer and effective data collection instruments for maximizing the learning.

USE OF OUTSIDE VERSUS INSIDE ORGANIZATION TRAINERS. Some managers ask the question: "Can't my training director do this kind of thing?" Perhaps he can if he himself has had extensive training.[12] Certainly he can handle some of the elements with proper knowledge and experience, such as information presentations and skill exercises. However, the sensitivity training group experience and the integration of all the elements of the training program into a meaningful experience require a great deal of specialized knowledge, skill, and experience.

These can be learned by many organization renewal leaders and training directors, but the expenditure in time, effort, and money is considerable. There is frequently the additional problem of the renewal stimulator being handicapped by operating within the organization and not being seen as a resource in this kind of developmental process. Most organizations, therefore, feel it is best to go outside the organization for professional guidance. The training specialist's job has so many responsibilities that frequently he cannot become an expert in this or other highly specialized areas of training if he is to most importantly serve as a consultant to the organization on how training can help management solve its problems.

Let us explore, however, some of the specific dimensions of the laboratory group leader's skills and methods that are required to effectively accomplish the goals of this type of learning. It is obvious to trainers using the sensitivity training concept that no two training groups or programs are identical. Part of this dissimilarity is accounted for by variations in the purpose, objectives, and nature of the overall program. In addition, differences in group composition, size, sophistication, motivation, training facilities, group leaders, and numerous other similar factors combine and interplay to bring into sharp focus the awareness that each group has a unique learning experience.

Any training program with its specific learning opportunities and participants is the result of background events, trainer background, participants' backgrounds and needs, and training location and program —all impinging on a given session at a given moment to produce a training event. Whether this event (silence, leadership struggle, conflict between two members, hostility, subgrouping, and so forth) will be utilized for appropriate learning will, in large part, be determined by the skill and sophistication of the trainer.

Figure 12–1 indicates some of the major forces of impact on a training program continuum to provide learning experiences and opportunities. Whether this rich and potent mix, culminating in a series of training events, will be the vehicle for meaningful learning discoveries, is heavily dependent upon the trainer.[13] Such a unique experience does not mean, however, that certain problems, sequential phases of group growth, and group behavior patterns cannot be predicted with a fairly high accuracy. It is this predictability that has enabled the laboratory method to evolve and to be translated into a useful training technique. From twenty years of intensive use and study, a significant body of "process" knowledge and desired trainer behavior has emerged. Drawing upon this accumulated data, let us examine some of the significant roles, problems, and qualifications of the effective group trainer.

Success in sensitivity training generally occurs only if there is a qualified professional trainer in the training group itself.[14] I am aware that in some trainer circles there is often a tendency to treat the role of a group trainer in a mysterious fashion. His interventions and behavior are often intangible and affected by the vagaries of the group's "here and now" needs. It is said that we can observe "what will happen and what should be done." It is my belief, however, that the trainer's role and the group processes with which his role is concerned are sufficiently known and predictable to be described and explained, and that guidelines can be established for useful trainer guidance and preparation.

The roles of a group trainer are multiple. Whether he works with a development group in a three-day or a four-week laboratory, he will be called upon to assume several roles that demand the utmost from his professional competency and responsibility. The execution of these roles will vary and will be conditioned by the following factors:

PURPOSES AND DESIGN OF THE TRAINING. The way a trainer carries out his role may be partially affected by the overall purposes of the training program. If the laboratory method is a part of a supervisory development program in which skills of working with employees are being practiced, and the general program focus is on supervision, this emphasis will affect the participants. On the other hand, if a trainer is

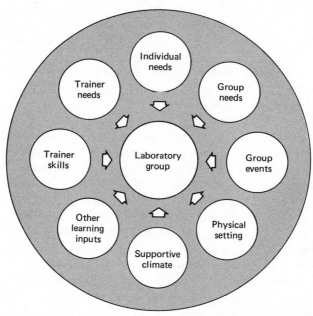

Pretraining influences	Learning applications
1. Purposes of program	1. Direct transfer to back-home situation
2. Training design	2. Cognitive and skill application to other situations
3. Trainee expectations and goals	3. Application of relevant how-to-learn ability to new situations
4. Planner's expectations and goals	
5. Past experiences of those at the conference	4. Reinforcement and follow-up with back-home training
6. Staff expectations and goals	5. Personal goals and achievement experiences
7. Cultural setting	

FIGURE 12–1

Factors Affecting Laboratory Group Learning

dealing with a homogeneous staff unit in an organization, his role may be quite different in terms of the need to protect certain standards within the group so that learning can take place without too much personal risk to any member of the group.

LENGTH OF TRAINING PROGRAM.   The duration of training will condition the different roles of the trainer. In a three-day program, a trainer normally needs to provide more structure than in a three-week program, if meaningful learning is to occur. This structure may be built through more emphasis on creating experiences within the group that are deliberately slanted to help it learn. In addition, the trainer may find it desirable to be more directive in the way he opens the group in terms of his suggestions for its entering into two-level learning processes.

GROUP COMPOSITION.   Another factor that will condition the way in which a trainer carries out his multiple roles is the composition of the group itself. For example, if a developmental group experience is being conducted in an organization for the first time, and there is little knowledge about its purpose or methods, the trainer may need to provide additional support in initiating the diagnostic process in the learning curriculum. In other cases, the group may be composed of members of an organization in which the concepts of laboratory training are known and practiced, with a resultant awareness on the part of each member of such training's purposes, objectives, and methodologies.

The factor of statuses within the group will also condition the trainer's role. It has been my experience that the higher the status of the individual members, the less free such individuals are to "let down their hair." This has real significance for the trainer's behavior and style.

Such matters as distribution of men and women, superiors and subordinates, disparity in ages, and similar aspects of group composition should also be considered.

PRACTICING PHILOSOPHY.   Different trainers have different approaches to sensitivity training groups. This usually results from different interpretations of the trainer role as it relates to the learning process, even though all apparently subscribe fundamentally to a similar philosophy of learning. In the continuum from "directive" to "nondirective" trainer functioning there will be numerous implications for the trainer role. Some trainers believe that the group should set its own standards and that the trainer should completely protect these standards. Even the most "nondirective" trainer, however, will respect the professional responsibility to be alert to any group standard which in any way really hurts an individual or sub-group.

EXPECTATIONS OF PARTICIPANTS.   The trainer's interventions will be affected by the participant's expectations of the kind of training to

which they will be exposed. If an improper expectation has been communicated, the trainer will want to assure himself that an adequate
explanation of laboratory education is provided. On the other hand, if
the group has received a valid orientation to the training, the trainer
can proceed more quickly to the diagnostic learning process. Seldom
does a participant have no formulated expectation—they run the gamut
from the valid to varying degrees of distortion.

EXPECTATIONS OF TRAINING PLANNERS.   The organization sponsoring
the training will anticipate certain results. The responsibility thrust
upon the trainer to achieve these results will influence the way he
conducts his training group. There should generally be a linkage between the manner in which the group training is conducted and the
expectations of the sponsoring organization. In some cases the sponsors may expect the group learning process to be related to the back-
home situation of the trainees. In other cases, they may want to have
the laboratory group learning process as divorced from the job situation
as possible.

ORGANIZATIONAL OR PERSONAL EXPECTATIONS.   The laboratory education process is usually utilized for a particular purpose in a training
design. A training design normally is based on fulfilling the needs of
an organization or the needs of those attending the program.[15] If the
needs evolved out of an organizational desire to improve the interpersonal competence of its employees because of a poor record of
labor-management relationships, the trainer needs to be fully cognizant
of the circumstances. But the training may be designed to provide improved skills of interpersonal communication for salesmen within a
company. The company's sales may be falling and the training is seen
as a step to improve sensitivity skills in contact with both the buyer
and the situation.

In some cases, the trainer will find personal needs very much in
evidence. A person will have come to the training program with expectations that the laboratory group process will solve one or many of
his personal problems. Knowledge of such expectations on the part
of either the individual or the organization are of prime importance
in determining the trainer's role.

INFLUENCE OF TRAINER'S PEERS AND HIS PROFESSION.   The trainer's
style will be conditioned both by the actions of his peers in a training
situation and his concept of his professional role. In most training situations, where more than one trainer is involved, a norm of trainer
behavior emerges that influences the use of methods and style. If a
norm develops during the training program that an "effective trainer"
is one who uses a highly nondirective approach, this will tend to influence the trainer to operate in that fashion.

In addition, professional training will also affect style. A clinical
psychologist may focus on the learning experiences for individuals in

the group, while a social psychologist may want to focus on the group learning aspects of the situations. An individual trainer whose background is mainly in the field of business or public administration may lean more toward relating the learning experience to the administrative or organizational process. The effects of these professional factors need to be honestly examined by all concerned.

CURRENT STATE OF RESEARCH. When sensitivity training was first introduced in 1946, research on group behavior and personal growth was limited. Since that time, however, a considerable amount of research has explored the behavior of people in groups and organizations. Numerous books and articles have been written on the dynamics of group behavior, the phases of group growth, the effect of leadership in groups, teamwork development, and the problems of group learning. There has been a rapid increase in knowledge about the learning process. Studies on group learning are readily available to the laboratory group trainer. The effects of feedback on group learning, the value of instrumentation, and numerous other methodologies are now available for review and assessment by a professional group trainer.

In addition, the history of some twenty-five years of work in the laboratory group field has provided a number of books and articles reporting research findings about education in the sensitivity training group. A well-informed group trainer will avail himself of these resources in assessing his approach, style, and intervention techniques. Each trainer will need to conduct himself in accordance with his own skills and abilities, but these can be based on validated principles and guidelines.

NEEDS OF THE TRAINER. Every individual brings his own needs to a learning process. This is no less true of the group trainer. In some circumstances a trainer may need to meet certain status needs with a particular group of trainees or other trainers. In another situation, the trainer may need to carry out some original experimentation relative to his research interests. Whatever the situation, it is imperative that the trainer be as insightful as possible to his own needs and assess their influence on his own behavior. One of the requirements of a professional trainer in the group learning process is that he not permit his own needs to interfere with the learning of others, but to recognize the reality of his needs and share them with the members of the group when appropriate, perhaps in order to diagnose their effect on the group process.

In exploring this form of training it has been indicated that the laboratory trainer has several roles to perform. There is no firm and fixed characterization to these roles, but at least six of them are readily identifiable.

It is the responsibility of the trainer to help the group see that its own processes and problems provide much of the "curriculum" for the learning experience. Initiating diagnostic procedures can be done in a "non-directive" fashion, as suggested in a paper by Roy Whitman; [16] or, at the other end of the continuum, a trainer may actually spell out his responsibility in a short training program where interpersonal laboratory training groups are being used.

For example, at the beginning of a sensitivity training session, the trainer might say something like this:

> This is the development group. We will be meeting in this room for five two-hour sessions during the next three days. Our purpose is to provide an opportunity for each of you to interact with one another in developing a group life, and to use these interactions as material for analysis, observation, and learning about human relations. As indicated in the orientation session, there are four things missing from this group that are usually found in a typical everyday group. This group does not have a stated agenda, a designated leader, agreed-upon procedures, or a common history. If this group finds these things necessary, it will provide them for itself as it sees fit. As the trainer, I see my function as helping the group to use its experiences to learn more about human relations. I do not see my function as the leader, and will resist being put into that role. It would handicap me from performing my trainer function—and prevent you from discovering emerging needs and processes.

Obviously, even this "more directive" introduction is not enough for the group to accept group diagnosis as its curriculum. In future sessions, no matter how a trainer begins the meeting, he will continue to carry out his role of initiating diagnostic observation. In many ways, the interventions used by the trainer will serve as a "prod" to the group to use diagnosis in its learning.

One of the major functions of the trainer is to make appropriate diagnostic observations to the group at such times as seem most appropriate for the group's learning and its ability to internalize. This does not mean that the trainer is responsible for all diagnostic observations. The goal of all laboratory trainers is that group members become their own diagnosticians.

At a number of points, however, for any one of several reasons, a trainer will find it desirable to make a diagnostic observation that might not appropriately be made by a member of the group because the group is not yet sufficiently sophisticated to make it or is neglecting this particular part of its learning experience. When the training groups are "family groups," or the training is taking place "on the company site," additional demands, sensitivities, and expertise are required.

As the group progresses, the trainer, in varying degrees, will assume his responsibility for initiating various techniques and methods to make possible a maximum learning experience. If the group does not know how to use a particular area of interest for its own learning, the trainer may set up a "testing situation." This might take the form of procedural suggestions such as role-playing to test out different approaches to the situation. It might be a suggestion that the group alternate group observers so that everyone in the group gets a chance to experiment with being analyzed.

There are a number of ways in which the trainer can, and should, use his own training resources to help the group. This does not mean, however, that the trainer should get "involved" at the task level of the group. The differentiation between innovating to maximize learning of a particular experience the group is having and becoming involved in the task is a fine distinction that requires astute judgment on the part of the trainer.

In the atmosphere of the training environment and in the work of the laboratory group itself, a number of standards will emerge. Such standards as diagnosing the "here and now" as against the "there and then" life of individuals will emerge. There may be times when the group will depart from this standard, and the trainer needs to be sensitive to whether his function is to protect it for the good of the learning experience.

Another standard that might well be protected by the trainer is the standard of "looking at the behavior" versus "looking at the prior determined motivation" of persons. This standard relates closely to the professional role of the trainer in terms of the differentiation between laboratory learning experience and that found in group therapy. In most instances the group will develop its own standards, but the standards most relevant to the role of the trainer will be those in the area of learning atmosphere and methods related to the training objectives of the program.

The trainer may have to initiate selected group standards but this function may be performed less often as the group matures. Nevertheless, there are times when an individual or sub-group may be getting hurt by the group, and the trainer may want to suggest standards to govern the level of diagnosis or personal attack. Of course, the vulnerability of an individual or sub-group to be hurt by the group differs widely according to the personality structure of the individuals in the group. It behooves the trainer to be sensitive to these different strengths and weaknesses of individuals.

Conversely, the group may be severely punished by an individual or individuals. The trainer may see some long-range consequences from such an attack, and here again may raise the question of a group standard. This may occur very rarely and, in a sense, it is the trainer protecting the group or individual from unproductive self-punishment. At such time, the need for professional training of the trainer becomes particularly important.

In some of the literature about sensitivity training, statements have been made that the trainer "never becomes a group member." I feel that this is an unrealistic interpretation of the psychology and reality of group life. The fact that the training group is a cultural unit implies that it has all the potential aspects of group identification, cohesion, and growth. The group builds expectations for all persons in the training situation, including the trainer. Each individual in the situation exerts and receives influence. The trainer meets, exceeds, falls short, changes, or frustrates the expectations of different members of the group. In doing this, he becomes a member whom the group must handle. The trainer may be a *unique* member, but as the laboratory group matures so does each member become unique in a number of different ways.

The trainer, of course, does not perform the typical membership function. It has been my experience that when a group has begun to "take over" its diagnostic function and begins to see the different contributions of the members, it identifies a point in its growth when it seems appropriate to overtly indicate that the trainer "is now a member of the training group." At the covert level, the trainer might have been a member of the group long before the group realized it. At another level, the trainer will never become the same kind of group member as the others, but does get group identification and membership to give the group its feeling of "wholeness" when it arrives at that point in its development.

The laboratory trainer is vulnerable to problems and traps that usually do not confront other kinds of trainers. As laboratory group trainers get together and share their experiences, several seem to occur most frequently. The following are especially noted and should be recognized, and provided against, when designing a laboratory program:

TRAINER BECOMES TOO DIRECTIVE. One of the major problems in leading a laboratory group is the temptation of becoming too directive and acting more like a teacher than a trainer. The teaching process is a seductive one, and frequently a trainer may find himself elaborating a diagnostic observation, when in reality the group itself could analyze the observation with greater learning impact. Self-discipline and commitment to the professional aspects of the training process are required.

TRAINER AND GROUP BECOME TOO CLINICAL. Another trap for many trainers is permitting the group to become too clinical in its diagnosis and learning. By "too clinical," I refer to the therapeutically centered diagnosis of motivational factors of individuals in the group rather than the behavior in the "here and now." The purposes of the training group, in terms of improving interpersonal sensitivity, increasing insight, developing membership skills, and other related knowledge in human and organizational relations, make it very easy for the emphasis to become clinical. The trainer needs to watch his own motivation and that of the group to prevent such personal and clinical emphasis from becoming too dominant.

TRAINER BECOMES TOO PERSONALLY INVOLVED IN THE GROUP. If the trainer permits himself to become involved in the work life of the laboratory group, he loses much of his ability to contribute to its purposes. As indicated earlier, the trainer *will* become involved in the life of the group, but he should avoid becoming involved at the emotional level of his own personal need. The trainer should guard against his personal "agendas" becoming a part of the group agenda. Obviously, the trainer will become a part of the "talk" of the group in its discussions, and they will deal with the trainer in terms of their dependency and leadership needs. This does not mean, however, that the trainer gets himself involved in the group life in a personal way.

TRAINING GROUP IS USED IN AN INAPPROPRIATE WAY. There are some settings in which the interpersonal focus in a sensitivity training program should not be used. Unless a group can have enough time for interpersonal and group learning and growth, for example, this kind of training should not be used. If the time is not adequate, a group does not have an opportunity, even with special provisions for a short program, to secure appropriate learning. Another example of an inappropriate setting occurs when there is no "emotional support" for the participants to utilize their learning and insights back home on the job. The use of the laboratory group should always be related to some specific organizational or trainee development purposes which are kept in mind in the design of the total learning experience. In addition, the regular conditions for effective learning should be maintained so as to realize maximum results from the use of the laboratory experience.[17]

MISTAKING FRUSTRATION AND FLOUNDERING FOR LEARNING. In the life of a training group, there will be numerous times when the group will grope aimlessly. On many occasions, this is a part of the group growth process. Such occasions are appropriate when the group uses this experience for its diagnosis and learning. If, however, the group does not learn, it is then inappropriate training. Some persons have incorrectly interpreted "exposure of behavior" as being synonymous with emotional disequilibrium in the training experience. Such disequilibrium is not an end in itself, but sometimes occurs in individuals as a means toward learning. It should not be allowed to occur, however, unless it is intricately related to the curriculum of the group as it studies its processes and learns from them.

The trainer's role in laboratory training frequently involves him directly in the learning experiences. He may be part of a "here and now" situation, involved in role play, a "member" of a discussion or diagnostic session, "leader" of a case study or group exercise, or an observer of the group and its processes. At such times he frequently is faced with the question "Should I intervene in the group discussion or activity, or should I let the group find its own way?" Seven guidelines will assist the trainer in making decisions about training interventions:

1. Intervention by the trainer has as its purpose, for the most part, the learning of the group about its processes.
2. Trainer interventions may be helpful to both the individual and the group in giving support to make possible the exposure of behavior for analysis.
3. Intervention by the trainer is helpful in encouraging the use of feedback among members of the group for both individual and group learning.
4. Trainer intervention may be necessary if, in the professional judgment of the trainer, a particular individual or sub-group is being excessively threatened by the analysis of the group. Individuals and groups vary widely in their ability to tolerate such feedback and perception.
5. As group members take over the observer function, the interventions by the trainer can become less frequent and at a different level from the observations being made by the group.
6. Training interventions may be of a procedural nature to maximize learnings within a group experience.
7. Near the end of the laboratory experience, there is frequently an expectancy on the part of the group members not only to share their feelings about one another and the ways they have seen one another, but also for the trainer to share with the group his feelings and observations about the group's growth, learning, and effectiveness. At this stage in the group's experience, such sharing is a legitimate aspect of intervention and "member-role" responsibility of the trainer.

These thoughts about the role of trainer interventions are suggestive of their relationship to the learning process. Although interventions are, basically, conditioned by the goals of the training process, they are constantly affected by the situation, time, and member and trainer needs. It is also likely that trainer interventions will be affected by the group's concept of the trainer's role—as experienced by the group and redefined at various points in the life of the group.

While there is no clear-cut set of standards for laboratory trainers, experience seems to indicate that a successful trainer will have most of the following characteristics:

SELF-UNDERSTANDING. A laboratory trainer needs a great deal of self-understanding to enable him to operate effectively in his role. This is necessary to prevent his own needs from interfering with the training process and to enable him to empathize with the interpersonal problems of others in the training group. Frequently, one of the major goals of a group is to increase self-understanding—the self-insight of its individual members. Therefore, it behooves the trainer first to secure his own self-understanding—through sensitivity training and such other experiences as are open to him—before he can hope to do an effective job in that role.

PERSONAL SECURITY. A laboratory trainer needs to have sufficient personal security to permit him to take a nonpunitive role in the training and to have genuine respect for other people. Such personal security is a prerequisite for effective educational leadership. Personal security will allow a willingness to share leadership roles with others and to relinquish authority in the learning transaction as training proceeds. Such personal security will also allow the trainer to participate adequately in the rather wide range of interpersonal situations that are inherent in a laboratory group, and to be able to deal with the many ambiguous and hostile situations which he faces.

PREVIOUS GROUP EXPERIENCE. A trainer in a laboratory group should be sophisticated and knowledgeable about group life. He should already have experienced the practical problems of working simultaneously as a group leader and a group member in a variety of settings. Such experiences, at both a theoretical and practical level, are imperative for effective diagnostic trainer skill.

PROFESSIONAL TRAINING. A background in the social sciences is highly desirable for an effective laboratory trainer. A professional, academic background in the fields of education, sociology, psychology, social work, psychiatry, personnel, philosophy, organizational administrative theories, and similar areas will provide a theoretical base on which the laboratory trainer will build his educational sophistication, philosophy, and expertise. Although a professional academic background does not guarantee training competence, the concepts and constructs that come from such study in the social sciences are indispensable qualifications.

ABILITY IN VERBAL COMMUNICATIONS. A laboratory trainer must be able to communicate effectively with others. One of the prerequisites for any trainer is to know how to communicate at the level of the particular group he is training, and with the appropriate words and imagery.

TRAINING SKILLS. With the proper personality, and educational and experiential background, most training personnel can learn the training skills needed to lead effective laboratory training programs. As a prerequisite, it is advisable that any potential laboratory trainer have experience as a member of a laboratory group. Specialized training skills can be acquired as a member of a training-for-trainers group, through an internship program, serving as a training associate in an action-learning laboratory, and finally as a group trainer under the supervision of a senior coordinator.

These criteria are suggestive of the kinds of things that should be considered when selecting and developing persons to lead laboratory training programs. Although too obvious to discuss in detail, the important areas of readiness, interest, and willingness to work with others are important basic dimensions. The philosophy that underlies the laboratory approach is a vital part of the necessary commitment. A penetrating concept of the laboratory approach and a thorough understanding of the conditions under which it operates are essential. As an important innovation in the field of learning, laboratory training philosophy, theory, and methods demand the highest caliber of professional competence and personal integrity.

Sensitivity training may have little to offer where management of the organization:

Is highly directive and intends to remain that way.

Is not concerned with public relations, even though publics are a major factor in its operations.

Is not concerned about the needs of employees being met, or not concerned about their becoming compatible and closely related to the organization's needs.

Is predicated on the assumption that men are motivated solely, or mainly, by money, promotional opportunity, threats, and rewards.

Believes that training is only for those in subordinate positions and is either anti-training or lukewarm toward training.

Sees the organization as composed of tight sub-units that have their own job to do and thinks that what happens elsewhere in the organization is none of their business.

Operates on a "hard-nosed" basis and is solely production-centered regardless of the means employed.

One of the dangers in setting down such a list is that most organizations will deny they have any of these attributes or characteristics. This kind of an organization will not find sensitivity training of sufficient benefit to warrant the investment of the required time and money. Other approaches to organization renewal, therefore, would have to precede the adoption of sensitivity training as a part of the development programs of this organization.

Management must see training as compatible with organizational objectives, understand the training objectives, and help managers see that management "buys" the philosophy of participative working with staff. Management should publicly endorse the program by its own way of behaving (men supervise as they are supervised—not as they are taught to supervise), be willing to finance the program adequately, and provide conditions that will allow men to put their learnings into operational practice.

There is always the risk that here and there an individual may be upset by sensitivity training. A not-too-well integrated person may be threatened by self-knowledge. It has not been demonstrated, however, that the experience will really do more than precipitate a personal situation that existed previously. There is the further risk that some managers exposed to this training may reach wrong conclusions about principles of behavior, and be less effective than before. This is usually the result of the wrong application of a principle, or the misunderstanding of what is learned. Specialists in laboratory training do not advocate that all decisions should be group decisions or that everyone in an organization needs to like each other, but a few participants in this type of training may draw the inappropriate conclusions that are a possible consequence of any form of educational endeavor. There is always the risk of seeing the training as a panacea for too many organizational ills. Sensitivity training does not guarantee results, it promises only more knowledgeable personal performance. It cannot substitute for a better product or service; or for organizational imperfections in such things as financing, advertising, or production. Nevertheless, sensitivity training probably is a desirable part of any organization renewal program, if properly utilized.

Robert J. House [18] has indicated his doubts about the value of many kinds of leadership development efforts, including sensitivity training, unless certain conditions exist:

> The consequences of leadership training depend on the degree to which the social influences in the trainee's work environment are viewed by the trainee as motivations to learn and the degree to which they reinforce the learned behavior during and after training. Specifically, the authority structure, the manner in which authority is exercised, and the norms of the trainee's primary work group can be analyzed into their motivational and reinforcement effects and assessed from: (1) their congruence with the prescriptions of the training, (2) the clarity of their relevance to trainee reward and punishment, and (3) their tendency to induce anxiety in the trainee.

The research by House that supports the need for organizational environment to support the change goals of training efforts is one of the keys to any organization renewal efforts.

One of the most publicized applications of laboratory training and sensitivity training is the work of TRW Systems in California. Sheldon

Davis [19] puts the contribution of this method into perspective when he comments:

> I think one important theme of the nearly four-year organizational change effort at TRW Systems is that of using laboratory training (sensitivity training, T grouping) clearly as a means to an end—that of putting most of our energy into on-the-job situations, and dealing with them in the here-and-now. This effort has reached a point where sensitivity training, per se, represents only 10 to 15 percent of the effort in our own program. The rest of the effort, 85 to 90 percent, is in on-the-job situations, working real problems with the people who are really involved in them. This has led to some very important, profound and positive changes in the organization and the way it does many things, including decision-making, problem-solving, and supervisory coaching of subordinates.

We can see in this situation that the sensitivity training method has been used to develop readiness and build team effectiveness, process, task awareness, and skill into all problem-solving efforts in the organization.

In closing this discussion, I think it is important to reiterate that sensitivity training in its varied approaches is only the best known of laboratory education methods, not the only method. Laboratory education can be practiced whenever the process of examining real life experiences is the basis of learning. This is the essence of knowing how to learn from all of life's failure and success experiences. This is the basis of any attempt at organization renewal. In the next chapter, I present some examples of organization renewal efforts.

NOTES

1. Edgar H. Schein and Warren G. Bennis, *Personal and Organizational Change Through Group Methods: The Laboratory Approach* (New York: John Wiley & Sons, Inc., 1965), p. 4.
2. Leslie E. This and Gordon L. Lippitt, "Managerial Guidelines to Sensitivity Training," *Training and Development Journal*, April, 1963, pp. 6–16. Reproduced by special permission. Copyright 1963 by the American Society for Training and Development, Inc.
3. Douglas McGregor, *The Human Side of Enterprise* (New York: McGraw-Hill Book Co., Inc., 1960), p. 221.
4. George S. Odiorne, "Managerial Narcissism—The Great Self-development Binge," *Management of Personnel Quarterly*, Vol. I, Issue 3, Spring 1962, p. 8 (Bureau of Industrial Relations, Graduate School of Business, University of Michigan).
5. Malcolm S. Knowles, *The Leader Looks at Self-development*, Looking Into Leadership Monographs (Washington, D.C.: Leadership Resources, Inc., 1961).
6. Sheldon A. Davis, "An Organic Problem-solving Method of Organizational

Change," *Journal of Applied Behavioral Science,* Vol. 3, No. 1, January–February–March, 1967, p. 5.

7. Rensis Likert, *Patterns of Management* (New York: McGraw-Hill Book Co., Inc., 1962).

8. A more complete discussion of the conditions for laboratory learning may be found in Leland P. Bradford, "The Teaching-Learning Transaction," *Adult Education,* Spring, 1958; and Selected Readings, Series No. 3, "Forces in Learning," National Training Laboratories, National Education Assn., 1961.

9. Harold Niven and Allen Zoll, "A Survey of Sensitivity Training for Industrial Managers," Boeing Airplane Co., Seattle, Washington, 1958 (unpubl.).

10. One example of the "family approach" to training is reported in Chris Argyris, *Interpersonal Competence and Organizational Effectiveness* (Homewood, Ill.: Richard D. Irwin, Inc., 1962).

11. Robert S. Blake and Jane S. Mouton, "The Instrumented Training Laboratory," *Issues in Human Relations Training,* National Training Laboratories, National Education Association, Washington, D.C., 1963.

12. Lippitt and This, "Is Training a Profession?" *The Journal of the ASTD,* April, 1960, p. 6.

13. Schein and Bennis, *op. cit.,* Chapter 14.

14. Most of the remainder of this chapter is taken from Lippitt and This, "Leaders for Laboratory Training," *Training and Development Journal,* March, 1967, pp. 2–13. Reproduced by special permission. Copyright 1967 by the American Society for Training and Development, Inc.

15. Blake and Mouton, "Initiating Organization Development," *Training Director's Journal,* Vol. 19, No. 10, October, 1965, pp. 11–20.

16. Roy M. Whitman, "Psychological Principles Underlying T-Group Process, in Leland P. Bradford, Jack R. Gibb, and Kenneth D. Benne, eds., *T-Group Theory and Laboratory Method* (New York: John Wiley & Sons, Inc., 1964), pp. 310–335.

17. This and Lippitt, "Learning Theories and Training Trends," *Training and Development Journal,* a two-part paper, April–May, 1966, pp. 12–18, 26–43.

18. Robert J. House, "Leadership Training: Some Dysfunctional Consequences," *Administration Science Quarterly,* Vol. 12, No. 4, March, 1968, p. 571.

19. Davis, *op. cit.*

13 ORGANIZATION RENEWAL IN ACTION

Bullfight critics ranked in rows
Crowd the Enormous plaza full,
But only one is there who knows—
And he's the man who fights the bull.[1]

ROBERT GRAVES, 1895–

Research theory and practice should be combined in any circumstance where a professional approach to progress and planned change is desired. I would like to report and discuss in this chapter, five actual cases of organization renewal in which I have been actively involved.

These examples have been selected because they represent different kinds of systems and different approaches to the process of organization renewal. Another rationale for the selection was to report on one case in which the renewal process existed over seven years, two situations which extended two years, one which is still an on-going process, and one which is a one-year project. In each case, however, the reader will find that confrontation, search, and coping serve as the core elements to the process.

THE CASE OF THE SEVEN-YEAR THRUST [2]

This case report on organization development will deal with a continuing change process within a large semigovernmental social welfare organization covering the period of 1953 to 1960. It had a national headquarters staff of 655 employees, and was organized on the basis of four regional operations and an overseas field of activity. There were 1,080 paid employees in regional offices under the supervision of a field staff of 350 who gave direct field consultation and program guidance to some 3,700 local units of the organization. It is estimated that the local units, and the regional and national offices, involved some 2,000,000 volunteers.

The presentation of this case study is my own; it has not been reviewed or cleared by the organization's officials. The existence of the report and its purposes were discussed, however, with appropriate persons in the organization. It was my privilege to work with Richard Beck-hard and Edward Moe as core consultants to this organization.

The basic feeling of need for renewal came out of a request by management personnel for the training staff to make a study of existing training practices and theories in industrial, educational, and voluntary organizations as these relate to managerial development.

To implement this survey, a representative task force of all levels of management from the vice president to local unit executives was selected. They were to study existing training needs and recommend to the management a program for meeting these needs. This step developed a readiness on the part of management at various levels to take a serious look at the best way to develop leaders in the organization; to examine ways in which the training office should become involved in the assessment process; and to select implementing levels.

The organization for many years had been carrying on a program of orientation training, on-the-job training, and specialized vocational skills training in particular program areas. A management survey, conducted in the organization in the early fifties, was an additional force in the "readiness phase." Although very few of the recommendations produced as a result of this survey were implemented in the organization's normal, day-by-day operation, it was recognized that some of them might be meaningful.

As a result of this interest in organization renewal, particularly as related to a management-training program, the organization, through its training office, contracted with the National Training Laboratories to consult with the organization's Study Committee to explore next steps in implementing the committee's recommendations. The helping relationship changed as the organization's needs grew and developed, and the need for its work in society changed. The relationship became defined in working with the organization:

CONSULTATION ON ORGANIZATION RENEWAL OVER A PERIOD OF TIME. The initial type of helping relationship involved a consultant to plan a management-training program. Working with the Study Committee, the consultant helped assess the basic needs for such training:

• That the basic skills needed to improve personal performance of management personnel are increased awareness of such performance and its effect on others, increased skill in diagnosing the work situation in which they operate; increased understanding of the nature of a modern, complex organization and of the action necessary to achieve its goals effectively.

• That the technical skills of the organization manager, such as budget-making and time-planning, can be effectively used only if the manager develops basic interpersonal insights, skills, and understandings.

- That the emerging body of information in the behavioral sciences about the nature of organization—how people behave in their work groups within the organization—must be a primary resource in the development of any curriculum. This implied the need for building in a continuous application of emerging social science knowledge about people in organizations and for developing the methods of training in these areas.

The Study Committee recommended to management that the organization enter into a renewal program on the basis of long-range planning rather than regard it as a panacea or a "grease gun" approach to training. On the basis of this recommendation, management decided to support a three-year initial program in the field of management development, with the thought that such a period of time would provide effective evaluation of the program, and an opportunity to see a real "test" of the methods and philosophy being used.

USE OF TRAINING SPECIALISTS IN CERTAIN FUNCTIONS WITHIN THE ORGANIZATION.   In planning the management school, the need was recognized for outside specialists in various fields of public administration, social work, business administration, sociology, psychology, and related fields who could be helpful in carrying out the program. Additionally, as the program progressed, strategic consultants were made available to such different levels of the organization as community units and regional offices in an effort to help them utilize training specialists. The latter, then, is an aspect of the use of consultants that developed through their use with the organization, and constitutes an additional definition of the helping relationship.

DEVELOPMENT OF THE CONCEPT OF "CORE CONSULTANTS."   Another phase of the helping relationship, which emerged after three years of experience in conducting the program, resulted from widening interest in organization renewal and a recognized need for a continuous relationship with the consultants. The organization hired a group of three core consultants, who together developed a philosophy, methods of consulting, and a close working relationship with one another. They were persons with skills from the fields of research, education, training, community organization, and management. Although the core consultants were frequently assigned to work on special projects as individuals, both they and the organization's training office maintained a common liaison and a "thinking through" process of the total needs of the organization.

The Study Committee's work with the consultant clarified a number of difficulties within the organization:

DISTANCE BETWEEN THE POLICY MAKERS AND THE IMPLEMENTERS. Questionnaires, interviews, and reports indicated that one of the existing problems was the factor of distance between the policy makers at the national level and the ultimate users of policy in the local units. This distance caused misunderstanding, resistance, and poor communication in the work of the organization at the community level.

PROGRAM ISOLATION AND COMPETITION AMONG VARIOUS PROGRAM UNITS. In such a multi-program type of organization, competition among various program units is almost inevitable. Here it was evidenced by a lack of intercommunication about programs, plus the inability of many participants at the local unit level to get a "total picture" of the organization and its work.

COMMUNICATION DIFFICULTIES BETWEEN PROGRAM SEGMENTS OF THE ORGANIZATION AND DIFFERENT LEVELS OF ORGANIZATION HIERARCHY. Four levels of hierarchy in the organization—national office, regional office, field staff, and local communities—posed numerous communication problems. Despite newsletters, management directives, and other means of communication, the amount of face-to-face communication among levels was limited.

PROBLEM OF REMOTE SUPERVISION IN LIGHT OF THE WIDESPREAD NATURE OF THE ORGANIZATION. The problem of remote supervision was most evident in the relationship between the field staff, constantly "on the road," and their supervisors in the regional offices. While this arrangement permitted a great deal of freedom, it prevented good communication, in-service development, and an effective relationship between supervisor and subordinate.

CONTINUING NEED TO BUILD A MORE EFFECTIVE RELATIONSHIP BETWEEN VOLUNTEER AND PAID STAFF. A real part of the organization's staff were the basic policy makers who were unpaid volunteers. It should be noted, however, that in spite of extensive organization renewal, the problems of perception, recognition, authority, and role relationship between paid and volunteer staff members persist, despite the organization's history of effective utilization of volunteers. This problem is, of course, typical of nearly every volunteer type of agency, but it is significant here that this organization caused extraordinary relationship problems in many personnel situations.

NEED TO DEVELOP STANDARDS OF TRAINING. Extensive training went on throughout the organization, particularly in the program service areas, with most of the program segments taking responsibility for training within their own area of specialty. With no common standards for the kinds of training being given, however, it was obvious to the Study Committee that a need existed to develop such standards and to exercise some control over the development of trainers.

NEED FOR ADDITIONAL TRAINERS IN THE ORGANIZATION TO MEET WIDENING TRAINING NEEDS. In the past, training personnel in the organization tended to be somewhat low on the totem pole. However, the widening interest in and need for training made imperative a broader base of qualified trainers in program units at various organizational levels. For future implementation, new programs would require the upgrading of existing training staff to even higher levels of proficiency.

NEED TO BUILD EFFECTIVE HUMAN RELATIONS THROUGHOUT THE ORGANIZATION. The assessment of the Study Committee indicated a need for improved interpersonal relationships at all work levels so as to meet more effectively the obligations of the organizational programs.

Although the original consultation process was initiated in connection with management-training possibilities, during its three-year period the need was seen for other specific organizational changes that could be aided through the renewal process.

As the organizational atmosphere became affected by management-training activities, a number of change possibilities presented themselves. Not only were managers returning to their responsibilities with a better concept of themselves and their working relationships with others, but also a new awareness of a potentiality of training was developing. This led to some breakthroughs in the program divisions. It indicated the developing status of the training function in the organization, and awareness of the role of the consultants and staff in the training office. As the everwidening change possibilities came into focus, a number of new activities and concepts developed:

THE MANAGEMENT-TRAINING PROGRAM WAS ESTABLISHED ON A CONTINUING BASIS. Following the three-year phase of the management-training program and the evaluation of its results, demands came from all parts of the organization to continue and expand such training to lower levels of supervision.

A FIELD STAFF TRAINING PROJECT WAS INSTITUTED. The change in organizational atmosphere, plus a study of local units, showed a need to train field staff personnel, some of whom consult with eight to twenty local organizational units. Since securing enough consultants was a financial impossibility, the decision was made to resort to "peers training peers." The program to train trainers in a centralized location in certain curriculum areas of field staff skills was developed to extend through a five-year period. Each year a group of thirty were to be trained as trainers to go back and train others in their region.

TRAINING PROJECTS WERE CARRIED OUT BY FOUR OF THE ORGANIZATION'S PROGRAM DIVISIONS. As a result of the increasing importance of organization renewal, four of the organization's program units developed training projects to meet their own operational needs.

A NATIONAL TRAINING COUNCIL WAS DEVELOPED TO REPRESENT THE WHOLE ORGANIZATION. Its members were from local units, regional offices, program areas, management, and the four highest agency officials. Founded in 1957, the council became a powerful force for initiating organizational change. With representatives of the policy-making and implementation areas gathered together in one large body of fifty persons, the council in a very real sense was recommending action to itself. Through the forming of a national training council, training at all levels to meet various needs was revitalized.

The generalization and stabilization of organization renewal assumed different dimensions:

EFFECTS OF THE MANAGEMENT-TRAINING PROGRAM AND ITS CONTRIBUTION THROUGHOUT THE ORGANIZATION. Interest was heightened in leadership training for most persons of the organization, both lay and professional.

IMPROVING AND STABILIZING THE FUNCTIONS OF THE NATIONAL TRAINING COUNCIL. The national training council met on an annual basis. In its first year it found itself somewhat hampered by the lack of subcommittee work in the interim. As a result of this, a number of program unit committees and interprogram task groups were set up to explore and carry out the recommendations of the national council.

STRENGTHENING THE REGIONAL TRAINING COMMITTEES. In each of the regional offices the regional training director had developed with the regional manager, an area training committee. Throughout the organization there was a revitalization of interest in the regional training committees. This tended to stabilize the responsibility for training and to give greater support for carrying out many activities.

UPGRADING THE ROLE OF THE TRAINING DIRECTORS. The importance of training and of the people who carried out this function was recognized. This process resulted in higher status for the training directors and the training office.

DEVELOPING AND WIDENING THE PROGRAM OF TRAINING TRAINERS. This program related to basic program needs as they developed and spread.

THE DEVELOPMENT OF THE PHILOSOPHY OF TRAINING. As a result of multiple training activities, it was necessary to continuously re-examine the philosophy of the organization as it related to training operations. Some of the basic elements of this philosophy reflected organizational change, and demonstrated the insight and understanding that had developed out of the consulting process in the organization. Some of the elements of this philosophy were as follows:

1. Action-oriented training to meet individual needs and some basic program needs.
2. Training should be given as close as possible to the situation for which training is developed.
3. Use of effective outside resources will aid in the creative development of people within the organization.

4. People who are to be affected by the training should be involved in the planning and the development of the training program.
5. Training is everybody's job—supervisor, volunteer, leader, manager, field staff.
6. Training must be decentralized.
7. A training program must remain flexible and adjustable to meet the changing needs of the organization in the society in which it finds itself.
8. Training is an active process—it should be situationally related and experientially based.

In the seven years' duration of the consulting relationship, a number of changes emerged:

CHANGES IN THE ROLE OF THE ORGANIZATION TRAINING STAFF. In the early phases of the consultation process, the training staff looked upon the resource consultants as "experts"; but the training staff soon developed for itself much of the technical know-how. This created less dependency on the technical assistance of the consultants and, as a result, the core consultants no longer worked with the organization on a continuous basis.

CHANGES IN THE ROLE OF THE CORE OF CONSULTANTS TO MEET THE CHANGING SITUATIONS IN THE ORGANIZATION. The core consultants tended to be "doers" in various training activities. As the organization developed more and more trainers, and as training spread throughout the organization, there was more need for the use of the core consultants in planning, in long-range development, and in thinking through organizational problems, rather than in the implementation of training activities.

DEVELOPMENT OF A RESOURCE NETWORK FOR UTILIZATION AT ALL LEVELS IN THE ORGANIZATION. By the early part of 1959, the organization recognized the need for resource consultants at various levels of the organization when appropriate. To this end, the organization developed a network of resources (in the universities, colleges, and organizations across the country that were geographically close to the local units of the organization) which were available to help at the appropriate time and under certain circumstances.

The brevity of this report forces omission of many of the subtleties and realities of a consultation process. The consulting process had no definite beginning and end. In this particular case, some very specific factors contributed to the development of a successful renewal process:

The enlightened and pioneering spirit of the training director of the organization. The training director, in this situation, was the key renewal stimulator.

Willingness on the part of top management to give training a chance to "work" over a sufficient period of time.

The strategic selection of appropriate inside and outside resource people to give assistance to the organization.

The constant awareness that people will support what they create, and the practice of the collaborative process at all phases of the renewal process.

An emerging philosophy of training that prompted the development of a national training council cutting across all levels of the organization.

Flexibility on the part of the consultants to change their role and to work in close conjunction with the national training office in developing a common philosophy about organizational growth and development. The organization moved forward into new areas of training and development as a result of this process, building commitment to the value of learning and renewal as contributions to organizational problem-solving.

THE CASE OF OPERATION ROADBLOCK

A large Midwestern paper company was involved in an interesting approach to organization renewal that was developed around the identification and solution of "roadblocks" facing the company. I was privileged to be associated with Douglas McGregor and Jack Gibb as consultants on the project.

The process began with recognition, by the president of the company and other top officials, of the need for improving personal, group, and company performance. It was decided to involve all members of management in all phases of the renewal process. To help build a readiness for the process, top management felt that the supervisors needed greater perspective; that they needed to look at their jobs in relation to the overall company effort, get more information about the company's plans for the future, and review the company's immediate and long-range problems in all phases of the business.

The supervisors were given this perspective in a preliminary undertaking called "Meeting the Brass." A team of the company's top officers visited the three divisions to talk with all members of management. The Finance Director, Sales Vice President, Research Vice President, Operations Vice President, and Industrial and Public Relations Vice President —each discussed the company's plans and problems as they saw them.

Given this insight into the organization, top management personnel began to identify the operating problems that stood in their way. The question asked in each work group was as follows: What are some of the roadblocks that prevent us from doing our most effective job for the company? And what can we do to remove these "roadblocks?" These were the perplexing problems that more than 500 supervisors undertook to identify and they held departmental meetings throughout the organization, from division managers on down. In these on-the-job group meetings, the supervisors studied work flow, space and equipment needs, problems of people, quality requirements, and many other factors that affect the work of their departments. Out of these discussions many key problems were developed. For example:

"We need better communication between technical and production departments."

"We should have a preventive maintenance program for such things as pumps, blowers, instruments."

"As supervisors, we must improve our leadership, organization, and planning."

"We need better quality control on coated paper."

In all, the supervisors listed some 1,500 of these roadblocks (there were duplications, of course) ranging from "improving order scheduling" to "reducing costs by improving cost consciousness." The supervisors put some of the problems up to top management for solution; the rest they thought "we, as individual supervisors, should be able to handle." In addition to the work groups identifying roadblocks, individual employees were asked to submit observations, comments, and suggestions. In this manner, over a period of a year, 4,000 additional roadblocks were identified. These two lists of roadblocks were then consolidated into truly major problem areas.

The stage was then set for problem-solving conferences. Top management personnel assembled in groups of about one hundred at a time for three-day training, confrontation, and problem-solving conferences. The conference design had three major features. First, small laboratory groups met with outside consultants in the mornings to develop human relations and teamwork skills. These sessions included inputs on certain behavioral aspects of management. Second, unit discussions were scheduled in the afternoons. The conference broke up into units of about twelve men each to discuss the roadblocks arising out of the departmental meetings. Each man was free to attend the unit which was discussing the problem that interested him most. Each unit tried to solve —or arrive at ways of solving—the problem they had chosen to study. In addition, the participants heard a talk by the company president. He reviewed the roadblocks that face top management, and outlined his plans for dealing with them in the coming year. Thus, this practical workshop tried to combine problem-solving with learning the human behavior skills involved in solving the problem. Each management group tried hard to find the answers to the practical, everyday operating problems. As one supervisor said: "This was an unusual and inspiring experience for me. I think all of us got a lot more out of this conference than either of the first two. We talked about our mutual problems—and we solved a few of them. We're taking home a lot of ideas about how to do a better job for ourselves, for our departments, and for the company. And we're going to do something about them. At least I know I am!"

Step four in the renewal process was the development of "Operation Follow-thru." The conferences were only a beginning; the real measure of the program's success was to be determined by performance on the job all year long. As the vice president said in his final talk at each conference, "Solving problems is a continuous job for all members of our organization. We have started to learn how to do it here at this conference. Now we have to implement these techniques day-by-day on the job. How well we do will indicate how well the organization will be able to compete in the months and years ahead . . . and if our company is going to be the company we want it to be, we must stay out in front!"

"Operation Follow-thru" was a means for all key persons to work together in acting on suggestions, ideas and information drawn from such sources as:

Opinion research survey
Five conference sessions
Employee complaints
Customer complaints
Safety meetings
Management planning reports
Employee suggestions

An overall Follow-up Task Force was appointed at corporate headquarters. At each manufacturing division and in the general office, full-time teams were organized to help supervisors expedite the work of doing something about all the ideas, criticisms, and suggestions that were advanced. "Operation Follow-thru" got underway only after some 6,500 roadblocks were gathered, classified, and discussed.

At the Materials Department, industrial engineering and production men dug into the job of improving the flow of materials through the mill . . . at another, plans were drawn up for a new cafeteria . . . at still another, staff employees pored over dozens of suggestions for improving its adult recreation program . . . at the general office, a better method of distributing technical reports was put to use. Throughout the company, hundreds of employees put their time and effort into solving some of the roadblocks that stood in the way of improved performance and better working conditions. Even more important, nearly all the employees of the organization participated in the problem-solving. Six months after the program was initiated, more than half of the 6,500 items had been reviewed; action was taken on almost 2,000 of them and some 1,700 more were under study.

Probably the greatest gain in this process was one which could be realized only in months and years to come—a method of working together to improve productivity and to make the company an even better place to work. Many departments began holding frequent meetings to pinpoint and solve problems as they arose. The company president observed, "As I have said many times, the important thing is to be sure that we work together in trying to identify, analyze, and solve problems. The way in which we do it is just as important as what we do. As roadblocks are disposed of, we ought to see improved performance and learn much more about how to deal with our problems."

The project continued for two years, but was somewhat curtailed by the sudden death of the president and a major situation that brought new dynamics into the situation. It proved to be, nevertheless, a significant venture in organization renewal that had some lasting effects.

THE CASE OF THE WEEKEND CONFRONTATIONS [3]

This case report concerns three different government agencies. Many top level executives in the Federal Government had been probing for practical means of developing better individual managers and of achieving, at the same time, a more closely knit management team. This need was identified by John W. Macy, Chairman of the U.S. Civil Service Commission,[4] who stated:

> The ability to exercise leadership in high-level executive positions does not spring naturally from routine or from long exposure to highly specialized single-project development. Its development requires deliberate, continuing stimulation through planned executive education.

This concern had been given additional impetus by President Johnson's demand that agency budgets "reflect economics from better management and higher productivity, from improved methods, procedures, organization and employee incentive." [5]

The seminars described in these three case studies were attempts to stimulate an organizational climate which fostered both individual executive growth and management team-building or, in other words, an attempt to stimulate organization renewal. In these extended weekend seminars, for which Drexel Sprecher and I were coordinators, the top executives of a single agency (or of a major bureau or division) partici-

pated throughout the learning experience. In the seven seminars which
provide the principal data for these studies, the sponsoring agency in
each case was assisted by a small team of organizational consultants.
The sponsoring agencies were the Post Office Department (three seminars, two at regional level), the General Services Administration (two
seminars), and the Small Business Administration (two seminars). I was
a member of the consulting teams which worked with these agencies.
The principal method used was the mutual identification of underlying
management concerns within each agency. The main target was organizational improvement through understanding the process of problem-
solving. In this respect, the purpose of the seminars related directly to
Warren Bennis' thesis [6] that "The process of problem-solving—of adaptability—stands out as the single most important determinant of organizational health."

These problem-identification and problem-solving seminars engen-
dered broad support from the leaders and training specialists of the
sponsoring agencies. The "Executive Seminar Report" of the General
Services Administration concerning the first of two such seminars states:
"The conference caused participants to evaluate themselves more than
they had ever done before. They became familiar with management
principles and techniques which they plan to apply to their own work
situations. In addition, they now have a positive feeling that they are
part of an agency team that has similar problems across operational
lines."

The Regional Director of the Washington Office of the Post Office
Department concluded his report to the Department Bureau of Personnel
as follows: "The association and participation of regional personnel have
resulted in better communications, understanding and teamwork to effect
our mission. . . . Without hesitation I can firmly state that the general
objectives of the seminar were successfully reached."

By way of providing additional data, this study will concern itself
with (1) the goals, process, and methodology employed; (2) some of the
principal questions asked about the conduct of these learning experiences; (3) the reactions of individual participants to various aspects of
the seminars.

The general goals were developed by a planning committee composed
of managers who later participated in the seminar. The need for confrontation of issues, problems, and concerns was the overall objective.
The specific purposes included the following:

Develop further the management team.
Identify and diagnose common concerns affecting organizational performance.

Explore some research-based principles of leadership and management applicable to the job of key executives.

Share ideas concerning ways to improve the work relations of the management group.

Develop plans to follow up the seminar back on the job.

Advance preparations for these seminars were extensive. In this connection, the many functions of the members of the planning committee were signally important. They assisted the agency and the consultants in general planning; they acted as a special communication channel for the other participants and helped interpret the seminar and its purposes to them; and they worked on evaluation procedures and follow-up plans.

Problem identification began well before each seminar. An early task of the planning committee and representatives of the consulting team was to examine major problem areas in the organization and to discuss methods most likely to stimulate a productive interchange at the seminar. This process was continued on the first day of the seminar when all the conferees, in small groups, developed a "problem census." The findings of each group were reported back in general session and the problems were discussed with the whole group. This census indicated a half dozen or more general areas which a considerable number of agency leaders felt to be especially urgent. In one of the seminars, for example, the broad "problem area" list was as follows (the figures in parenthesis indicate the number of participants who ranked the general areas as of paramount importance):

Planning, goals, direction, priorities (11)
Supervision, leadership, teamwork (9)
Communication (5)
Motivation and morale (5)
Authority and delegation (4)
Decision-making (4)
Resistance to change (3)

The value of this list was *not* the novelty of the topics; indeed, with some variation, these are fairly predictable. The value lay in the probing and confrontation process which produced many consequences other than the list itself, including a climate for the entire seminar and a foundation which influenced the ensuing process, including presentations, small group work, and discussions. Following the initial problem census, the resource consultants and steering committee reappraised the tentative agenda and made a considerable number of revisions in both content and method.

Considerable emphasis was placed on experience-centered learning and action-oriented methods of instruction. Several assumptions caused this emphasis. First, of course, a recognition that the individual and collective resources of the conferees were very considerable. The process of the seminar was designed to bring out these resources in a variety of of ways. A second principle was the importance of peer learning.

Matthew B. Miles [7] states:

> Practical experience in training programs suggests this generalization: When the primary motivation for improvement comes from an individual's concern about what "outsiders" want him to do, the changes in his behavior are apt to be confused, transitory, un-integrated, and irrelevant to the demands of the job. When primary motivation for improvement comes from the strong desires of the person—aided by "insiders" who are members of the same training group—to improve his own ways of working with others, then the changes in his behavior can become increasingly systematic, permanent, integrated, and job-related.

We can learn many things more readily from appropriate interactions with our associates than we can from the best of instruction by our superiors or by the experts.

A third assumption was that organization renewal is most likely to occur when higher managers, as a group, work at becoming more sensitive to the essential conditions and climate for organizational growth. This involved a mutual examination of the underlying nature of many management problems, including the motivation of available human resources and the release of latent creativity within the organization.

Presentation by the trainers occupied roughly one-fourth of the total time of the seminar. Part of this time was directed towards setting the stage for a particular small group session, or in drawing out possible meanings from earlier sessions. The consultant faculty were members of the seminar from beginning to end, not a series of experts who came in to cover particular subjects and then depart after a brief interaction with the group. Often their approach was more one of dialogue and probing into the significance of particular observations. Considerably less time was spent on lectures than is normal in the more conventional management courses. The faculty gauged its inputs in terms of total on-going process, rather than as segments of a structured group.

Small groups were used for many purposes: problem identification, analysis of experience, observation and other skill practice, planning and problem-solving, and experimentation with a range of methods which can be employed back on the job. A continuing objective was to evoke a substantial number of "live incidents" which appeared as "helps" or "hindrances" in accomplishing the mission of the agency. These incidents took on personal meaning to the participants because of their part in identifying them. The small group work was reported, discussed, and analyzed in general sessions. The consultants, by reference to similar or analogous situations, frequently brought in outside data. But the group "listened" within their organization as a frame of reference.

With few exceptions, the small group activity received favorable mention in the open-ended evaluations at the end of the seminars. In speaking of what he liked best, one participant wrote of the "use of small group sessions to initiate and discuss problems. Also, the use of such group sessions to suggest solutions considered. Use of true-life situations in the organization." Another noted "the role-playing and the small group work with time for analysis in the general session. I think the role-playing actually broke the ice and established a better attitude."

It is important to note that some of the interactions in both the small group and general sessions were not all sweetness and light. Differences in experiences and perceptions frequently led to disagreement and occasionally to open conflict. The pace of the "digging" at times caused impatience and some yearning for a more structured process of instruction. Concerning the small group work, one participant wrote in his evaluation: "The small group discussions were the most difficult sessions of this conference. These discussions were not the least valuable, but certainly were the least pleasant of the conference. . . . At least a knowledge and awareness of our interaction in small groups is recognized."

A part of every manager's job, of course, is listening perceptively and patiently to observations he may think are not as well or as succinctly phrased as he would like or which are not in agreement with his own. One of the functions of the consultant was to help the conferees cope with the differences and frustrations which are part and parcel of this kind of learning experience. Thus, such "difficult" experiences offered great learning potential in these seminars.

Part of the function of the consultants has already been noted. Another element was the briefing of the small groups in their various assignments. Frequently, a consultant would sit in on a small group session as an observer, but in this role he declined any typical leadership role. He may have helped to clarify the assignment, or he may have made a few selective observations on a point producing particular difficulty for the group. A related task was that of setting guidelines for the reporting sessions which followed most of the small group sessions. The consultants rotated in chairing the reporting sessions, drawing out and helping to organize the observations of the reporters and the others who commented.

One goal of the consultants was to achieve something approaching peer status for all the conferees for the *duration of the conference*. The services of a professional resource person tended to reduce the inhibitions against a free interchange of ideas. Many of these inhibitions are outgrowths of the usual hierarchical and functional divisions of a large organization, and they do not disappear simply because "the boss" invites open discussion.

Consultants for this type of work conference need to be well versed in management practice, organizational theory, interpersonal relations, group process, consulting skills, and action learning design. It is useful if some of them have had first-hand managerial experience.

Questions are frequently asked about the minimum and the optimum number of consultants for this kind of in-house organizational seminar. My experience and that of my associates tended to two conclusions. First, it was unwise to try to get along with less than two consultants, even when the group was relatively small (twenty to twenty-five). When there were more than thirty participants, we recommended adding another special resource person for each additional fifteen participants. The reasons are these: It is too wearing for a single consultant to assume the many and continuing responsibilities of the faculty in a seminar of this kind. Two or more consultants can give each other support in alternating presentations, watching carefully for participant reactions and interactions, revising the flexible agenda to emerging needs, etc. In the larger seminars (thirty or more) the additional consultants are especially important in making the small group work more effective, in securing additional information on individual problems, and in maintaining close relationships with the participants throughout this intimate learning retreat.

The seminars had certain characteristics common to all "off-the-job" meetings of managers. These spring from a conviction that occasionally there is real value in a common exodus from the usual work setting. This gets busy people away from the demands of daily operations, thus providing an atmosphere permitting concentration without interruption, and deliberation without routine pressures. Most of these conferences are held in a rural area at a facility which offers the necessary conference rooms and equipment, and which also provides opportunities for individual recreation and reflection. One of the seminars was held at a hotel in a large city some distance from Washington. The nearly universal reaction of participants and faculty was that this location was a limiting factor and that its choice was an error.

The seminars spanned a weekend, beginning on a Thursday or Friday and continuing until Sunday afternoon. The conferees included the top management team of the entire government unit, either the agency or a division of the agency. No agency felt it practical or possible to spare so large a group for more than two days of the usual work week. In fact, in one case it was felt mandatory for one of the top administrators to remain behind on Friday to handle possible emergencies and otherwise to hold the shop together. There are two other reasons why these seminars have included a Saturday and a Sunday. First, the cost to the Government was reduced, since no compensatory time had been suggested. Second, this enabled the participants to contribute two days of their own time to a program that has important dimensions for individual growth as well as for organizational improvement.

The schedule of the seminars included evening sessions which lasted from two to three hours. To avoid excessive crowding, some topics had to be curtailed, or even excluded altogether, and more could have been accomplished had there been more time. The question of the amount of time and its best use is always a complex matter, but the almost unavoidable demands upon the top echelons of a government agency were inescapable. It might be better to have conducted each seminar in two stages, the first separated from the second by several weeks or more.

How many participants should there be? What is the proper cutoff point? The answers to these questions depended upon the number of executives of the agencies with direct and substantial influence in policy-making and implementation. The main object was to have a group which can function as peers concerned with major management problem-solving. Final selection was made by the chief executive of the agency, or his deputy, after consultation with the planning committee and representatives of the consulting team. A great deal depended upon the organization's peculiarities. Still, the size of the organization does not affect the learning and the action-taking quality of this kind of learning experience.

In the seven seminars, the range was from nineteen to sixty participants. For this type of seminar, the number should not exceed sixty. If management believes that its top management group exceeds forty-five, I would be inclined to recommend holding two or more seminars rather than one large one.

Assuming proper goals, the ultimate criterion in evaluating a training program is the extent to which it achieved them. Although depth research would have been preferable in measuring results, the fact is that the immediate post-program responses of the trainees was relied upon in judging the success or failure of the training effort. The reliability of these reactions was increased greatly by including written questionnaires which were carefully phrased, open-ended, and anonymous. The data obtained were relied upon very considerably in developing the official reports on these seminars.

A common criticism of many management programs is that management functions are treated as entities rather than as integral parts of the total management picture. In situational training of the kind discussed here, more emphasis was placed upon improved organizational performance than upon increasing individual competence. Several of the declared goals of the seminars spoke to this point, and many of the seminar participants directed a considerable part of their evaluations to teamwork. One participant said: "As a whole, these sessions have welded the primary staff into a better team. This will assist us in effecting our mission." Another felt one result would be "to secure a closer, more intimate knowledge of the areas where conflict and duplicating effort are now existing." One felt the experience "should be of definite value in establishing an improved teamwork concept."

Several mentioned closer understanding of other team members as a valuable consequence of the joint learning endeavor: "A better understanding between each of us. Those who can learn together can work together." "We are now more of a unit. We have more knowledge of ourselves and our colleagues and of our roles."

Nothing in the evaluations suggested that the stresses of some of the interactions had a deleterious effect on teamwork. On the contrary, the respect of the participants for one another appeared to be increased. In this vein one participant said: "I better understand the other members of our organization. Some bore out to a greater extent my past opinions of them while some completely surprised me (pleasantly, that is) when I got to know them better."

The participants readily took to grappling with a number of the common concerns affecting organizational performance which cross divisional lines. Traditionally, government agencies place considerable stress on clearly defined delegations among the various bureaus, divisions, sections, and branches. Necessary as this may be for most purposes, it produces many difficulties and concerns for executives and administrators with program responsibilities which transcend the formal compartmentalization of the agency.

Such fractionalization of functions requires government managers to invest much time and energy in coordination, in establishing or disestablishing special task forces, in cutting across divisional lines, or in otherwise avoiding the restrictions of rigid or ingrained "divisionalism." A second consequence identified in this seminar was the loss of potential contributions and individual creativity. Leaders in the division often felt it to be awkward, difficult, or unsafe to take substantial initiative, except through well-established organizational channels. Often they were not quite certain what appropriate channels are, and they had some reservations about the means, such as informal communication, which are used to shore up the organization. Many able line and staff people felt only partly used, with varying consequences to their morale.

In these seminars there was much identifying and diagnosing of common concerns, particularly in the small group and report-back sessions. Some examples of actual small group assignments from a number of the seminars indicate the range of subjects which were explored:

How can we provide time and opportunity to develop improved staff
    relations?

How can we develop more effective leadership at mid-management and division head levels?

How can we further develop our own leadership?

When are different styles of leadership appropriate or inappropriate in our agency?

How can we improve the planning and goal-setting aspects of our job?

How do we improve communication between headquarters and regional offices; with middle managers; between superiors and subordinates?

What are the driving and restraining forces which affect the image of our particular agency?

How can we help improve poor employee attitudes?

How can we help reduce staff turnover?

How do we keep the most qualified personnel?

How can we effectively orient and train personnel?

The findings under such assignments were not all practical nor were all of them adopted by the agencies, but a better consensus and a better problem-solving process developed. One participant observed: ". . . attitudes of our relationship with organizational personnel have been changed during this conference. Better understanding of the complexities of our organizational structure have been accomplished. . . . A new approach to our problems and management attitudes has been recognized and even demonstrated."

Another wrote that the seminar: ". . . should provide a means of improving the handling of problems not only between personnel concerned and divisions involved, but expedite possible solution thereto."

A great many participant evaluations referred to the job-oriented and experience-centered emphasis of the seminars and to the combination of theory and practice: "This is the first time I have attended a seminar that combined directly leadership theory and our organization. Up to now they seem to have been distinctly separate." One liked best "the opportunity to think and express theory." Still another found the greatest value in the "experience of objective, uninhibited criticism and comment upon the various managerial and administrative procedures."

In answer to the question on "Which experiences (or topics) do you consider to have been most valuable?" one participant said: "Perhaps the greatest single advantage to the whole program is the realization of the many techniques for leadership which have become available during the last decade and which will necessitate further study and thought." A great many participants declined to indicate a preference for individual topics, stating that all were valuable and essential. Most participants, however, did indicate two or more topical preferences. Communication and the problem-solving process (or decision-making) usually run ahead of other topics in these ratings.

Of communication, one participant said, "This topic and discussion have enabled me to come up with new ideas and approaches to assist in the follow-up program to improve communication. I have always thought this was our weakest link." Another found most worthwhile "an improvement in my communication to others and an awareness of the possible 'blocks' or 'faults' in communication I receive."

Under the question on what was of least value, individual topics were mentioned only about one-fourth as often as those mentioned as of most value, and no clear pattern emerged. Many participants expressly declined to answer this question. Some were not satisfied with the adequacy of this practical application of theory. One said: "I believe there should be more actual demonstrations of the practical side of the theory. The theory was presented very well. The problems and the pitfalls were pointed out, but there was very little suggestion as to how to avoid the problem or pitfall." Some also indicated that more time should have been spent—or made available—on some of the more "difficult" areas. The search process should have been more complete."

The number of evaluations which specifically mentioned work group relations makes it clear that this is an important concern of top management people. One participant concluded: "I believe the greatest value to the organization to be the breaking down of barriers between individuals compartmentalized on a functional basis by reason of the informal and uninhibited manner in which the seminar was conducted, and by removal of the conference to the pleasant and remote environment in which this course has been conducted." Another wrote that the experience would help him "in securing greater cooperation from my staff and workers—in furnishing clear cut goals and objectives for my organization." Others said: "I believe a more flexible approach to my everyday problems will result in benefit to the organization." The seminar should "create harmonious working relations between divisions toward the accomplishment of all projects and programs." The experience "brought people closely together in an atmosphere of thought expressions that cannot exist in day-to-day work. It enables a better understanding of people with whom one seldom comes in contact. I have gained a broadened concept of management-employee relations."

Developing plans to implement learnings from the seminars, back on the job, was discussed at an early meeting of the planning committee— and of course it was the principal topic for the wind-up session. The individual notebooks of each participant contained pertinent literature and a bibliography as helpful resources for individual development after the seminar. However, the evaluations showed considerable concern for what is likely to happen in the organizational setting after the conference was over.

One participant wrote: "At follow-up sessions, which have already been planned, these role-playing and problem-solving conferences have indicated various weak areas where it is possible to help individuals to improve and develop themselves." Another stated that the seminars "will cause some reassessment of past handling of problems, and probably result in broader views of problems, particularly in relation to other divisions of the organization." Some wrote more generally: "The final results of this conference will be demonstrated in the months to come."

Others were less sanguine about the long-term results. In speaking of the value of the seminar in which he participated, one wrote: "For a while an attempt [will be made] to develop both individually and as a team. But without nurturing this may gradually die out." Still another showed a similar concern: "This cannot be a 'one shot' affair as this type of conference is like 'a shot in the arm,' a rededication, an awakening, a realization that we begin to slip after some time. Having refresher conferences would maintain the degree of enthusiasm and keep everyone stimulated." In reporting to his department on a regional management seminar, the Regional Director concluded with a paragraph on follow-up: "Plans have already been developed and implemented to follow up the seminar and to emphasize management improvement and individual self-development as continuing tasks." One agency later set up a "follow through" committee to implement some of the suggestions which came to the fore at the conference. Post-training slippage is a continuing concern of good managers, training directors, and organizational consultants, and no simple answers are available. Hopefully, these seminars pointed in the right direction. They were designed as a part of the on-going processes of the management group itself, their focus was on meanings which relate to everyday management, and they endeavored to make follow-up an integral part of the goals of the learning experience.

Each of the seminar goals discussed above was keyed to organizational improvement. Still, each agency worked only through its human resources, and these are individual persons. In the final analysis, the insightfulness of individual managers concerning themselves and the organization was what counted. It is striking, therefore, that so many of the assertions in the evaluations dealt with different aspects of self-insight and self-improvement. Each of the following quotes is from the evaluation of a different participant in one of the seminars:

"It [the seminar] has caused me to reflect on my role and to take a look at my own shortcomings."

"It has served to cause me to know myself and others better. It has especially caused me to take a self-analysis of my own weakness and shortcomings."

"By opening your mind to self-analysis, you see faults in your personality that undoubtedly keep you from becoming as good a leader as you might become if you are willing to be flexible enough to change your tactics and approaches to cope with various problems and situations."

"It has awakened a determination for occasional self-evaluation."

THE CASE OF NEW PLANT TEAMS

A large, well-established company with corporate offices in Pittsburgh had reached a mature stage of organizational functioning. Knowing, however, that such maturity cannot be automatically transferred from a corporate entity to its divisions or units, the leaders of this company developed an organizational development process where manpower planning and the creation of new plants was concerned.

The basic approach in the process was an analysis of the overall manpower development requirements of the new plant organization; identification of the specific training needs of the various groups, with consideration for individual member needs; and the preparation of a well-integrated plan tailored to the new operations. This plan was concerned primarily with developing management and professional people and providing them with the essential training prior to the completion of the plant building. The general objective was to provide the knowledge, skills, and positive attitudes essential to the development of an effective management team capable of putting the new plant "on stream" in a new environment, within the time and financial limits designated, and of maintaining a corporate related and represented plant.

The starting of a new plant afforded management a unique opportunity for organization renewal, beginning with a nucleus of top management people, and provided effective development opportunities as additional levels of management were identified and selected.

In each of these new plants there usually were three different manpower groups that required different knowledge and skills to carry out their job.

GROUP 1.   The six top managers (the plant manager and his five key managers) of the new organization. This was a highly experienced, knowledgeable, and skilled group with differing backgrounds of experience and temperament.

GROUP 2.   The middle managers with company experience who would serve as line superintendents, general line supervisors, and key staff managers.

GROUP 3.   The third group consisted of the first-line manufacturing supervisors (normally called foremen) to be recruited in the new plant area. This group would not have company experience and would vary considerably from the standpoint of previous work experience and education. Moreover, their exposure to industrial practices and manufacturing technology was sure to be limited.

The training and development needs of each of the foregoing groups were quite different, particularly Group 3, although the objective of the personnel development plan is the same—effective management. An organization renewal plan was designed to meet the needs of each of the three groups with due consideration for both individual and teamwork needs. This plan is presented below briefly in outline form. The New Plant Manpower Development Plan consists of two distinct programs:

1. Participation in on-going courses, presented at headquarters by the Training and Development Department, in accordance with each person's individual needs.
2. Organization renewal through courses presented exclusively for new plant management.

These programs are tailored to fit the needs of each of the three groups, as follows:

I. PERSONAL DEVELOPMENT PROGRAM FOR GROUP 1
   1. Those of the top six who had not participated in the Corporate Policy Course, Business Management Courses, and Profit Planning and Financial Statements Workshop presented at headquarters were encouraged to do so at the earliest possible date.
   2. Participation of the plant manager was provided for in a problem-solving and decision-making skills course scheduled for all division managers.
II. ORGANIZATION DEVELOPMENT PROGRAM FOR GROUP 1 AND GROUP 2
   1. *Organization development workshop—effective team relations* (one week). The workshop was focused on such matters as (a) the human relations problem of starting a new plant, (b) developing positive attitudes in management of people in the new plant environment, and (c) self-understanding and development of interpersonal and intergroup skills. This workshop was presented by the Training and Development Department under the direction of a highly competent trainer-consultant. It is a live-in program held at an appropriate location away from the plant site.
   2. *Problem-solving and decision-making* (five days).
   3. *Management by objectives* (six two-hour sessions). This course coordinated the objective-setting process so that individual objectives would be in line with the objectives of the division. The mutual establishment of objectives by managers and their subordinate managers provided involvement of all members of the

management team; and thus secured commitment. An integral part of this process was a realistic basis for performance appraisal and individual performance improvement.

III. ORGANIZATIONAL DEVELOPMENT PROGRAM FOR GROUP 2

1. *Management principles, policies, and practices* (three days). This course was designed to orient the middle managers with the policies and practices to be established at the new plant.

2. *Effective communications* (five two-hour sessions). This was a well-designed, color film, discussion course, presented by local leaders who had participated in a Leader Training Institute. It not only provided skills in communications but also focused on the important fact that meanings are in people, not in words. This was significant in that company-experienced managers and new supervisors employed locally may interpret the same words and instructions differently.

3. *Conducting small group meetings with subordinates and work place meetings.* Consisted of the principles and techniques of conducting group meetings. This course was presented by the local training supervisor or line manager.

IV. TRAINING AND DEVELOPMENT FOR GROUP 3. The training of the first-level supervisory force living locally required special approaches. Since they would undoubtedly be selected over a period of weeks, a time interval would lapse between the selection of the first man and the formation of an optimum group for conducting training sessions. Following proper orientation by the man's superior, the supervisor was scheduled to participate in the next presentation of "Manufacturing Management—Principles and Application" or "Management Techniques," presented periodically by the Training and Development Department at headquarters. This course was presented under the direction of the Training and Development Department with the assistance of a trainer-consultant and the industrial relations manager and training supervisor of the new plant. When a sufficient number of the first-line supervisors had been employed, the following courses were presented at the new plant:

1. *Management principles, skills, and techniques course* (three days). This course was designed to provide the first-level line supervisor with an understanding of the work of a manager. Areas of discussion included the functions and responsibilities of a manager with particular emphasis on the development of skills in human relations and the motivation of people. The objectives of the course were the improvement of supervisory performance in the attainment of results and the maintenance of good employee relations.

2. *New plant policies and practices course* (three days). This course, similar to that presented to the middle managers, was tailored to

the needs of the first-level supervisor. Its purpose was to provide the new supervisors with specific information on the policies and practices under which the new plant would operate.

3. *Management by objectives workshop* (three half days). This workshop was a variation of the program presented to Groups 1 and 2. It aimed to provide the first-level line supervisor with an understanding of the concept of management by objectives and the process he would be involved in with his superiors. It was presented by local top management with the assistance of the training supervisor.

The foregoing three local courses provided a new supervisor with an overall understanding of three dimensions of his job; namely, management of people, specific new plant policies, and the concept of management by objectives. Upon completion of these courses, he needed training in greater depth in certain aspects of his job:

Job instruction training
Effective communication
Conducting small group meetings
Wage payment plan
Accident prevention
Budgets and shop accounting

Upon completion of the organizational development courses outlined above, individuals were scheduled to participate in appropriate headquarters courses presented by the Training and Development Department. While it was highly beneficial for the new plant supervisor to work with other members of the immediate team in a learning design, it was also deemed advantageous to get a broader perspective through association with their counterparts in other company divisions in programs presented by headquarters.

The presentation of the various elements of this new plant manager development plan was sequenced to coordinate with workloads and with the overall plans of the new plant management.

The key resource in this plan of developing effective new plant organizations rested with the Training and Development Department. This department provided special services to the management of new plants:

1. Consultation, identification of needs, and the development of a plan for the training of management and professional personnel.
2. Program design and course preparation tailored to fit the needs of the new plants.
3. Standard programs designed to meet a wide range of needs. Certain of the courses were designed for local presentation; others were

presented at headquarters by the Training and Development Department.

This organization renewal process has been put into action in nine new plants. Comment by plant management, corporate management, and Training and Development Department staff indicates that such a program is creating renewal potential in new sub-systems of a large corporation.

THE CASE OF THE ELUSIVE RELEVANCE

The purpose of this organization renewal process is to identify the crucial forces and directions of society for the nineteen-seventies and to determine the organizational implications of these future developments.

A face-to-face consultation was held in which members of the organization research council and key lay and staff leaders, together with the social scientist consultants, reacted to projections of the future program direction. The consultants will not make decisions, but rather will seek to clarify the various alternatives which will confront the organization in the next ten years, and to identify the program directions implied in each alternative. Following this consultation, two pamphlets were published, describing the results of the steps to date. One pamphlet contains the social scientist consultants' projections and their identification of crucial issues in American society for the nineteen-seventies; the second pamphlet summarizes the work of the consultation, clarifying the alternatives confronting the organization in the next decade and the programmatic implications of each alternative.

The national board of the organization is vitally concerned that its total organizational resources be committed to producing programs that are relevant to the fast changing needs of its constituents. This means giving high priority immediately to analyzing the factors of change, to testing present program emphases in the field, to making long-range decisions based on projections for the future, and to marshalling all available resources for effective planning and implementation of new program directions in the seventies.

In planning the kind of an organization it will be in the nineteen-seventies it is important that the organization not only consider the problems that it will face in that decade, but also enumerate its own best responses to these problems on a national basis and how to start on them. It will be necessary to:

Identify changes in the social order which do or may affect the organization's basic values and traditional roles.

Determine, by discovery or design, the most effective organizational responses, in terms of program and services, to these changed conditions.

Recommend ways in which 1,725 local units of the organization can work most effectively with their own potential constituencies, using all available relevant resources in terms of programs and services.

This renewal project will include five key elements: (1) analyzing current and future projections and exploring implications to the organization of crucial issues in American society, (2) examining roadblocks, resources, and capabilities in program services and organizational functioning which effect relevant organization response, (3) evaluating existing and potential program and organizational innovations, (4) setting targets for local unit self-renewal and improvement, and (5) securing directives from local units as to possible goals for the total organization in meeting national issues and concerns. It will involve members and staff in all sub-systems, from metropolitan as well as smaller communities.

This project was undertaken with some basic assumptions about an organization with 4,000,000 members and operating in fifty states being capable of renewing its direction, program, and spirit:

1. The organization has the potentiality and capability within its own membership, if properly released, to bring about organizational change.
2. The organization will realize this change only if it adopts a process of confrontation, search, and coping with its many constituent groups.
3. Such a process will demand creative utilization of the process of inquiry and reassessment that will be based on sound means of involvement, communication, and concern.
4. The issues to be faced by the organization in this process shall be those that are seen as the most relevant future concerns of the society of which the organization is a part.
5. Such a process of renewal shall utilize key laymen, specialists, and staff members in all phases of organizational programs and services.
6. The 1969 Convention provides a point in time that could be used as a part of the search phase of this renewal process.
7. Such a process should identify some deadlines for target changes, so that while the process of search is neverending, it does not lead to fruitless coping.
8. Some research on the effects of this process could be built in so as to evaluate the value of the process.
9. This renewal process establishes a format, a process, and a way to function so as to keep the organization continuously a viable institution responding to the needs of society.

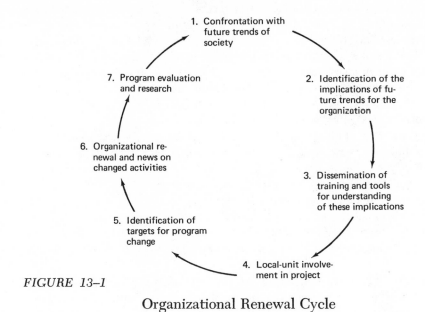

FIGURE 13–1

Organizational Renewal Cycle

These assumptions began to see action in a renewal cycle indicated in Figure 13–1.

The first step was to analyze projections of the future and to explore their implications for the organization. The input for this analysis came from a project, co-sponsored by the research department and the program department, which identified the crucial issues of the nineteen-seventies, and utilized resources from the physical and social sciences, as well as key organizational leaders. This step focused upon: (1) the critical forces in the field of education, religion, welfare, government, industry, and labor that need attention and are related to the future mission of the organization; and (2) the value questions facing the organization in terms of which issues and areas it should focus upon and respond to in the future. The essential task in this step was to develop a clear definition of goals in light of future trends in the modern and changing world. In carrying out this plan, the resources of the Center for Research on the Utilization of Scientific Knowledge of the University of Michigan were utilized. A task force from inside the organization received the predictions of the future and identified the implications for this nationwide, youth-serving agency.

The second step consisted of examining roadblocks, resources, and capabilities in the area of program service and organizational functioning which affect organizational response to social change. In this step, critical account was taken of the perceptions, readiness, and capacity of the organization to meet changes in the social order which affect its basic values and traditional roles. A process will be employed, e.g., Force Field Analysis, in order to see both sides of the picture and to provide a mechanism for tackling the problem and making changes for the future. Through this process the value alternatives and potentials will be confronted and examined for new directions for the organization in all phases of its program and organizational resources.

The third step of the project is aimed at locating program innovations and evaluating their usefulness in improving conventional programs and establishing new programs. It will consist of a systematic retrieval of program experimentation carried on by local units as well as other organizations which might provide clues as to what the organization should be and the directions in which it should go. An objective will be to identify the creative deviants "who are taking the present in hand and changing it" in attempting to respond more relevantly to changed conditions.

Step four will utilize a system of partner units of the organization, pairing local units of similar size and fairly close geographical proximity. Under competent direction and through a designed process including both group and individual involvement, present program innovations will be located and studied, and targets set for self-renewal and improvement at both local and national levels. These will include programs that involve teenagers and sub-teenagers, young adults and adults, as well as services to specialized groups such as students and the armed services. It will also include locating new organizational patterns and evaluating their usefulness in improving program performance. Testing will be carried on in small cities as well as in large metropolitan centers. Major emphasis will be placed on programs in the urban centers where the organization is committed to long-term, continuous service.

A project planning task force will develop background material and a series of probing questions to assist local units to become aware of the importance of the decisions for the future.

The partner system will be used to identify and screen existing innovations in present program practice for on-site evaluation by the project task force. This process will utilize self-study instruments which will help local units analyze current and future projections and explore their implications. It will also help set targets for local program renewal. A consultant was engaged to help develop the resource materials and design the process.

In June 1969, the organization will hold its first national convention, at which the focus will be upon the nineteen-seventies. It is expected that the convention will present some of the critical problems the organization will face in the next decade. In addition, how the organization could begin to respond to these problems will be indicated; and the data produced by this self-study process will be analyzed and interpreted by the staff of national headquarters. The local units will share their findings and targets for program change.

Thereafter, the targets set by local units will be implemented and put into action. In this connection, the competencies and resources of all divisions and departments of the national board and its regional organizations will be made available. Experimental models, based on the nineteen-seventies, will be developed, tested, and presented to all local units for adaptation to their local communities wherever appropriate.

This organization renewal project is seen as extending over two and one-half years and will present an excellent opportunity for the leadership of the organization, both lay and professional, to begin examining the present course upon which the organization is directed, and try, at least to some degree, to make some choice of direction. In addition, it may be possible to exercise some measure of control, thus attempting to shape the nature of future program development rather than have it shaped by conditions over which it exercises no control.

SUMMARY

In each of these cases we see major attempts to initiate planned change in the way an organization functions, achieves its objectives, and grows to a potentially higher level of maturity. Each situation involves a realistic "facing up" to the problems in organizational life. Without such direct problem-solving, these examples would not qualify as examples of organization renewal. In reporting another exciting example of the renewal process in the organization, Sheldon Davis [8] says:

> There is no real growth—there is no real development—in the organization or in the individuals within it if they do not confront and deal directly with their problems. They can get together and share feelings, but if that is all they do, it is merely a catharsis. While this is useful, it has relatively minimal usefulness compared with what can happen if they start to relate differently within the organizational setting around task issues.

In each of these cases the people in the organization are trying to cope with real problems. Other practitioners and social scientists have seen the implications of team building, a task group, problem-solving, and confrontation as the necessary ingredient in organization renewal. Such authors as Robert Golemblewski and Arthur Blumberg [9, 10] have related this process to complex organizations. Robert Blake [11] has indicated the value in the extended application of his grid approach, and Richard Beckhard [12] has reported experiences in which confrontation to initiate organizational change can occur in a relatively short span of time.

In all cases, however, some one person or group has to be the stimulus at the right time, in the proper manner, and with appropriate resources. If an organization is struggling for birth and survival, it may not be ready for the renewal process, although the dynamics of survival could very well be aided by reality confrontation. Conditions for renewal seemed appropriate in the examples cited.

NOTES

1. Robert Graves, in *The Daily Express,* London, 1961. Reprinted by permission of Collins-Knowlton-Wing, Inc. Copyright © 1961 by Robert Graves.
2. This portion of the chapter is taken from Gordon L. Lippitt, "Consulting With a National Organization: A Case Study," *Journal of Social Issues,* Vol. XV, No. 2, 1959, pp. 20–27.
3. This portion of the chapter is taken from Drexel Sprecher and Lippitt, "Management Development in the Federal Government," *ASTD Journal,* April, 1964, pp. 8–16. Reproduced by special permission. Copyright 1964 by the American Society for Training and Development, Inc.
4. The Hon. John W. Macy, Jr., "University-Federal Cooperation in Career Development," *Higher Education,* January–February, 1962.
5. Statement to the Cabinet, December 11, 1963.
6. Warren G. Bennis, "Toward a 'Truly' Scientific Management: The Concept of Organizational Health," Yearbook of the Society for General System Research, Vol. VII, 1962.
7. Matthew B. Miles, *Learning to Work in Groups,* Columbia University, New York, 1959, p. 38.
8. Sheldon A. Davis, "An Organic Problem-solving Method of Organizational Change," *Journal of Applied Behavioral Science,* Vol. 3, No. 1, January–February–March, 1967, p. 5.
9. Robert Golembiewski and Arthur Blumberg, "Confrontation as a Training Design in Complex Organizations," *Journal of Applied Behavioral Science,* Vol. 3, No. 4, October–November–December, 1967.
10. Golembiewski and Blumberg, "The Laboratory Approach to Organization Change: Confrontation Design," *Academy of Management Journal,* Vol. II, No. 2, June, 1968.
11. Robert Blake and Jane S. Mouton, *Grid Organization Development* (Houston, Tex.: Gulf Publishing Co., 1968).
12. Richard Beckhard, "The Confrontation Meeting," *Harvard Business Review,* March–April, 1967.

PART FIVE

Resources For Organization Renewal

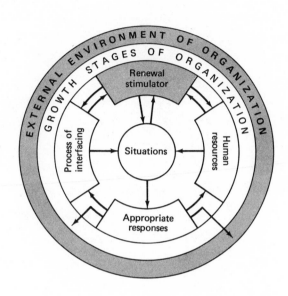

Resources for organization renewal revolve about initiative, commitment, courage, time, professional skills, creativity, and energy.

In Chapter 14 the role and function of the renewal stimulator is discussed. Chapter 15 suggests that the professional qualifications needed by specialists in organization renewal are numerous. In Chapter 16 there are expressed some of the hopes and challenges for organization renewal.

14 ROLE AND FUNCTION OF THE RENEWAL STIMULATOR

The routine of custom tends to deaden even scientific inquiry; it stands in the way of discovery and of the active scientific worker. For discovery and inquiry are synonymous as an occupation. Science is a pursuit, not a coming into possession of the immutable; new theories as points of view are more prized than discoveries that quantitatively increase the store on hand. It is relevant to the theme of domination by custom that the lecturer said the great innovators in science "are the first to fear and doubt their discoveries."

JOHN DEWEY, 1859–1952

The success of any organization renewal effort depends to a great extent on the qualifications and performance of the personnel doing the initiating and the planning.

Any individual or group that assumes responsibility for initiating, stimulating, and planning for organization renewal will be carrying out various roles and functions in the process. Whether the renewal stimulator is a key manager, supervisor, staff specialist, a special organizational development task force, or a concerned group of board members, the courage and skill of initiating renewal will require a professional approach mixed with a sense of need and commitment. The needs of modern organizations are producing an enlarging role and increased responsibility for training directors and others skilled in manpower and organizational development. In an article written by Leonard Nadler and myself [1] we explored some of the functions of the modern training director. Four major roles are performed by him in modern organizations (see Figure 14–1):

1. As a planning leader.
2. As an information and communications link.
3. As a learning specialist.
4. As a consultant to management.

It is my feeling that each of these functions requires somewhat different skills and abilities. In a small organization the renewal stimulator may perform all four functions, whereas in a larger organization the "head of a division" might well be the consultant to management for initiating change, but others will be involved in planning, data collection, and a potential learning design. It is my feeling that every renewal stimulator should exercise the initiative to be professionally prepared in *all four* roles and functions.

PLANNING LEADER.   As organizational complexity has increased, the administrative role of planning has begun to demand a major portion of the time, skill, and energy of the renewal stimulator. In this role he must apply all the administrative skills. He will need to recruit, select, and involve others in the organization; plan meetings; set up the process of coordination and communications; carry out any financial plans related to the planning for change; and all of the other functions of a leader:

The [renewal stimulator] should know the principles and practices used in the administration of programs. He should also know the concepts of management principles, including areas such as problem solving, the dynamics of organization, controls and reporting procedures.[2]

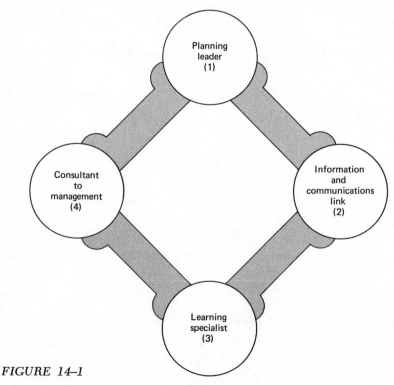

FIGURE 14–1

Key Roles of the Renewal and Development Person

But this requirement for managerial skills should not be frightening:

There is nothing esoteric or mysterious about planning as such. It is simply a description of what we want to accomplish in the future and agreement on the means for achieving it. It is an effort to arrange for the use of our resources in an orderly, economical and goal-assuring way.[3]

Dr. Lowell Hattery[4] points out in his monograph, *Planning for Achieving Goals*, that these are the eight steps in the planning process:

1. Agreeing on and understanding the goals of the organization.
2. Gathering information on the nature of the current situation, prospective available resources, and future requirements (forecasting).
3. Involving others in the process.
4. Diagnosing needs and setting planning goals.
5. Choosing alternative courses of action.
6. Agreeing upon responsibility for action.
7. Preparing the final plan.
8. Getting the plan approved.

The planning function is increasing in importance within large organizational systems, and it is a critical area of skill for the sophisticated renewal stimulator.

INFORMATION AND COMMUNICATIONS LINK. In this function the renewal stimulator must serve as a seeker of information, clarifier of information, synthesizer of information, reality tester of information, provider of information, and as a communications "link" in the organization. Let us examine these functions in more detail:

1. As a *seeker* of information the renewal agent must discover the goals and expectations of his organization for the changes to be confronted. He must learn from those who are key leaders what objectives and results are desired, and who is to participate. He will want to request certain information from those who will be involved and guide the renewal efforts. He will need to seek out information from those who know about the changes to be proposed, the program to be suggested, the goals to be achieved, and whether other input-output information is necessary so that the renewal stimulator can perform the proper functions.

2. As a *clarifier* of information, he will impart to the involved people the multiplicity of ideas and information that has been collected. A renewal process in which there is no common understanding of intentions, plans, and objectives is doomed to failure.

3. As a *synthesizer* of information, he will put into a proper frame of reference the different ideas and information which he obtains,

bringing it all into focus so that the goal of renewal is not a "hodge podge" of conflicting ideas and parts, but becomes an integrated target with a proper sequence of events around a basic need.

4. As a *reality tester* of information and communication, he should always help his superiors, or the planning group, to see that the plans they approve are feasible, workable, and realistic. The expectation of management may not always be realistic in light of the allocated resources, or the number of persons to be involved may not make possible the proposed learning goals. Whether or not he is a professional, the renewal stimulator must assume responsibility for bringing reality into the renewal process.

5. As a *provider* of information, he will give proper information and communication to those in the organization. From his own experience and training, he should present ideas, opinions, and concepts that will be helpful in planning a successful renewal process. If he cannot do this, he is a "functionaire," and not a professional member of the management team.

6. As a *communication link* in the organization, he is the pivot for management, departmental and technical personnel, the organization specialists, and all others participating in the process. Obviously, he must be an effective communicator. To be effective, he will need to:

Be *accessible* to those who are working on the renewal process, or who will participate in it.
Develop *trust* between himself and all others concerned.
Level with people on plans and problems.
Keep the *goals* clearly in mind, and help others to do the same.
Define the *responsibilities* of others.
Develop his *listening skills.*

In this way he will find his role to be essential and one which contributes to the greater assurance of a highly successful renewal process.

LEARNING SPECIALIST. An important aspect here is the ability to use learning theory and effective educational methods to meet the needs of a renewal process in which people will learn from their experiences. People in an organization contemplating renewal will not be inspired or motivated to change, "buy" an idea, or re-look at their own functioning unless they *learn* something from having done so. In a recent paper about this need for learning sophistication, it was stated as follows:

Since the [renewal stimulator] is concerned with learning, it follows that he should be concerned with learning theory. [Renewal planners] often talk about the learning theory that underlies their efforts. However, most of us do not have a good understanding of learning theories and their application to our development efforts.[5]

The behavioral sciences in the last two decades have made major contributions in the area of learning theory, learning methods, and learning skills:

Research by the behavioral sciences in the learning process is also contributing to the successful practice of management. Recognizing that people come into a learning situation with an image of themselves as self-directing and responsible persons—not as dependent individuals—is one of the important realities to a superior trying to develop his subordinates. Also we know from behavioral science research that there are different levels of change in the development process. We know that people can increase their knowledge, insight, understanding, skills, attitudes, values, and interests; and we know that different methods are involved in developing different levels of these skills or knowledge.[6]

The responsibility of an enlightened and effective renewal stimulator is to assure himself that one or more persons engaged in the planning process is knowledgeable in the field of learning principles and practices. This should be a prerequisite for effective renewal efforts and designs, and preferably, this knowledge should be held by the renewal stimulator himself. In addition, of course, he should be knowledgeable about the tools and methods of learning to implement the goals of the renewal process. This will include the direction of certain activities, coaching the key renewal leaders, selecting correct learning targets, and utilizing the best in human and technical resources. And it goes without saying that he should always examine and improve his own skills as they relate to helping others learn how to learn. One of the great challenges to the renewal stimulator function, therefore, is the increased sophistication required in making use of the rapidly growing body of knowledge about how people learn and change, and relating this to the best of renewal efforts and resources.

CONSULTANT TO MANAGEMENT. I come now to the function I feel is the most important one in the portfolio of the renewal stimulator when he serves as a problem-solving consultant.

We have always recognized the need for management to support the renewal effort. It is not, however, the support of renewal that is the major need. The major need is for renewal to be recognized as needed and used as a valuable tool for management problem-solving, which is itself a learning process. The renewal function should serve as an example and a resource to management in the solution of problems.

The new challenge for the organization's renewal stimulator, then, is to develop his skills and role in the organization as an internal organizational consultant on problem-solving, change, and organizational development. The following are among the activities involved:

1. Helps management examine organizational problems (e.g., organizes a management meeting for problem-identification in the problem relationships between home and field office personnel).
2. Helps management examine the contribution of the proper dialogue to these problems (e.g., in relation to home and field office problems, explores with management how a conference on communication blocks might lead to problem-solving).
3. Helps examine the long- and short-range objectives of the renewal action (e.g., involves management in refining objectives and in setting goals).
4. Explores with management alternatives to renewal plans.
5. Develops, with management, the renewal plans (e.g., based on the objectives, works with a task force to develop a process with built-in evaluation rather than simply submit an independently developed plan to management for approval).
6. Explores appropriate resources to implement renewal plan (e.g., provides management with a variety of resources both inside and outside the organization. The renewal stimulator must help management to understand what each resource can contribute to effective problem-solving).
7. Provides consultation for management on evaluation and review of renewal process (e.g., evaluation must be in terms of problem-solving; working with management, the renewal stimulator must assess the current status of the problem, rather than check whether or not certain activities have been conducted).
8. Explores with management the follow-up steps necessary to reinforce problem-solving and outputs from the renewal process (e.g., encourages management to look at the implications of the steps taken so far, and to assess the current status of the organization in terms of other actions that might be necessary to follow up on implementation of the renewal process).

This "internal consultant" role is important for the changing organizations of today's society. This role will require increased professionalization and skills in the organizational development field:

In a sense everyone is a consultant. Everyone has impulses to give advice, information, or help. Teachers, parents, and friends are consultants. Specialists in management, human relations or finance are consultants. Also, everyone at times feels the need for help. In order that the consultantship between the helper and the recipient optimally meets the needs of both parties, appropriate relationships must be built. It is necessary that both

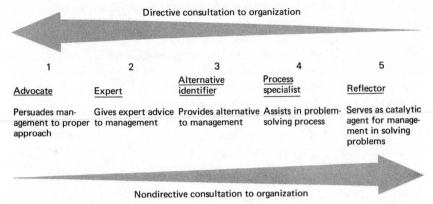

1	2	3	4	5
		Alternative	Process	
Advocate	Expert	identifier	specialist	Reflector
Persuades man-agement to proper approach	Gives expert advice to management	Provides alternative to management	Assists in problem-solving process	Serves as catalytic agent for manage-ment in solving problems

FIGURE 14–2

Multiple Consulting Approaches of the Renewal Stimulator

parties have certain kinds of skills, knowledge, and awareness in order to establish these relationships.[7]

It is my feeling that more attention needs to be given by management to selecting and developing specialists who have the necessary skills. As Richard Beckhard [8] puts it:

> The consultant (or person in a helping role) always enters such a relation-ship as a person with authority achieved either through position or role in the organization or through the possession of specialized knowledge. To achieve an effective consultative relationship, it is essential that he under-stand the nature of this power and develop skills to use it in a way which will be viewed as helpful by the person receiving the help.
>
> A person entering a consulting or helping relationship must have the ability to diagnose the problem and goals of the person being helped, and be able to assess realistically his own resources to help in the particular situation.

In carrying out a "helping" relationship to management, a renewal stimulator will find himself operating along the continuum of consulting roles shown in Figure 14–2. Here I have illustrated some of the major helping relationships from directive to primarily nondirective consulta-tions.

POSITION 1: ADVISES MANAGEMENT OF A PROPER APPROACH.   In cer-tain circumstances management may be attempting to solve a problem by using a medium or method which the renewal stimulator, from his professional experience, feels will not work. He may need to use his best persuasive skills, especially if time is short, to convince manage-ment not to use that particular approach.

POSITION 2: GIVES EXPERT ADVICE TO MANAGEMENT.   There will be occasions when organizational management will expect the renewal stimulator to answer a technical question; for example, a question about the value of a certain kind of activity and its utilization to the organization in moving toward the next stage of its growth needs.

POSITION 3: PROVIDES ALTERNATIVES TO MANAGEMENT.   The renewal stimulator may offer alternatives to management in the solution of a major organization problem. The situation is not one in which he is the implementer of a solution, but one where he recognizes the values of identifying alternatives for management in confronting the learning aspect of a problem and the various implications for organizational functioning.

POSITION 4: ASSISTS IN PROBLEM-SOLVING PROCESS.   In this situation, the renewal stimulator serves as a process specialist and consultant to management. He does not get involved in the "content" of the problem, which may be outside his area of competence. Rather, he helps management maintain the quality of its process, problem-solving, and planning through his skill as a specialist in the area of interpersonal relations.

POSITION 5: SERVES AS CATALYST FOR MANAGEMENT PROBLEM-SOLVING. In this last category, the renewal stimulator may only ask questions for management to take into account as it considers a certain direction, action, or policy.

The choice of which position to take at any given time as a consultant to one's own management is conditioned by these factors:

THE RENEWAL STIMULATOR AS A PERSON.   His skill as a consultant may be related to his academic background, knowledge of certain aspects of management, experience in the present organization, or interpersonal skills. The latter is related to his own self-concept and personal sincerity. Effectiveness as an internal consultant can be blocked by:

- *Overeagerness.* The need to establish one's credentials as a helper may precipitate helping action prior to clarification of the problem or before management is ready to confront the need for organization renewal.
- *Blowing off.* Sometimes as a reaction to his own uncertainty regarding his expertness, or for his own gratification, the internal consultant makes a great display of his talents but fails to aid his organization.
- *Competition.* If there is someone in the group who can help or do the appropriate thing as well or better, one is tempted not to accept such a person, or to find a fatal flaw in what he does.

These natural blocks are very human, but very disastrous to effectively initiating this renewal process. They often keep a renewal stimulator from choosing the appropriate consultant role.

THE RELATIONSHIP BETWEEN MANAGEMENT AND THE RENEWAL STIMULATOR. The choice of which response is appropriate to a particular consultation situation is affected by the status of the internal consultant in the organization, his previous role in organizational problem-solving, and his previous successes and failures in working with various elements of the organization. Some of the reactions from others in management that may block effective utilization of the renewal stimulator might be as follows:

- *Competitive.* Even though management might have taken the initiative in seeking assistance, the organization's leaders may feel compelled to demonstrate that they have been successful by rejecting suggestions or otherwise denying the need for help.
- *Challenging.* Often management experiences feelings of guilt at having to seek help and responds by posing unanswerable questions.
- *Fearful.* In many consultation situations, management must confide in people in the organization, but does not trust them enough to "open up."
- *Passive.* Sometimes the managers of an organization feel and express their discomfort at being placed in the position of needing renewal by reacting in a completely uninvolved and uncommitted way. This demonstrates to others and to themselves that nothing can be done without their collaboration.

These adverse responses are typical in the organization where the need for renewal is not recognized, but they also involve the ability of the renewal stimulator to develop a readiness for confrontation, search, and coping.

Some of the factors affecting the choice of consultant roles will be related to the nature of the need for organization renewal. If the basic problem is one which might require a long process of help, the consulting role might be more to the right on the continuum shown in Figure 14-3. If it is a problem that requires immediate confrontation, a more direct response may be called for. In addition, the internal consultant's knowledge about the major issue will govern the appropriate role response. If an organization must confront the possible use of corporate funds to meet certain social responsibility needs, a renewal stimulator who is not a corporate financial expert may contribute as a process specialist, but not as an expert.

In summary, I see the consultant role of the renewal stimulator as one in which a concerned specialist sets out to help his own organization as a client with a problem. His aim should be to contribute to the solution of the problem to the end that the organization's own resources have been fully used.

I have tried to present an inclusive view of the multiple roles of the renewal stimulator. With the greater demands for organizational change, increased specialization of management processes, and the increased needs of organizations, I feel all these functions are needed. In many cases, management is not aware of the potential help it has available from a competent specialist in renewal planning. It should be said, however, that many of those attempting to give leadership to organization renewal have not been creative, innovative, or professional enough to see and fulfill all four roles and functions.

NOTES

1. The present chapter is an adaptation of an article by Gordon L. Lippitt and Leonard Nadler, "Emerging Roles of the Training Director," *Training and Development Journal*, August, 1967. Reproduced by special permission. Copyright 1967 by the American Society for Training and Development, Inc.
2. Leslie E. This and Lippitt, "Learning Theories and Training," *Training and Development Journal*, April and May, 1966, p. 14.
3. Lowell H. Hattery, *Planning for Achieving Goals,* Management Series Monographs (Washington, D.C.: Leadership Resources, Inc., 1966), p. 2.
4. *Ibid.,* pp. 11–13.
5. This and Lippitt, *op. cit.,* p. 16.
6. Lippitt, "Implications of the Behavioral Sciences for Management," *Public Personnel Review,* July, 1966, p. 46.
7. Jack R. Gibb, "The Role of the Consultant," *Journal of Social Issues,* Vol. XV, No. 2, 1959, p. 1.
8. Richard Beckhard, *The Leader Looks at the Consultative Process,* Looking Into Leadership Monographs (Washington, D.C.: Leadership Resources, Inc., 1961), p. 7.

15 PROFESSIONAL QUALIFICATIONS

> The point is to simplify and to order knowledge. The profession I'm part of has as its whole function the rendering of the physical world understandable and beautiful. Otherwise, you have only tables and statistics. The measure of our success is our ability to live with this knowledge effectively, actively and, eventually, with delight. If we succeed, we will be able to cope with our knowledge and not create despair.
>
> ROBERT OPPENHEIMER, 1904–1967

As indicated previously, the process of organization renewal can be initiated almost anywhere by concerned leaders in a variety of divisions, departments, or units, but it will not get very far if it does not quickly involve and link up with other individuals and groups in the organization. Nevertheless, some individual must serve as the initiator, stimulator, or spark to set the process in action. It may be a key executive, the personnel or training director, or the marketing or systems manager. What are the qualifications required in this person? Does he have to be a behavioral scientist? Will he need to be an expert on communication systems? Does he have to be so courageous to personally strive to initiate change, at risk to his own job, that it requires a person with unusual psychological maturity? These questions are logical and understandable, and I will try to answer them.

Whoever is responsible for initiating organization renewal will need to manifest *professional* behavior and leadership. Let me point out a distinction between a profession and professional behavior. In a pamphlet issued by the Society for Personnel Administration,[1] this difference is elaborated by two definitions:

> PROFESSIONAL. A person who is in an occupation requiring a high level of training and proficiency. This person has high standards of achievement with respect to acquiring unique knowledge and skills. A person who is committed to continued study, growth, and improvement for the purpose of rendering the most effective public service. The level of training, proficiency, and ethical standards are controlled by a society or association of self-governing members. These people maintain and improve

standards and criteria for entrance and performance in the field of work or
occupation.

PROFESSIONALISM.   High level competence exhibited in action by people
in a field of work. This behavior stems from an effective integration of a
person's knowledge, skills, and attitudes which are derived from high
standards of education and experience.

It would be a prerequisite for effective renewal efforts that those giving it leadership manifest professional behavior. To understand this behavior, however, we need to see how certain professions such as
medicine, law, education, and others have tried to achieve a professional
status. In an article written by Leslie This and myself,[2] we discussed
this issue in relation to training directors.

The literature in the field of management repeatedly gives evidence
of the yearning of many management personnel for professional status.
Statements, ranging from "Wouldn't it be nice to wear a gold pin indicating membership in the Association of Mystic Management Leadership?" to impassioned, learned pleas, can be found in the pages of
professional journals, books on management, various study groups and
committees, and convention speeches. Some of the critics [3] of those in
the training and education part of management have made jibes at such
a yearning on the part of this group:

> Educationists are morbidly self conscious about the standing of their pro-
> fession. They exhort one another to be "professional minded" and each
> feels his pulse from time to time to make sure it has the right professional
> beat. Beneath it all, however, is a frightened uncertainty concerning the
> exact nature of a profession, and a desperate longing for palpable tokens of
> salvation.

Part of this mutual exhortation, of course, comes from three usually
unspoken motivations:

> Desire for financial security which professional standing promises to
>   enhance.
> Recognition and status.
> Lack of acceptance that certain jobs in management are seen as pro-
>   fessional by "outsiders" and the necessity to find solace, compassion,
>   understanding, and assurance of worth from fellow sufferers.

Too often there unfortunately seems to exist some sort of naive faith
among various management leaders that a cataclysmic change in public
opinion, an enlightened act of legislation, or a scrooge-like change in the
vice president to whom those who are engaged in training or organizational development report, will miraculously create a professional status
for them. If there is action, it usually is in the form of passing a resolution
typically worded something like this: "These are desired personal char-

acteristics, knowledges, skills, and attitudes in a specialist in organization renewal. This group affirms that we believe in them—have them—and with their passage management and the public will hereafter treat us with dignity and respect—and raise our salaries."

This phenomenon, of course, is not peculiar to those engaged in organization renewal; it is the problem of every new or emerging profession. A group striving for professional recognition recently drew up a list of desired qualities, skills, and knowledges for a credit manager, and honestly believed that when they submitted the statement to their company presidents it would make them accepted as professionals. Somewhere, at this writing, there undoubtedly is a group of sadly disillusioned and frustrated credit managers.

Those of us engaged in the field of organization renewal and development, fortunately, are now beginning to realize that we will have professional status only to the extent that we create it for ourselves. As we review many professions, we find that professional recognition frequently stems from four sources:

Persons in the profession who have skills and/or knowledges that take years to acquire, that are recognized by the public as being highly desirable and needed, and that are possessed by few in the population. Examples are the lawyer, doctor, and civil engineer.

Persons in the profession who have skills and/or knowledges that are in short supply, with the number of newcomers entering the profession rigidly limited. Certain crafts and unions are examples.

Persons in an activity that has a long history of being called a profession. The auctioneer, chimney-sweep, and circus barker are examples.

Persons who excel in any field—such as football and baseball players, jugglers, salesmen, automobile mechanics, garbage collectors, well diggers, and yoyo twirlers.

Such definitions, however, hardly serve us in trying to answer our question, "What is a profession?" The National Education Association's Division of Field Service [4] has suggested that a profession has eight criteria:

1. Involves activities essentially intellectual.
2. Commands a body of specialized knowledge.
3. Requires extended professional preparation.
4. Demands continuous in-service growth.
5. Affords a life career and permanent membership.
6. Sets up its own standards.
7. Exalts service above personal gain.
8. Has a strong, closely-knit professional organization.

Another attempt [5] to appraise the characteristics of a profession lists these criteria:

Does the profession have a well-defined function, the scope of which can be identified?

Does the profession have a philosophy, code of ethics, and other means of self-regulation which assure that its practice transcends the bounds of political, sectarian, and economic self-interest?

Does the profession have a unified pattern of organization that can speak for it with one voice?

Does the compensation received by the professional practitioners indicate that the public is willing to pay them as skilled and responsible professional workers?

Is the practice of the profession limited, or tending to be limited, to persons with approved general and professional preparations?

Is there, in fact, a recognized systematic body of knowledge, skills, and attitudes which can be identified and transmitted as a regimen of professional preparation?

Is the regimen of professional education recognized as a quality appropriate for inclusion in the graduate and professional offerings of a university?

Flexner [6] suggests that professions have still other criteria:

They involve essentially intellectual operations.
They derive their raw material from science and learning.
They work up this material to a practical and definite end.
They possess an educationally communicable technique.
They tend to self-organization.
They are becoming increasingly altruistic in motivation.

One other resource to which we might turn to help us identify the criteria of a profession is to define it. One dictionary [7] offers the following:

The occupation, if not commercial, mechanical, agricultural, or the like, to which one devotes oneself; a calling; as, the *profession* of arms, of teaching; the *three professions*, or the *learned professions*, of theology, law, and medicine.

Other criteria may need to be added to meet the peculiarities of the organizational development type of endeavor. For example, criteria to demonstrate conclusively that the development process does have a very real dollars-and-cents and quality payoff. As noted earlier, this is an area in which the training and development field is trying many approaches. Another example might be tangible demonstration that a renewal process led by a person with professional qualifications is generally more successful than when change efforts are initiated by a person with no applicable background or skills. One of the difficulties we face is that organization renewal deals in a large part with human relationships and other intangibles, and everyone in almost every organization considers himself an expert in these fields. Opposing concepts are difficult to prove or disprove because people in organizations have a way of learning dramatically even in unplanned or unorganized situations.

Current usage of the term "professional" seems to be quite casual. Anyone who specializes in a job and does it better than anyone else today seems to be entitled to the term, but such usage does not have the element mentioned above: "activities essentially intellectual." Accordingly, it seems erroneous to speak of professional football players, professional baseball players, professional rug cleaners, or professional cesspool cleaners.

The problem becomes even more frustrating when we find much evidence that employers follow this same pattern. When organizational training and development positions open, employers reach down into supervisory ranks and come up with an employee who seems to be able to do an ambiguous something better than any other supervisor—and we then have an organizational development director or training specialist. What it is this supervisor can do better than any other supervisor no one really can identify.

Unfortunately, as one of the criteria suggests—*Does the compensation received by the professional practitioner indicate that the public is willing to pay him as a skilled and professional worker?*—the customers who control the destiny of development specialists are not the public. Specialists have to sell themselves to vice presidents, company chairmen, and other organization leaders. What they possess must be seen and recognized by management as being something unique and worthwhile, and in achieving this, those nearest to true professionalism probably have a long way to go, for example, witness much of the activity that shows how more standard types of training activity can be measured and proved to be cost-reducing. Too often, management sees those who espouse organization renewal as only self-termed experts who would put new wine in old wineskins.

I should like to address myself to the one criterion that appears in each of the definitions quoted: *The profession has a body of specialized knowledge.* It is my feeling that those involved in organizational change have had too limited a concept of the content encompassed in doing such a complex job. I remember the time when mastery of role playing, the "buzz session" method, and Job Instruction Training were considered pretty adequate background for a training director. Although the training profession has come a long way from those early days, it has not yet come up with an acceptable outline of educational background for persons in the training and development field. It seems to me that the following are essential areas of professional competence for the renewal specialist:

1. The ability to utilize appropriate findings from behavioral sciences.
2. An understanding of organizational dynamics and growth.
3. A working knowledge of informational and structural systems.
4. The understanding of a working knowledge about personality growth and development.
5. The ability to develop learning experiences based on research findings.
6. The ability to design change-growth-type learning experiences.
7. The ability to accomplish further research on the organizational change.
8. The development of a philosophy of organizational change and growth related to our present knowledge of the individual, the group, the organization, and the community in which we live.
9. A good working knowledge of accepted methods and techniques, and the ability to utilize them effectively in the design of an organization renewal process.
10. The ability to plan and work with people in the organization on effective, immediate, and long-range organization renewal efforts.
11. The ability to do—to teach, train, develop others. It is particularly important, I think, to be able to train trainers who can spread the development and renewal process throughout the organization.

If these areas are accepted as being essential to professional competency, we ought then to take a look at some of the significant contributions the behavioral and management sciences can make:

PSYCHIATRY.   An understanding of individual dynamics, derivations, and the limits of training for the "average" and "normal."

GENERAL PSYCHOLOGY.   An understanding of personality growth and development.

SOCIAL PSYCHOLOGY.   An understanding of interpersonal relationships, leadership, group behavior, and change.

EDUCATIONAL PSYCHOLOGY.   An understanding of learning research, method, and theory.

BUSINESS AND PUBLIC ADMINISTRATION.   An understanding of the dynamics of organizations, systems, concepts, and the importance of policy formulation.

POLITICAL SCIENCE.   An analysis of social systems, use of power, and conflict resolution.

SOCIOLOGY.   An understanding of the forces in social systems and the role of an organization in the larger community.

ANTHROPOLOGY.   An understanding of the function of a culture and
the place of organizations as sub-cultures.

Being knowledgeable in such an array of areas may strike some renewal specialists as too unrealistic and broad an educational background.
However, there is much evidence to indicate that most of management's
disenchantment with past training and development efforts has been
created by persons who turn knobs and pull controls without adequate
understanding of the forces and factors they are trying to use. I envision
the professional renewal stimulator of the future, no matter what he may
be called, as a trained specialist of broad comprehension and ability,
rather than merely a manipulator of established methods.

Such a person will need to be competent in the four roles of planning,
communicating, consulting, and learning discussed in Chapter 14. These
roles will require a sophistication of background and experience in organizational relations that is more than "common sense" or just "book
learning." The last role as a learning specialist is stressed because if
organizational change is to be maintained, the ability to learn how to
learn must become a way of life within the organization. The renewal
stimulator, therefore, should be both comfortable and familiar with the
following knowledge about learning:

THE NATURE AND SCOPE OF THE LEARNING PROCESS.   It is much larger
than we usually assume—considerably larger than mere formal training. It embraces formal education, supervisory training on the job,
job experience itself, reading, family living, and other life experiences
where confrontation, search, and coping are involved.

THE FACTORS THAT CONDITION LEARNING.   The dissatisfaction of the
individual, group, or organization with existing behavior, readiness for
learning, supportive learning atmosphere, opportunities to get "feedback" in learning, opportunities to practice new learning, and transfer
of learning are all factors which affect the learning process. A renewal
stimulator needs to be aware of factors as they relate to the designing
of an organization renewal process, whether of a weekend management retreat or a two-year plan of diagnosing roadblocks to organizational growth.

THE FACTORS AFFECTING RESISTANCE TO LEARNING.   Threat to self-
concept about present performance, cultural inhibition about "expos-
ing inadequacies," need for emotional support during learning, and
numerous other factors give meaningful diagnostic dimensions for
persons planning change.

As can be seen from the field of learning alone, we must be up to date
on the recent studies of learning, and the effects of group size in training,
concepts of mental health for the individual and the organization, and

numerous other aspects of behavioral science research that affect this important endeavor of organization renewal.

In all our endeavors we must become *professional* in our ability. To act as a professional demands some specific standards. While there is no clear-cut set of standards for persons who assume responsibility for organization renewal, experience indicates that those who are likely to be successful will have some of the following characteristics:

PROFESSIONAL BACKGROUND.   Often people with professional preparation in one of the following fields will have attained insights helpful in preparing for the role of renewal agent: sociology, psychology, business administration, educational psychology, public administration, personnel administration, and adult education. However, because of the wide variance of skills required in organization renewal, professional preparation does *not* guarantee competence, and conversely, people can be competent without such conventional academic training. Nonetheless, some knowledge in these fields is essential to a well-rounded renewal stimulator, whether self-taught or academically learned.

GROUP EXPERIENCE.   In addition to the professional background of some kind, the renewal stimulator must meet the practical problems of learning to work successfully as a group leader. Experience with groups, however, might simply have firmed up old habits of wielding authority and afforded practice in ineffective work habits. Experience then, can be helpful or harmful, depending on its quality. Nevertheless, much of the renewal process will take place in task groups, project groups, functional units in organizations, and other similar settings.

SELF-UNDERSTANDING.   This is an absolute essential in the role of the renewal stimulator. He must have sufficient understanding of his own motivations and sufficient control of his own defense mechanisms to prevent his own needs from interfering with the renewal process and to enable him to empathize with the interpersonal problems of others in the process of change. It is also a prerequisite to be an effective internal consultant to an organization.

PERSONAL SECURITY.   Along with his organizational experience, a renewal stimulator must have sufficient personal security to permit him to take a relatively nonpunitive role in initiating change, to be accepting in his relations with others, to have a genuine respect for them, to have a willingness to share leadership roles, and to relinquish authority as the renewal process proceeds. In short, sufficient personal security to allow him to participate adequately in a rather wide range of interpersonal situations where confrontation, search, and coping is involved, will be an indispensable requirement.

MULTIPLE PROFESSIONAL SKILLS. With the proper background and maturity, one probably can learn enough planning, communication, learning, and consulting skills to carry out the complex functions involved in organization renewal. This assumes, of course, that in his professional background the person has acquired a working knowledge of the process of scientific problem-solving and social change. These skills can be acquired. Obviously, the wider his range of skills, the more effective the renewal stimulator can be in applying them appropriately in the organization renewal process.

DEMOCRATIC PHILOSOPHY. If a person can meet to a modest degree each of the above criteria, he will probably also have as part of his behavior a democratic philosophy of leadership and work. He will be able to encourage a renewal process in which persons learn for themselves. Such a philosophy will also imply a set of ethical norms that go with a democratic or collaborative planned change effort.

ABILITY TO CONCEPTUALIZE. Tackling a process with such varied forces at work will require that the renewal stimulator be able to see the larger situation, to see the organization in its totality and to see how the human, technical, structural, and economic forces interrelate. The broad prospective is a prime asset.

Organization renewal does require professional skills and behavior, but as long as it can be accomplished by persons with different and unqualified backgrounds, we cannot think of the field as *being* a profession. But there is ample indication that organization renewal, ill-defined as it is, is receiving increased acceptance. Sometimes the need for organizational change is basically accepted by management; more frequently, however, it resembles a product display I once saw. Not only was the manufacturer's line shown, but also that of each of his competitors. It was reasoned that by featuring the whole industry all manufacturers benefited more. When I asked whether there was evidence to support this rationale, I was told, "Oh, we don't know. Frankly, we're afraid to stop because we might find out that it is valid."

We in the organization renewal field cannot too long rest our professional case on this sort of evidence. Out of our huddling together, mumbling training, development, and organizational change lingo in one another's ears, and stoutly maintaining in a blunt tone, "We *are* professional," must come some beginnings, some actions, some planned charting, that will advance our efforts to make the complete arena of change and organization renewal a place where only the professionally qualified will be recognized as fully prepared to tread.

NOTES

1. Jack Epstein, *Personnel Professionalism Challenges the Status Quo* (Washington, D.C.: Society for Personnel Administration, 1965).
2. This portion of the chapter (pp. 284–291) is adapted from Gordon L. Lippitt and Leslie E. This, "Is Training a Profession?" *ASTD Journal*, April, 1960. Reproduced by special permission. Copyright 1960 by the American Society for Training and Development, Inc.
3. Arthur Bestor, *The Restoration of Learning* (New York: Alfred A. Knopf, Inc., 1955), p. 269.
4. Institute on Professional and Public Relations, "The Yardstick of a Profession," *The Association*, National Education Association, Division of Field Service, 1948, p. 8.
5. Ernest V. Hollis and Alice L. Taylor, *Social Work Education in the United States*, report of a study made for the National Council on Social Work Education (New York: Columbia University Press, 1951), pp. 109–110.
6. Abraham Flexner, "What are the Earmarks of a Profession?" in B. Othanel Smith and others, *Readings in the Social Aspects of Education* (Chicago: Interstate Printers and Publishers, Inc., 1961), pp. 553–556.
7. Webster's New Collegiate Dictionary (Springfield, Mass.: G. & C. Merriam Co., 1961), p. 674.

16 ORGANIZATION RENEWAL:
A HOPE AND CHALLENGE

We travel together, passengers on a little space ship, dependent on its vulnerable supplies of air and soil . . . preserved from annihilation only by the care, the work, and I will say the love, we give our fragile craft.

From the last speech of ADLAI STEVENSON, 1900–1965

One of the most difficult things to accomplish is the act of self-examination that can lead to self-renewal. It is a primary need, difficult to satisfy. Whether we take Socrates' admonition that "the unexamined life is not worth living," or a recent statement of HEW's former Assistant Secretary, Francis Keppel, who said, "Education is the only profession which has not had the guts to look at itself," we must recognize the universal need for renewal, including the renewal of most of man's organized efforts.

It is desirable for us to examine the ways in which organizations can increase and maintain their relevancy to the needs of the latter third of the twentieth century, ways in which organization renewal can be initiated, maintained, and evaluated. Such a process is not simple. I feel the reason more organizations do not undertake such an effort is that there exist some false assumptions about organizational change.

It is generally believed, for example, that the promotion of "good human relations" among employees is synonymous with increased morale, productivity, and effectiveness. Research finds no grounds for this assumption. Even when our intentions are right and understood, others may not like them or may consider them opposed to their own interests. Nor should we assume that face-to-face meetings and personal association will necessarily engender loyalty and mutual accord. This idea somehow survives despite persistent reports of abrasive collisions between unions and management, and despite the obvious fact that some units of an organization which constantly deal with one another also fight with one another frequently.

Such broad assumptions are an inadequate base upon which to rest decisions; for example, to expand an organization's services or to spend limited resources on a new project, we must be more specifically concerned with the total organization, where it goes, what it does, and why it does it. Organization renewal, I believe, ought to produce concentrated and continuing efforts to relate the organization's technology, structure, and people to the problems confronting the organization as it relates to the changing environment.

Organizations are caught up in the massive forces that are changing the political, social, economic, and religious life of the world today. To ignore these forces would be folly. To respond to them by executing the same old programs and services would be to ignore a responsibility. To rush into ill-conceived programs is wasteful and to be opportunistic is shallow. Any real attempt at organization renewal will need to fully comprehend the complexity of organizational life. As Harold Leavitt [1] puts it:

> This is not to say that the complexity of the organization is so great that we can never tell what will happen when we do something. It is only to say that an organization is complex enough to make any simple *structural* or *technical* or *human* model inadequate. But we have made a lot of progress in understanding the complexities in the last few decades. We now know a good deal more about ways of acting on structure or people or technology; and we know somewhat more about how they are wired to one another. There is real progress in the organizational world.

While I have attempted to give credence and reality to the interrelationship of technology, structure, and human resources, it is my contention that organization renewal should begin with a renewal stimulator who can create the climate and process in which change in the tripartite nature of organizational functioning may take place. This thesis has been well stated by others, including Eli Ginzberg: [2]

> Only men and women can develop the ideas that serve as the foundations for scientific and technologic process; only men and women—even in an age of giant computers—can manage organizations; only men and women can operate and repair the new machines which produce the goods which we desire; only men and women can provide services to the young and old, to the sick and well, to those seeking education, or recreation. Only men and women, not financial grants or ballistic missiles, determine the strength of a country.

When people in organizations become agents of change, however, they find themselves caught up in many dynamic forces and new problems. These often occur while they are still in some phase of solving the problems created by earlier changes. This is the story of every man, and it is equally the story of every organization. Both man and his organizations can tolerate variations and modifications philosophically, even gladly; crises of greater or lesser importance develop when these things result in dislocations.

No man or group of men, however empowered, can prevent change from occurring. At best they can only hasten or delay it. More importantly, they can cope with change at all only if they are aware of its nature and probable effects. In this sense, those responsible for the management of our organizations are faced with extraordinary difficulties in being always correctly informed and situationally knowledgeable. Organizational changes faithfully reflect the needs and interests of *some* of the people, but not necessarily all of them; therefore, they inevitably produce inequities. Since everything is the result of a change, the competent managers cannot afford to overlook any change whatsoever, because every change is a seed from which some part of tomorrow's organization will grow.

In presenting a conceptual model for organization renewal, illustrated in Figure 1–7, p. 20, I have focused on the circular process of appropriate problem-solving. In this model, an appropriate problem-solving response to a situation will have the following effects:

Strengthening and further developing the human sub-systems.

Furthering the use of the confrontation, search, and coping nature of the interfacing process.

Contributing to the next growth stage of the organization in its sub-unit.

Responding to the environmental forces interacting with the organization life cycle.

In planning the organization renewal effort to achieve this kind of positive recycling, some principles about planned organizational change can be formulated. Organization renewal will be most likely to succeed if the top policy-making group is involved early in the process. If they don't want change or renewal, it will be difficult, if not actually foolish, to attempt very much real change. The sanction of those high in the hierarchy lends necessary legitimization to the renewal effort. In a very real sense, the leadership for renewal should come from this group even though some of the needed technical, fact-finding, and development skills for the process may be furnished by others in middle management. In periods of rapid change, a characteristic of our present era, organizational leaders must continually study the needs and interests of the people they serve as well as those who serve them in the organization, and assess the extent to which existing organizational efforts, programs, and responses are effective in relationship to these needs and interests. They must also revise, adapt, or create new efforts to meet foreseeable new requirements, and attempt to anticipate emergencies so as to plan ways to meet them.

The responsibility of the organizational leader to determine changing organizational concerns requires channels of communication and methodical evaluation. A broad general analysis can be accomplished by using surveys, reports, statistical data, and research findings, but it is well to keep in mind that these sources are subject to arm's length interpretation which can be misleading. The wise leader will want to get closer to the major issues by consulting professionals and specialists, by taking field trips, and by being involved in appropriate formal and informal groups. Often overlooked are the sometimes significant revelations of change that come to light in careful analysis of the complaints and requests of individuals in the organization.

Once a meaningful change is tentatively indicated by any means of systematic observation, it might be verified or found to be nonexistent by informal personal contacts with the people of the organization likely to be affected. No harm is done and little expense is involved if these contacts are made to range from new to older employees of both sexes, and from the shoeshine boy to the most senior officer. It is essential, however, that such informal probes be conducted by those who can talk the particular language of the interviewee's economic position and overall outlook, and who can report accurately the tenor of comment. Certainly, true readings can be obtained only in an atmosphere of trustful rapport.

The art of organizational management is largely the ability to make accurate evaluations, to sort out true need for change from the mere chaff of minor problems—and to take timely action. Timely action requires not only the recognition of change, but informed judgment as to its likely effects, readiness of the organization to adjust to it, and adequate resources to deal with it. Management may be well aware of change, and still unable to do anything much about it for want of resources, skills, or other circumstances beyond their control. But this is quite different from being ignorant of change, and thus unable even to advise of its approach until it has perhaps resulted in real crisis.

Organizational change can frequently be initiated best where some stress, conflict, and strain exist, and organization renewal is most frequently needed when a dissatisfaction with the *status quo* is felt by individuals and groups. In this time of demonstrations, sit-ins, and other anti-establishment attempts to enforce change, we see the extreme of confrontation. The concern or problem becomes a motivating factor for change in the system. In diagnosing the possibility of change, it is almost always desirable to assess the degree of stress and strain at points where change is sought; but the renewal stimulator should evaluate whether beginning change at the point of *greatest* stress is the most effective initiating point.

A significant overcoming of resistant forces will be achieved once the workers in an organization agree to partake in investigation and shared fact-finding regarding their mutual working problems and interpersonal relationships. Although this will be enhanced by the use of professional resources from without the organization, participation by those to be affected by resultant change is essential and it increases the likelihood that new insights will be formed and that the goals and methods of planned change will be accepted. In this light, professional diagnosis and prescription is usually more accurate and beneficial if the people who are to be affected by change can also be trained in fact-finding and fact-interpreting methods prior to the introduction of actual problem-solving processes. The process of search is added to confrontation.

One question frequently asked is whether it is reasonable to expect that meaningful change *can* be planned. Are not those involved more often the unaware victims or beneficiaries of unplanned change in the situations in which they work? Are they not even unaware of the very factors that affect the direction of change? Are not most of these factors, even when recognized, beyond their control, originating in changes in the larger societal system of which their organization is only a part?

To some extent, of course, this is all too true. But change—or resistance to change—sometimes may stem from the members themselves, as well as from the personality of leadership, unknown to both. And there are personality factors which can be remodeled, although this frequently requires therapeutic processes not ordinarily available. Nevertheless, conceding these facts, the members and leaders of organizations owe it to themselves to know what causes change, and to adjust to those factors that cannot be controlled. The dynamic forces of science, technology, and intercultural relationships make change unavoidable, but this does not mean that change cannot be brought into more planned perspective and dealt with rationally, in a planned fashion.

It is one of the characteristics of ineptly planned change that it is often directed toward the alteration of a sub-system without adequate consideration of the relevant aspects of the whole system. Normally, the result is lowered morale. Diagnosis and preplanning demands a deeper examination. Similarly, diagnosis must look at the informal as well as the formal organization, at the network of cliques and groupings which extend powerful influences for or against change initiated by higher authority. No lasting change is likely to be effected unless this power is successfully harnessed, but this requires the particular knowledge, skills, ingenuity, sensitivity, and flexibility more often found in the professional renewal stimulator than in the average manager.

Two examples will serve to illustrate the effect of, first, changing a sub-system within an organization and, second, changing only one level of a hierarchy:

> The manager of the central office of a large school system wants to increase the efficiency of the secretarial forces by placing private secretaries in a pool. It is the manager's hope that the new arrangement will make for

better utilization of the secretaries' time. In this situation at least two driving forces are obvious: fewer secretaries can serve a larger number of sub-executives; a substantial saving can be expected in office space and equipment. Among the restraining forces are the secretaries' resistance to a surrender of their personal relationship with a status person, a relationship implicit in the role of private secretary; the possible loss of the prestige implicit in the one-to-one secretary-boss relationship; the prospective de-humanization, as the secretaries see it, of their task; and a probable in-crease in workload. Acceptance of this change in role and relationship would require accompanying changes in other parts of the subsystem. Furthermore, before the private secretaries could wholeheartedly accept the change, their bosses as well as lower-status clerks and typists in the central office would have to accept the alteration in the secretarial role as one that did not necessarily imply an undesirable change in status. The secretaries' morale would surely be affected if secretaries in other parts of the school system, secretaries to principals in school buildings, for example, were not also assigned to a pool.

Thus, to plan changes in one part of a subsystem, in this case in the central office of the school system, eventually involves consideration of changes in overlapping parts of the system—the clerical force, the people accustomed to private secretaries, and others as well.[3]

Shortly after World War II, the United States Army decided to change the role of the sergeancy. The sergeant was not to be the traditional tough driver of men but a supportive, counseling leader. The traditional view of the sergeant's role was held by enlisted men, below the rank of sergeant, as well as by second lieutenants, above the rank of sergeant.

Among the driving forces for change were the need to transform the pre-war career army into a new peacetime military establishment com-posed largely of conscripts; the perceived need to reduce the gap between military life and civilian status; and the desire to avoid any excesses in the new army that might cause the electorate to urge a return to the pre-war volunteer military establishment.

Among the immediate restraining forces were the traditional authoritarian role behaviors of the sergeancy, forged by wartime needs and peacetime barracks service. These behaviors were in harmony with the needs of a military establishment that by its very nature is based on the motion of a clearly defined chain of command. Implicit in such a hierarchy are orders, not persuasion; unquestioning obedience, not critical questioning of deci-sions. Also serving as a powerful restraining force was the need for social distance between ranks in order to restrict friendly interaction between levels.

When attempts were made to change the sergeant's role, it was dis-covered that the second lieutenant's role, at the next higher level, also had to be altered. No longer could the second lieutenant use the authority of the chain-of-command system in precisely the same way as before. Just as the sergeant could no longer operate on the principles of unquestioning obedience to his orders, so the second lieutenant could no longer depend on the sergeant to pass orders downward without question. It was soon seen that, if the changed role of the sergeant was to be stabilized, the second lieutenant's role would also have to be revised.

The role of the enlisted man also had to be altered significantly. Inculcated with the habit of responding unquestioningly to the commands of his superiors, especially the sergeant, the enlisted man found the new permissiveness somewhat disturbing. On the one hand, the enlisted man welcomed being treated more like a civilian and less like a soldier. On the other hand, he felt a need for an authoritative spokesman who represented the army unequivocally. The two needs created considerable conflict. An interesting side effect, which illustrates the need of the enlisted man for an authoritative spokesman for the army, was the development of greater authority in the rank of corporal, the rank between private and sergeant.[4]

In Chapter 1, I discussed my "E" Concept of leadership which is based on the existential nature of the capable professional manager. In subsequent chapters I discussed the role and qualifications of those responsible for organization renewal. The same person may perform both functions concurrently. Warren Bennis and Caroline McGregor titled the book they edited for Douglas McGregor, *The Professional Manager*.[5] They describe the challenge to the role of the modern professional manager in the following manner:

> For the professional manager, the magnitude of role conflict is likely to increase in one way, for the environment of the modern manager is more dynamic, turbulent, and clogged than that of his counterpart operating in the relatively stable and more certain world of the nineteenth century. More is expected of him. Not only is he expected to operate an efficient enterprise at a reasonable profit; he is also expected to possess interpersonal competence and extensive skills in a wide variety of management sciences, such as statistics, economics, and linear programming. In another way, the conflict is more bearable precisely because management is emerging as a well-defined profession based on the behavior and management sciences. The new role of the professional manager, anchored in many disciplines, can help to provide security, and continuity in a rapidly changing world.

This kind of managerial role as a professional is a continuing challenge for the individual, but there is also another challenge I would like to offer for consideration. This challenge is related to why an organization should strive through the continuing renewal cycle to achieve the maturity stage of organizational growth—that is, the stage concerned with the contribution of a socio-technical system to the larger society, including one's own field or industry and the community, state, nation, and world community.

One of the major reasons for organization renewal is the continued growth of the organization to maturity. In my mind, the need for the organization to be relevant to its environment requires that continued growth. A major factor of relevancy in the modern world is the *social responsibility* of the organization. Many a leader is now recognizing that the total society is the environment in which an organization exists. Modern problems call upon it to be relevant to the solution of these problems. As one leading businessman [6] put it:

> A new kind of corporate statesmanship is required. The new corporate statesman does not believe that it is his job to manipulate his community into meek acceptance of the corporation's private and selfish goals. Rather, he accepts his full share of responsibility, not only for the products he markets, but for the schools we operate, the air we breathe, the water we drink, the government we support, the pictures in our museums, the music in our concert halls, the health of our citizens, the peace and tranquility of our neighborhoods, the health and viability of our communities—in short, he accepts his share of responsibility for the environment in which he operates. And he brings to all these community needs the full weight of his company's knowledge, experience, and resources—knowing that tomorrow's balance sheet cannot be separated from the quality of our community life.

We all face relatively large or relatively small problems within our organization, but we cannot be concerned solely with so narrow a world. Each community, national and international situation, private and public, justifies recall of the words of the poet John Donne: ". . . *I am involved in Mankind: And therefore never send to know for whom the bell tolls; It tolls for Thee.*" It may be well worth our while to examine a few of our acts on this broader stage.

For an organization renewal effort taking place in a professional organization, The American Society for Training and Development, a task force of which I was co-chairman, developed a list of some of the key issues that confront society and their implications for modern organizations:

> AFFLUENT SOCIETY.   The per capita income of a family in the United States was $2,940 in 1966—about $1,000 higher than it had been ten years earlier. The Gross National Product in 1966 amounted to about $740 billion, as compared to about $400 billion in 1955. A high percentage of American citizens have never had any adult experience with a severe depression.
>
> CHANGES IN VALUE SYSTEMS.   Individual values are shaped by the kinds of experiences people have. The affluent society, the world climate, and technological developments all have influenced the value system of members of our society.
>
> GAP BETWEEN AFFLUENT AND POOR.   Despite the fact that we are an affluent society, there is still a sizeable portion of our population not

in the mainstream of this affluence. For example, the U.S. Riot Commission reports that "Negro family income is not keeping pace with white family income growth. In constant 1965 dollars, median nonwhite income in 1947 was $2,174 lower than white median income. By 1966, the gap had grown to $3,036." In spite of our affluent society, thirty million people still have inadequate income for a proper living standard.

GROWING IMPORTANCE OF YOUNG PEOPLE AND MINORITY GROUPS. Fully one-half of our population is now under age twenty-five. In recent years we have thus had more and more young people entering the work force. The growing importance of minority groups is related to the desire of these groups to become a part of the mainstream of American economic and social life. Thousands of firms who have never hired blacks before are now hiring blacks at a rapid rate. This past summer the National Alliance of Businessmen, under the leadership of Henry Ford, II, began sponsoring a program to hire 500,000 hardcore unemployed by June 1971. This development creates some sizeable challenges for training and organization renewal.

INFLUENCE OF LOCAL, STATE, AND FEDERAL GOVERNMENTS. Influence of governments in part results from the growing complexity of our society. The problems are so vast and encompass so many kinds of people that governments must almost inevitably become involved in their identification and solution. The problems cut across industry functions, and even geographical units.

GROWTH IN NUMBER AND KIND OF POWER CENTERS. Society is characterized today by bigness—governments, businesses, colleges, and universities. Everything is vast. This creates concentration of power, which significantly demands an on-going attempt to achieve organization renewal.

INFLUENCE OF MASS MEDIA. The influence of mass media, and particularly television, has had an impact on the energizing environment. Probably this development has shaped the value systems discussed above. The mass media has enabled us, for better or worse, to witness in recent months and years the assassination of our leaders, to go through the agony of burial, and to witness with what amounts to a front row seat a war that is taking place thousands of miles from home.

SHIFT FROM PRODUCTION TO SERVICE ECONOMY. In 1956, for the first time in any industrial society, the number of white collar workers outnumbered the employees in blue collar jobs. This trend has continued. Service occupations are increasing in percentage while production occupations are declining.

TECHNOLOGICAL CHANGE. The impact of technological change is evident from the amount of money spent on research and development; in 1965 this amounted to about $20.5 billion as compared with about $6.3 billion spent in 1955, ten years earlier.

CONTINUING EDUCATION. The idea is growing, and properly so, that education is not just for the young. Symbolizing this changing concept is the fact that centers for continuing education are being established at schools throughout the country, and that there is today a greater demand for adult education programs. Professional people require the latter to avoid technological obsolescence. Others need it to prepare for a new role in a changing society, and many others are simply interested in self-improvement. But it is becoming abundantly clear that education is a lifetime proposition.

INCREASED INTERNATIONAL INTERDEPENDENCE. The major aspect of the international environment now is that events taking place in one nation have a profound influence on nations elsewhere. For example, the gold crises in the United States caused widespread repercussions in Europe; and the French riots in the spring of 1968 were of deep concern throughout the world. Further, many American companies have become internationally involved. *Life* Magazine (November 24, 1967) reported that "American-affiliated firms have three-quarters of the European computer market, produce one-half of France's telecommunications equipment, own one-third of Germany's oil refinery capacity. In Britain, one out of every 17 persons works for a U.S.-controlled company."

CONTINUATION OF EAST-WEST CONFLICT. We are in for at least fifty years of cold war tension, according to those who have studied these matters closely. We are not going to soon resolve the East-West issue. This will continue to be an era of tension. What does this mean for organizations? Again, we are going to be a part of living history. There will continue to be people who are fearful of atomic war, because it will be a threat for a long time. People must become more aware of what to expect from themselves and others. Never has the need been so great for knowledge of behavioral sciences and religion, in order that man may better understand and cope with himself in physical, mental, and spiritual balance.

TECHNOLOGICAL REVOLUTION. The ability of man to store and retrieve information, to solve problems, and to automate routine jobs through the computer is but one of the examples of the modern marvels of science. Such advances project many potentials and problems, including a reassessment of the very concept of work.

These trends are not a complete listing of forces at work in the community of man. But they provide a background for examination of the prospective nature of the modern organization's social responsibility. An organization that is struggling for survival or putting in systems to maintain the organization will not have much of an opportunity to be immediately concerned about these issues. This is why the process of organization renewal is of high priority—so that organizations can examine themselves, their growth, and their role in the problems of their environment. The more mature the organization, the more it can contribute to the social need and not just react to the forces at work on it. Let us examine these trends for implications in carrying out organization renewal:

INCREASED NEED FOR PROFESSIONAL MANAGEMENT OF THE SOCIAL SYSTEMS IN SOCIETY.   More and larger institutions will develop in government, business, health and welfare, and religion. These expanding organizations will require effective managerial leadership, but the dearth of trained manpower will inhibit desirable growth. Training and development for effective management of these organizations will be increasingly important.

GREATER NEED FOR ORGANIZATION RENEWAL AND THE USE OF INNOVATIVE EDUCATIONAL METHODS.   To achieve social and industrial progress will require much more education. The problems of hard core unemployment and cultural adaptation will be a challenge to the ability of educational specialists to perform their tasks responsibly. It behooves organizations to examine their educational methods and procedures to see if they are the most effective for the responsibilities that lie ahead.

NEED FOR THE TRAINING OF TRAINERS.   It is quite apparent that organizations themselves will not be able to meet the need for organization renewal specialists. A high priority must be placed on the "training of trainers." Any organizational change program should have as its core responsibility the multiplication process: continuous education through transmission of experience to other persons.

NEED FOR THE PROCESS OF CONFRONTATION, SEARCH, AND COPING.   The programs of organization renewal should not be seen as a means of merely solving one vexing organizational problem. It should be seen, I believe, as a *process* of helpful confrontation, search, and coping by people so that they may learn from the solution of their own problems. Persons throughout an organization can help each other through interfacing; but interfacing is meaningful only if it involves shared confrontation.

NEED FOR EVALUATION OF ORGANIZATION RENEWAL EFFORTS.   While the process of organizational change has been carried out for many years, there has been all too little evaluation of these programs. Those involved in such experiments should examine ways to make more from their research, effort, and money.

UTILIZATION OF MULTIDISCIPLINARY AND MULTIPLE EXPERIENCE TEAMS.

The nature of today's organizational problems requires an interdisciplinary approach to their solution. In too many cases, teams of specialists focus on their own specialties and do not take advantage of the variety of experiences that could be brought to bear on the problems they confront. It seems to me that for maximum effect organization renewal efforts should represent various disciplines and backgrounds.

FOCUSING ON THE PROCESS OF CHANGE.   In planning for organization renewal, we need to apply our understanding and knowledge of the processes of change, and of the learning process. In many cases, the methods we use to initiate and manage planned change do not include our knowledge of how human beings learn, or how they are motivated, or how they change. We are not conducting renewal efforts just for the creation of good will or even of understanding through dialogue, but to bring about a favorable change in the lives of those participating as individuals, groups, and organizations. The challenge for those of us planning organization renewal is to discover capabilities for developing meaningful action which will really make a difference to the organizational systems we serve.

As never before, the world needs creative organizational leadership that is looking for new paths, new methods, and new approaches and the search for innovations that are yet to come. To accept modern technology and to use it rather than be afraid of it is essential. To see such technologies as tools to improve mankind, not to control man, is the proper attitude.

In conclusion, these words of William Faulkner are appropriate:

> What's wrong with the world is, it's not finished yet. It is not completed to the point where man can put his signature to the job and say, "It is finished. We made it, and it works."
>
> Because only man can complete it. Not God, but man. It is man's high destiny and proof of his immortality, too, that his is the choice between ending the world, effacing it from the wrong annals of time and space, and completing it. This is not only his right, but his privilege, too.
>
> Like the Phoenix, it arises from the ashes of its own failure with each generation, until it is our turn now in our flash and flicker of time and space which we call today . . . to perform this duty, accept this privilege, bear this right . . . .

Here then, is the hope and challenge of organization renewal both for ourselves, our organization, and all of the people with whom we share the earth. We will, as individuals, find the ways of interfacing best suited to ourselves. When we do, we can bring—out of the experiences of today and tomorrow—effective coping, comprehension, and confrontation for the growth of both ourselves and our organizations.

NOTES

1. Harold Leavitt, *Managerial Psychology*, 2nd ed. (Chicago: University of Chicago Press, 1964), Chapter 21.
2. Eli Ginzberg, *Human Resources* (New York: Simon and Schuster, Inc., 1958), pp. 169–170.
3. *Summer Reading Book in Human Relations Training*, National Training Laboratories Institute for Applied Behavioral Science (Washington, D.C.: NEA, 1968), p. 67. The papers for the *Summer Reading Book* were originally prepared for theory sessions at NTL's laboratories.
4. *Ibid.*, p. 68.
5. Douglas McGregor, *The Professional Manager* (New York: McGraw-Hill Book Co., Inc., 1967), p. 55.
6. Charles Y. Lazarus, a speech before a joint meeting of Beta Gamma Sigma, the American Association of Collegiate Schools of Business, and the Council of Professional Education of Business, April 20, 1968.

ANNOTATED BIBLIOGRAPHY

The references listed below are some of the books related to organizational behavior and change which I have found helpful.

APPLEWHITE, PHILIP B., *Organizational Behavior,* Series in Industrial Engineering and Management Science. Englewood Cliffs, New Jersey: Prentice-Hall, Inc., 1965, 168 pp.

Reviews the literature in organizational behavior and attempts to integrate major research findings into a meaningful whole. The vast number of topics include job satisfaction, morale, and the relationship of morale and job satisfaction to other variables; group standards; *resistance to change;* decision-making; communications; leadership; supervision and control, including supervisory orientation and the span of control. Chapters conclude with bibliographies.

ARGYRIS, CHRIS, *Integrating the Individual and the Organization.* New York: John Wiley & Sons, Inc., 1964, 286 pp.

This book is an outgrowth of Chris Argyris' earlier book entitled *Personality and Organization.* The author gives a revised view of his earlier book and then presents a preliminary theory on redesigning organizations to take human potential more fully into account. The term "psychological energy" rather than "mature" and "immature" is proposed as a more effective way of conceptualizing the individual. The author's main emphasis is how this psychological energy can be increased to serve both organizational and individual effectiveness.

ARGYRIS, CHRIS, *Some Changes of Organizational Ineffectiveness Within the Department of State.* Washington, D.C.: Center for International Systems Research, Occasional Papers No. 2, Department of State, 1967, 52 pp.

The author, as a member of an advisory committee composed of business leaders and behavioral scientists, examines the causes of effectiveness and ineffectiveness within the Department of State. Argyris analyzes this organization as a "living social system" rather than a collection of individuals. He looks at the norms and values held by Foreign Service personnel, and proceeds to analyze and evaluate these in terms of organizational effectiveness. He summarizes discussions held with Foreign Service personnel and outlines several problem areas. Eight recommendations are made for changes and alterations in the "living system" based on behavioral science research.

BASS, BERNARD M., *Organizational Psychology*. Boston: Allyn and Bacon, Inc., 1965, 459 pp.

Chapters on attitude toward work, rewards of work, motivation, supervisory behavior, working in groups, industrial organization, communications and conflicts in industrial organizations, and psychological aspects of executive decision-making.

BENNIS, WARREN G., *Changing Organizations*. New York: McGraw-Hill Book Co., Inc., 1966, 223 pp.

Part 1 identifies some important evolutionary trends in organizational development. Part 2 focuses on the ways behavioral scientists can illuminate and *direct processes of change*. Bibliographic notes at the end of each chapter.

BENNIS, WARREN G., BENNE, KENNETH D., and CHIN, R., *The Planning of Change*. New York: Holt, Rinehart and Winston, Inc., 1961, 765 pp.

A comprehensive series of readings by various authors on subjects related to planned change efforts.

BENNIS, WARREN G., and SLATER, PHILIP E., *The Temporary Society*. New York: Harper & Row, Publishers, 1968, 139 pp.

The authors make a convincing case of the need for temporary affiliations, inside and outside existing systems, with social groups that serve specific needs. Since rapid changes in contemporary society make it difficult for institutions as structures to keep pace with needs, temporary structures become necessary.

BLAKE, ROBERT R., and MOUTON, JANE S., *The Managerial Grid: Key Orientations for Achieving Production Through People*. Houston, Texas: Gulf Publishing Co., 1964.

A comparative treatment of managerial theories, offering descriptions of each and ways to change from one system of management to another, either individually or as an organization.

BLAKE, ROBERT R., and MOUTON, JANE S., *Corporate Excellence Through Grid Organization Development*. Houston, Texas: Gulf Publishing Co., 1968, 355 pp.

These two leaders in the managerial grid method have extended their six phases of change into a so-called Grid Organization Development approach where the achievement of the "9.9 model of excellence" is the goal.

BRADFORD, LELAND P., GIBB, JACK R., and BENNE, KENNETH D., *T-Group Theory and Laboratory Method: Innovation in Re-education*. New York: John Wiley & Sons, Inc., 1964, 498 pp.

Collection of essays which describe general development of laboratory training with emphasis on the Training Group. Of interest because of its recognition of value of findings and methods of behavioral sciences in effecting and reinforcing behavioral change.

DAIUTE, ROBERT JAMES, *Scientific Management and Human Relations*. New York: Holt, Rhinehart and Winston, Inc., 1964, 183 pp.

The author presents a historical look at some of the contributions of key leaders to management thinking and then relates this to the present state of the art.

DICKSON, WILLIAM J., and ROETHSLISBERGER, FRITZ J., *Counseling in an Organization: A Sequel to the Hawthorne Researches*. Boston: Graduate School of Business, Harvard University, 1966, 148 pp.

Two of the original researchers in the classic Hawthorne Study examine the resultant "counseling program" that operated for twenty years. Their analysis may be viewed as a cause study in administration with implications for the theory practice of management, personnel administration, supervision, counseling, clinical psychology, industrial psychology, and the behavioral sciences generally. Partial contents include: An Overview of Counseling and the Problems of Evaluating It; Employee Concerns at Work; Contributions of Counseling; The Ambiguity of the Counselor's Role; and The Systemic Problems of Counseling.

Education for Innovative Behavior in Executives (Cooperative Research Project No. 975). Chicago: Chicago University Center for Advanced Study in Organization Sciences, 1962, 112 pp.

Papers resulting from examination of creative executive behavior. Purpose was to: (1) study cognitive and personality variables and organizational climate as related to innovative behavior, and (2) develop experimental education programs to encourage change in behavior. Participating administrators were federal executives of grades eleven to seventeen.

FABUR, DON, *The Dynamics of Change*. Englewood Cliffs, New Jersey: Prentice-Hall, Inc., 1967, 190 pp.

This collection from a series of issues of the Kaiser Aluminum News is a well-done presentation of the changes confronting modern man.

FIEDLER, FRED E., *A Theory of Leadership Effectiveness*. New York: McGraw-Hill Book Co., Inc., 1967, 265 pp.

An excellent presentation of the author's research on leadership over a period of fifteen years.

GARDNER, JOHN W., *Self-renewal: The Individual and the Innovative Society*. New York: Harper & Row, Publishers, 1963, 141 pp.

Points to urgent need for creative people and for renewal of aging institutions and organizations to prevent bringing ". . . our civilization to moldering ruin." In discussing problems of growth, decay, and renewal, the author considers questions of educating generalists or specialists, versatility, innovation, and the conditions and obstacles of renewal.

GELLERMAN, SAUL W., *Motivation and Productivity*. New York: American Management Association, Inc., 1963, 294 pp.

The author has synthesized many studies by psychologists who have conducted research in business and industrial organizations. He has translated the findings of these studies into language more applicable and intelligible to executives. Generalized concepts about the complex motives of people are given to aid the executive in understanding some of the widely accepted conclusions relevant to motivation and productivity in business and industrial organizations. These understandings are essential for any change effort to be successful.

GOLEMBIEWSKI, ROBERT T., and GIBSON, FRANK, *Managerial Behavior and Organization Demands: Management as a Linking of Levels of Interaction*. Chicago: Rand McNally & Co., 1967, 430 pp.

An excellent collection of readings which links various approaches to management functions and organizational behavior.

GUEST, ROBERT H., *Organizational Change: A Study in Leadership*. Homewood, Illinois: Richard D. Irwin, Inc., 1962, 160 pp.

A case study presentation in which change in a situation is effected by a new plant manager.

HAIRE, MASON, *Psychology in Management*, 2nd ed. New York: McGraw-Hill Book Co., Inc., 1964, 231 pp.

This book is geared to giving the manager the most significant facts, concepts, and principles which the behavioral sciences can provide on the philosophy of human relations on the job. The principal theme is the employee's self-concept and the way he perceives his role.

HANEY, WILLIAM V., *Communication and Organizational Behavior*, rev. ed. Homewood, Illinois: Richard D. Irwin, Inc., 1967, 533 pp.

A well-written book on communication with illustrative case examples. The author presents both a logical and psychological approach to communication problems in organizations. Selected portions of the book are articles by other leading specialists in communication.

HARRIS, CHESTER W., *Problems in Measuring Change*. Madison, Wisconsin: The University of Wisconsin Press, 1963, 192 pp.

This volume contains the proceedings of a conference sponsored by the Social Science Research Council. An integrated set of twelve papers is presented which analyze the problems of assessing change and deal with various models that may be employed in resolving the problems.

HILL, WALTER A., and EGAN, DOUGLAS, *Readings in Organizational Theory: A Behavioral Approach.* Boston: Allyn and Bacon, Inc., 1966, 645 pp.

This collection of readings tends to focus on the effect different social systems, goals, and environmental factors have on the manner in which the administrative process is implemented.

HOFFER, ERIC, *The Ordeal of Change.* New York: Harper & Row, Publishers, 1963, 120 pp.

This dynamic man puts some of the world, social, community, and organizational changes into clear perspective. He pictures the hardships to be encountered in revolution and change.

HOUSE, ROBERT J., *Management Development: Design, Evaluation, and Implementation.* Ann Arbor, Michigan: University of Michigan, 1967, 125 pp.

This book provides an excellent frame of reference for critically examining many of the management development efforts now being advocated in the organization field.

JENNINGS, EUGENE E., *Executive Success: Stresses, Problems, and Adjustments.* New York: Appleton-Century-Crofts, 1967, 205 pp.

This very readable book develops some profiles of successful executive behavior out of some case examples of executives in crisis. The categories are stimulating and thought-provoking.

KATZ, DANIEL, and KAHN, ROBERT L., *The Social Psychology of Organizations.* New York: John Wiley & Sons, Inc., 1966, 498 pp.

Describes and explains the organizational processes; shifts from an earlier emphasis on traditional concepts of individual psychology and interpersonal relations to stressing systems concepts. Discusses organizations and systems concepts, the characteristics of social organizations, the development of organizational structures, organizational effectiveness and roles, power and authority, policy formulation, decision-making, leadership, and organizational change.

LAWRENCE, PAUL R., and LORSCH, JAY W., *Organization and Environment: Managing Differentiation and Integration.* Boston: Harvard Business School, 1967, 246 pp.

The authors present field research data from three industries and then compare the data with certain organizational characteristics, with particular reference to the environment in which the organization functions. This latter emphasis makes this a unique contribution.

LEAVITT, HAROLD J., *Managerial Psychology: An Introduction to Individuals, Pairs, and Groups in Organizations.* Chicago: University of Chicago Press, 1964, 437 pp.

The author integrates new ideas about people in organizations. He covers recent developments in information-and-communications theory and in decision-making models. The author believes that revolutionary concepts are needed in the theory of organization.

LEVINSON, HARRY, PRICE, CHARLTON R., MUNDEN, KENNETH J., MANDL, HAROLD J., and SALLEY, CHARLES, M., *Men, Management, and Mental Health*. Cambridge: Harvard University Press, 1963, 203 pp.

An enlightening report of studies done by the Menninger Foundation on some of the mental health problems occurring in industry and the means taken to solve them.

LIKERT, RENSIS, *The Human Organization: Its Management and Value*. New York: McGraw-Hill Book Co., Inc., 1967, 235 pp.

A leading authority in organizational behavior extends his earlier report of twenty years of research at the Institute of Social Research, University of Michigan.

LIPPITT, RONALD, WATSON, JEANNE, and WESTLEY, BRUCE, *The Dynamics of Planned Change*. New York: Harcourt, Brace & World, Inc., 1958, 298 pp.

A clear presentation of the phases of planned change with emphasis on the relationship between the "change agent" and the "client system."

LITTERER, JOSEPH A., *Organizations: Structure and Behavior*. New York: John Wiley & Sons, Inc., 1963, 416 pp.

A book of readings by various authors. The stress is on the interrelationship between the formal and informal organization. Chapter IV deals with organizational adaptation.

LITTERER, JOSEPH A., *The Analysis of Organizations*. New York: John Wiley & Sons, Inc., 1965, 460 pp.

An excellent overview of some of the concepts and methods managers would find helpful in solving organizational problems. Part Four of the book is devoted to change and adaptation.

LUPTON, TOM, *Industrial Behavior and Personnel Management* (Industrial Relation Series). London: Institute for Personnel Management, 1964, 59 pp.

Considers contribution of the behavioral sciences to understanding human behavior in organizations and their implications for the personnel administrator as a change agent. Includes Personnel Management—Applied Science or Ideology; Personnel Management and Ideology; Behavioral Science and Industrial Behavior; A New Role for the Personnel Manager.

MARROW, ALFRED J., BOWERS, D. G., and SEASHORE, STANLEY, *Management by Participation*. New York: Harper & Row, Publishers, 1967, 228 pp.

This volume gives a report and analysis of the Harwood Manufacturing Company story. It deals with the methods and effects of the employee participation activities encouraged by the company management. A case study in organization development.

McGREGOR, DOUGLAS, *The Professional Manager.* New York: McGraw-Hill Book Co., Inc., 1967.

This book, edited by Warren Bennis and Carolyn McGregor, is an extension of the author's thinking since writing *The Human Side of Enterprise.* It emphasizes that Theory "X" and Theory "Y" were not intended to be managerial style, but underlying assumptions. Stress is placed on the professional aspects of managerial leadership.

MORRIS, ROBERT, BINSTOCK, ROBERT H., and REIN, MARTIN, *Feasible Planning for Social Change.* New York: Columbia University Press, 1966, 169 pp.

Selected contents: Chapter IV, The Dynamics of Goal Development, Chapter V, Organizational Resistance to Planning Goals; Chapter VI, Overcoming Resistance Through Influence; Chapter VII, Evaluating the Feasibility of Goals; Bibliography.

O'CONNELL, JEREMIAH, *Managing Organizational Innovation.* Homewood, Illinois: Richard D. Irwin, Inc., 1968, 183 pp.

This is a case study of a change effort in a large insurance company. The data make possible an evaluation of the success of the consultant in the situation.

PRICE, JAMES L., *Organizational Effectiveness: An Inventory of Propositions.* Homewood, Illinois: Richard D. Irwin, Inc., 1968, 212 pp.

Author uses an inventory of propositions to present what behavioral sciences now know about the effectiveness of organizations. Effectiveness is defined as goal-achievement.

RUBENSTEIN, ALBERT H., and CHADWICK, J. HABERSTROH, *Some Theories of Organization,* rev. ed., Irwin-Dorsey Series in Behavioral Science. Homewood, Illinois: Richard D. Irwin, Inc., 1966, 722 pp.

Selected articles. Focuses on organizational theory as an approach to the systematic study of organization behavior. Illustrates a variety of conceptual approaches and research methods. Emphasis is on nature and structure of organizations, leadership and morale, communicational control and evaluation, decision-making, and field study techniques. This revised edition contains a *new section on planned change.*

SAYLES, LEONARD R., *Managerial Behavior: Administration in Complex Organizations.* New York: McGraw-Hill Book Co., Inc., 1964, 42 pp.

Departing from the stereotyped views of management theory and of human relations perspectives, the author proceeds from a review of the behavioral studies of what managers actually do, supplemented by his intensive investigation of managerial behavior in a large corporation. On the basis of his research findings, he constructs a series of interrelated concepts that more closely conform with the reality of the manager's job in contemporary organizations. With these interrelated concepts, the manager can deal with problems of leadership, interdepartment relations, the introduction of change and controls—all in operational terms that are derived from the underlying structure of the organization. The conclusions are based on actual observations of behavior rather than responses to questionnaires or imputed motivation. Hence, the patterns of work associated with successful managers become learnable and trainable skills rather than a set of "correct" attitudes.

SAYLES, LEONARD R., and STRAUSS, GEORGE, *Human Behavior in Organizations.* Englewood Cliffs, New Jersey: Prentice-Hall, Inc., 1966, 492 pp.

Authors attempt to integrate various human aspects of organizations into a holistic view. Practical applications and examples are given to help the reader.

SCHEIN, EDGAR H., *Organization Psychology.* Englewood Cliffs, New Jersey: Prentice-Hall, Inc., 1965, 108 pp.

A very readable treatment of some of the major elements of the new field of organizational psychology.

SCHEIN, EDGAR H., and BENNIS, WARREN G., *Personal and Organizational Change Through Group Methods: The Laboratory Approach.* New York: John Wiley & Sons, Inc., 1965.

The authors present research theory and applications of the laboratory method as it relates to the change process. The descriptive detail of some methods help clarify a field that is frequently discussed but seldom clearly understood.

SEASHORE, STANLEY E., and BOWERS, DAVID G., *Changing the Structure and Functioning of an Organization: Report of a Field Experiment.* Ann Arbor, Michigan: The Institute for Social Research, University of Michigan, 1963, 113 pp.

This monograph deals with procedure and policy problems in the introduction of experimental change, and concludes that reliance upon the organization's resources rather than external control by research workers can bring about positive changes in interpersonal relations. This study is based on a three-year field study involving 800 factory workers.

SOFER, CYRIL, *The Organization from Within.* London: Quadrangle Books, 1962.

Reports on a change situation in a research unit of a hospital, a department of a technical college, and a small company.

TANNENBAUM, ROBERT, WESCHLER, IRVING R., and MASSARIK, FRED, *Leadership and Organization: A Behavioral Science Approach.* New York: McGraw-Hill Book Co., Inc., 1961, 456 pp.

The authors believe the way to build leadership skills is through the use of sensitivity training. They hypothesize that leadership, influence, and organizational effectiveness hinge on improved human capacities to diagnose interpersonal situations and to act effectively on the basis of the diagnosis.

THOMPSON, JAMES D., *Organizations in Action*. New York: McGraw-Hill Book Co., Inc., 1967, 192 pp.

The author focuses on the uncertainties in organizational life and how they may be met. Points up the reasons why various organizations differ in design, structure, coordination, decision-making, and control.

WHYTE, WILLIAM, *Man and Organization: Three Problems in Human Relations in Industry*. Homewood, Illinois: Richard D. Irwin, Inc., 1959, 196 pp.

This well-known author gives three case examples from his own experiences where the morale or interpersonal factors were major factors in organizational functioning. His three cases indicate that the "human relations" is not easy, and is unique for each organization.

ZALEZNIK, ABRAHAM, and MOMENT, DAVID, *The Dynamics of Interpersonal Behavior*. New York: John Wiley & Sons, Inc., 1964, 520 pp.

Scholarly examination of interpersonal and group behavior in an organizational setting. Partial contents: Productivity; Satisfaction; Leadership; Change. Includes extensive bibliography.

ZOLLSCHAN, GEORGE, and HIRSCH, WALTER, eds., *Explorations in Social Change*. Boston: Houghton Mifflin Co., 1964, 816 pp.

A collection of papers, articles, and case examples of different types of social change, including economic, cultural, psychological, historical, and institutional.

INDEX